The Beeching Legacy
Volume I
The West Country
New revised edition

The line from Exeter to Okehampton was not listed for closure in the Beeching Report. The service was nevertheless listed for modification with the closure of the intermediate stations at Bow, North Tawton and Sampford Courtenay. In the event all passenger services were withdrawn on 5 June 1972. The survival of the line itself was due to its use by stone trains from Meldon Quarry.

Since 1984 'Dartmoor Rambler' trains subsidised by Devon County Council have run from Exeter calling at Sampford Courtenay and Okehampton on certain summer weekends. The Dartmoor Railway also runs heritage trains from Okehampton station.
(Further details are given on page 69)

BRITISH RAILWAYS BOARD   TRANSPORT ACT 1962

PUBLIC NOTICE

PASSENGER SERVICE

EXETER – OKEHAMPTON

In November, 1970, the Secretary of State for the Environment gave his consent to the withdrawal of the railway passenger service between Exeter and Okehampton involving the closure of the stations at Okehampton, Sampford Courtenay, North Tawton and Bow.

The terms of the consent, which has been published, require the provision of certain additional omnibus services. Road service licences authorising the provision of these services have now been granted by the Traffic Commissioners and the services, details of which are reproduced hereunder, will be brought into operation with effect from Monday, 22nd May 1972.

ADDITIONAL OMNIBUS SERVICES TO BE OPERATED ON AND FROM 22 MAY 1972
Operated by W. J. O. JENNINGS LTD. 8. QUEEN STREET, BUDE.

		WEKDAYS				
Okehampton (West St.)	dep.	09 01	11 11	14 16	16 08	18 24
Exeter St. David's	,,	10 01	12 11	15 16	17 04	19 24
Exeter (Coach Station)	arr.	10 06	12 16	15 21	17 09	19 29
Exeter St. David's	dep.	10 30	13 30	15 30	17 30	20 10
Exeter (Coach Station)	,,	10 35	13 35	15 35	17 35	20 15
Okehampton (West St.)	arr.	11 35	14 35	16 35	18 35	21 15

The above service operates to or from Bude. Details of intermediate timings between Okehampton and Bude can be obtained from the Operator.

Operated by W. T. & W. R. PHILLIPS, EXETER STREET GARAGE, NORTH TAWTON

		WEEKDAYS			
Exeter (Coach Station)	dep.		08 30	14 30	17 45
Exeter St. David's	,,		08 35	14 35	17 50
Crediton	,,		08 55	14 55	18 10
Copplestone	,,		09 05	15 05	18 20
Bow	,,		09 15	15 15	18 30
North Tawton	,,	07 30	09 25	15 25	18 40
Sampford Courtenay (New Inn)	,,	07 40	09 35	15 35	18 45
Sampford Courtenay (Station)	,,	07 45	09 40	15 40	18 55
Okehampton	arr.	07 55	09 50	15 50	19 05
Okehampton	drp.		10 00	16 10	17 30
Sampford Courtenay (Station)	,,	07 10	10 10	16 20	17 40
Sampford Courtenay (New Inn)	,,	07 20	10 15	16 25	17 45
North Tawton	,,	07 30	10 25	16 35	17 55 arr.
Bow	,,	07 40	10 35	16 45	
Copplestone	,,	07 50	10 45	16 55	
Crediton	,,	08 00	10 55	17 05	
Exeter St. David's	,,	08 20	11 15	17 25	
Exeter (Coach Station)	arr.	08 25	11 20	17 30	

Notice is hereby given that, on and from MONDAY, 22nd MAY 1972, the passenger train service between EXETER and OKEHAMPTON will be withdrawn and the undermentioned stations closed:

OKEHAMPTON, SAMPFORD COURTENAY, NORTH TAWTON, BOW

The stations at YEOFORD, CREDITON, and NEWTON ST. CYRES will continue to be served by the passenger train service between EXETER and BARNSTAPLE.

Paddington Station
May, 1972

F. M. WRIGHT
General Manager

The Beeching Legacy
Volume I
The West Country

New revised edition

Philip Horton

Silver Link Publishing Ltd

First published in 2010
New revised edition 2019

British Library Cataloguing in
Publication Data

A catalogue record for this
book is available from the
British Library.

ISBN 978 1 85794 546 1

Silver Link Publishing Ltd
The Trundle
Ringstead Road
Great Addington
Kettering
Northants NN14 4BW

Tel/Fax: 01536 330588
email: sales@
nostalgiacollection.com
Website: www.
nostalgiacollection.com

Printed and bound in the
Czech Republic

Acknowledgements

The Author would like to thank the many people who have helped produce the Second edition of this book 'The Beeching Legacy – The West Country'. Most of them have also helped with all five of my 'Beeching Legacy' volumes. I have again used photographs taken by Terry Gough, Frank Hornby, David Mitchell, Neil Carter, Owen Mogg and the late Peter Gray. In this new edition my thanks go to Ian Bennett who has allowed me to use colour slides taken by the late M E J Deane and Geoff Radley for his photographs taken at Barnstaple Town and Braunston stations. Five photographs have been reproduced courtesy of Colour-Rail. The maps produced by Steve Edge for the first edition have been checked and revised by him to ensure that they are still up to date.

A large number of books and articles have been referred to while writing this book. In particular RVJ Butt's 'The Directory of Railway Stations' (Patrick Stephens Ltd, 1995) and Hugh Longworth's 'British Railway Steam Locomotives 1948-1968' (OPC, 2005) have been particularly valuable in providing dates of station closures and the building and withdrawal dates of steam engines respectively. The text of the book has again benefited enormously from the early proof-reading and editing carried out by my wife Susan. I must also acknowledge her help and support in accompanying me on my forays to photograph railways around the country. Finally I would like to acknowledge yet again the help and encouragement received from Peter Townsend and Will Adams of Silver Link Publishing Ltd.

Tickets and luggage labels

Many of the luggage labels and tickets illustrated in the book were either collected or used by the author. In two cases these were printed by the pre-nationalisation railway companies but were still in use at BR stations in the mid-1960s.

Philip Horton
Castle Bytham, Lincolnshire
August 2019

A Silver Link book
from
The NOSTALGIA
Collection

Contents

○ Introduction ○

The first edition of this book was published by Silver Link in 2010, 47 years after the publication by Her Majesty's Stationery Office of Part 1 of the report *The Reshaping of British Railways* by Dr Richard Beeching, then Chairman of the British Railways Board. Since then controversy surrounding his Report has if anything intensified. Its 50th anniversary in 2013 focussed attention from both the public and the media on the 'Beeching legacy'. This in turn led to the broadcasting of several TV programmes together with the publication of other books on the subject. In addition, the increasing pressure on the nation's transport infrastructure has led to demands to reopen some of the lines he closed. Across the country as a whole such pressure has led to the reopening of many of the stations and a few of the lines. In the West Country the closure of the former SR route from Exeter to Plymouth via Okehampton has been bitterly regretted every time the sea wall at Dawlish is breached together with the adjacent main-line railway. If Beeching were to return today, the situation would surely give him food for thought, yet, as contemporary interviews show, he remained convinced that he was right to close around a third of our railway network. When asked towards the end of his life if he regretted anything about his time with BR, he replied that his only regret was that he had not been able to close more of it!

In this second edition, the opportunity has been taken to correct several errors that crept into the first, and to update the text in terms of the Train Operating Companies that are now involved. In addition, the number of photographs has been increased, many of them reproduced from colour slides taken by the late M. E. J. Deane. These are now in the care of Ian Bennett, who has kindly agreed to their publication in this book.

Like the first edition, this book records how passenger services in the West Country were affected by the ruthless implementation of the Beeching Report over a ten-year period. Since then, despite the introduction of modern high-speed rolling stock and much track rationalisation, the extent of our rail network has remained basically the same. Train services today are therefore still very much Dr Beeching's legacy. The passenger rail network in the West Country before and after Beeching is shown in Maps 1 and 2 respectively. The area covered by this book includes the counties of Devon and Cornwall, together with parts of west Somerset and Dorset.

To understand the Report it is worth considering the development of railways in the West Country and their condition immediately prior to the Report's publication. Chapter 1 therefore describes how, despite the 'Railway Modernisation Plan' of 1955, operating methods and the service provided to passengers had changed little in the decade and a half since nationalisation of the railways in 1947. By 1960 British Railways' Western Region (BR(WR)) had already closed a number of little-used branch lines, but there is no doubt that there was still plenty of dead wood in the network that required pruning. (A list of the lines closed prior to publication of the Report is given in Table 1.0). BR(WR) also made an early start on replacing steam haulage of its trains with diesels.

For passengers travelling on BR's Western Region from the North via Bristol or from London Paddington, Taunton was the gateway. By 1972 when this photograph was taken the Beeching cuts were virtually complete. Taunton had lost its train services to Yeovil Pen Mill (line 3.1), Chard (line 1.1), Barnstaple (line 3.11) and Minehead (line 3.18). In addition all but one of the intermediate stations between Taunton and Exeter were closed (line 2.2).

The track layout at Taunton was much simplified and the semaphore signals swept away in 1986, leaving it with just two platforms. Its middle, island platform, from which this photograph was taken has since had to be reinstated. In the distance to the left is a reminder of the past and portent of the future. Ex-GWR 'Small Praire' tank No. 5542 was withdrawn from Taunton shed in December 1961. After thirteen years in Barry scrapyard it was rescued for preservation and has since worked on the West Somerset Railway to Minehead and on other heritage lines around the country.
M E J Deane collection, courtesy of Ian Bennett

In contrast, on the lines then operated by BR's Southern Region (BR(SR)) the service offered had seen little change since the end of the 19th century. Despite an influx of new steam locomotives after the Second World War, its ageing fleet included tank engines that dated back to 1874 – a joy for enthusiasts but a nightmare if you wanted to operate an efficient, modern railway. It could therefore be argued that by 1963 the time was ripe for a review of rail services in the West Country. However, few expected the radical solutions proposed in the Beeching Report.

Chapter 2 considers the impact on each of the lines listed in the Report as 'Passenger Services to be Modified'. These include virtually all the main lines in the West Country. While they were not directly threatened with closure, the Report had revealed that most of the smaller wayside stations were losing money. As a result many of these had been listed for closure, leaving only stations where there were major conurbations. In some cases the proposals were too extreme even in 1963 and were not implemented, while in two others the passenger services were withdrawn altogether. Another service to be 'modified' was the former BR(SR) line from Waterloo to Exeter via Salisbury. The Report questioned 'the need to maintain separate main-line services to Exeter via both the Southern and Western routes'. Details of what happened to each of these services is given in Chapter 2, while a full list of the lines and stations affected is given in Table 2 and Appendix 2.

The Report showed that virtually all the branch lines in the

West Country were carrying fewer than 5,000 passengers per week, while the cut-off point for a line, operated by a diesel multiple unit (DMU) service, to be profitable was set at 7,000 passengers per route mile per week. The list of 'Passenger Services to be Withdrawn' for the West Country contained in the Report was, needless to say, a long one. The debate in the West Country was sharpened by an event unrelated to the Report. The winter of 1962/63 was the most severe for many years. Rural communities had, for a few weeks at least, suddenly become dependent on their railways again and were horrified by the prospect of not having a rail service to fall back on.

Chapter 3 includes a brief history of each line with its route illustrated by a map. Contemporary timetables indicate the rail service available prior to closure. Details are also given of the type of trains in use in the lines' final years. In the few cases where the passenger services survived, a summary is given of the present-day timetable, while any subsequent use by a heritage railway is also recorded. It should be noted that this book deals exclusively with the withdrawal of passenger services; the dates of closure given in the text and on the maps therefore refer to the withdrawal of these services. In a few cases the lines remained open for freight traffic at least for a year or two. The branch lines affected and their dates of closure are given in Table 3.

Most people have their own opinions of the Report. Many believe that it was heavily weighted against the railway industry by the Government of the day, which was perceived as being in the pocket of the road transport lobby. After all, the Conservative Transport Minister, Ernest Marples, who had appointed Dr Beeching as Chairman of the British Transport Commission in the first place, was the 'Marples' of Marples Ridgway, a road construction company. The Report and its implementation therefore provided a field day for conspiracy theorists. Certainly the outcome of the inquiries, held to consider the closure proposals, left many feeling dissatisfied. Objectors were frequently able to put forward strong arguments against closure, including successfully challenging the financial case advanced by BR. In almost every case their views were either considered to be outside the scope of the inquiry or were simply brushed aside. The question remains as to whether the closures would have occurred without the involvement of Dr Beeching. The answer is almost certainly 'Yes'. Extensive line closures were probably inevitable whoever was in charge of British Railways. Without Dr Beeching it is, however, tempting to speculate that these would have been undertaken in a more measured and sensitive way.

Dr Beeching resigned from the British Railways Board in 1965. He had just produced Part 2 of his Report, *The Development of the Major Trunk Routes*, which would have further reduced the country's railway network, a report that the Labour Government of the day failed to back. He was made a life peer as Baron Beeching of East Grinstead in the Birthday Honours of 1965, and died in 1985. Two years earlier the radical proposals in Beeching's Report Part 2 had been resurrected by Sir David Serpell. Two recent publications by Chris Austen and Richard (Lord) Faulkner ('Holding the Line' & 'Disconnected', OPC 2012 & 2015) have illustrated the depths of skullduggery which went on between the publication of Beeching's 2nd Report in 1965 and the Serpell Report of 1982/83. Plan after plan was hatched by top civil servants, ministers and

For several years after nationalisation BR(WR) continued to build GWR-designed engines and coaching stock at Swindon Works. An example was 'Castle' Class 4-6-0 No 7030 *Cranbrook Castle*, seen approaching Exeter St David's with an up express in August 1961. No 7030 was built in June 1950 and was withdrawn in February 1963. The last BR-designed coaches, ten new 'B' set non-corridor coaches, were built at Swindon for BR(WR) in 1954, Nos W6276W to W6285W (see the photographs on page 22). *M. E. J. Deane collection, courtesy of Ian Bennett*

sections of the BRB to decimate the country's railways. On each occasion their plans, including the Serpell Report, were leaked to the national press by railway supporting 'whistleblowers' who risked prosecution to do so. Fortunately, faced with a deluge of adverse publicity, the governments of the day always backed down.

To end on a positive note, there have been some unforeseen benefits from the closures, although it would be argued by some that these do not make up for the loss of the railway. Although many of the old trackbeds have been returned to farmland, others have become footpaths, cycleways and nature reserves. It is interesting to speculate that without the Beeching closures we might no longer be able to enjoy the sight and sound of branch-line steam on the West Country's heritage railways. Most of the standard-gauge heritage lines in the West Country occupy routes closed as a result of the Report, while at least two narrow-gauge railways and one tramway, the Seaton Tramway, now run on the routes of former branch lines. The fact that these working lines exist is a testament to the hard work of both volunteers and professional staff together with their many supporters. These present-day amenities are therefore also a part of the Beeching legacy. Details of the political background to the Report are given in Appendix 1.

Map I: Passenger-carrying lines in the West Country prior to the publication of the Beeching Report

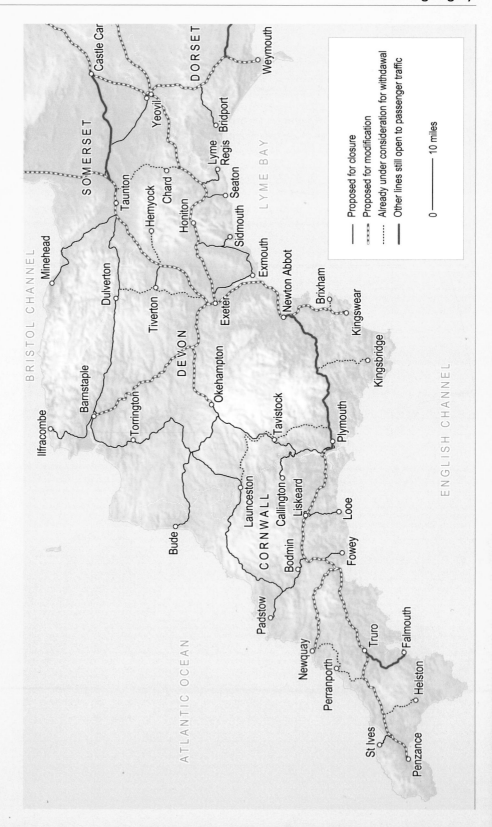

Proposed for closure
Proposed for modification
Already under consideration for withdrawal
Other lines still open to passenger traffic

0 ————— 10 miles

Map 2: Passenger-carrying lines in the West Country after implementation of the Beeching Report

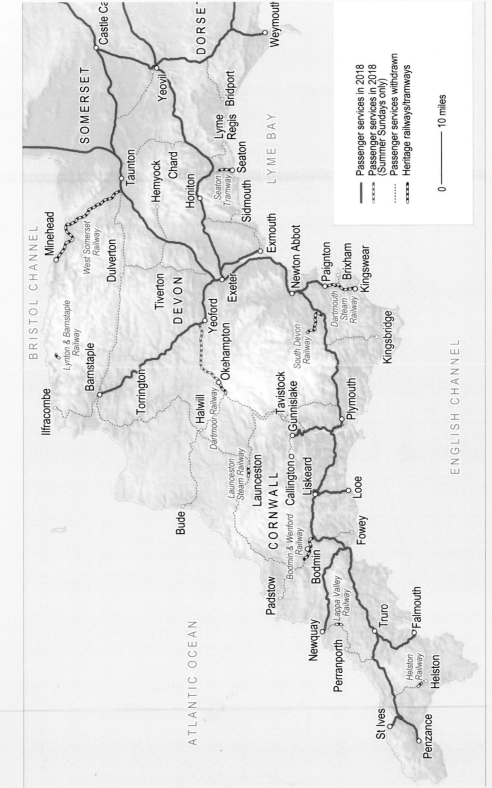

1 • West Country railways before the Beeching Report •

The History

Horse-drawn tramways had been a feature of the West Country for more than 100 years before the first public railway opened in 1834. This was the Bodmin & Wadebridge Railway, which ran from Wadebridge to Wenfordbridge, with a branch to Bodmin. It was the first steam-worked railway in Cornwall, and one of the first in Britain to carry passengers.

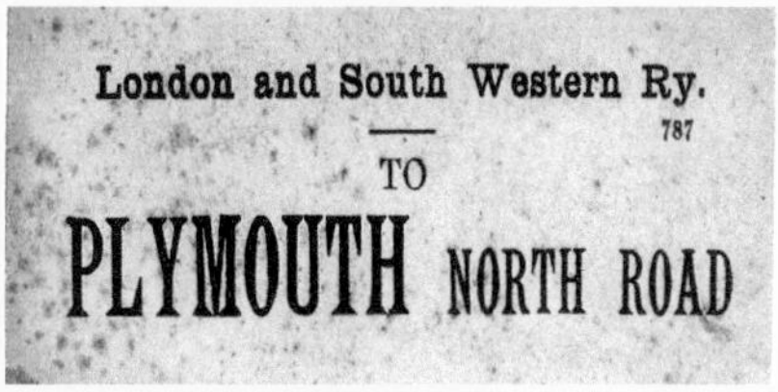

London and South Western Ry.

787

TO

PLYMOUTH NORTH ROAD

By 1884 two companies dominated the rail network of the West Country: the Great Western Railway (GWR), which still ran on its original broad gauge of 7ft (the last broad-gauge train ran in 1892), and the standard-gauge London & South Western Railway (LSWR). The year 1923 saw the grouping of Britain's many private railways into four major companies: the London & North Eastern (LNER), London Midland & Scottish (LMS), Great Western (GWR) and Southern (SR). While the GWR was little affected by this change, the LSWR found itself within the Southern Railway, together with the South Eastern & Chatham (SECR) and the London Brighton & South Coast (LBSCR). Once things had settled down both the GWR and LSWR did their best to attract holidaymakers to their respective lines, but progress was interrupted by the outbreak of the Second World War, when all railways were put under Government control.

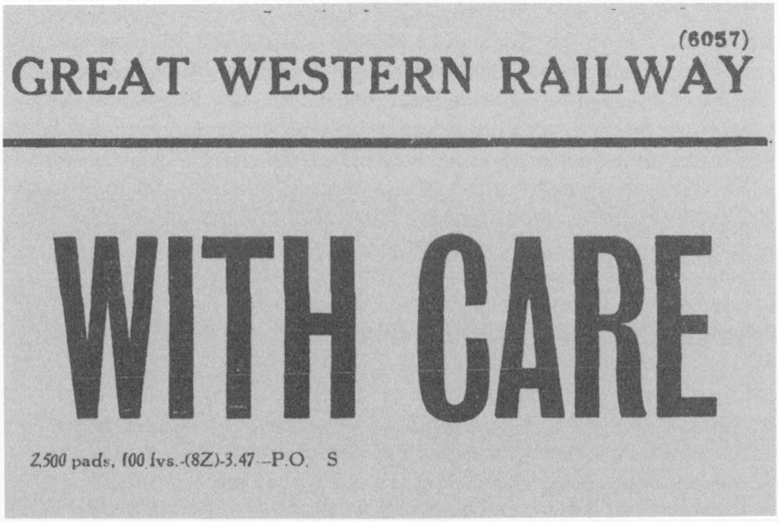

(6057)

GREAT WESTERN RAILWAY

WITH CARE

2,500 pads, 100 lvs.-(8Z)-3.47.-P.O. S

BR(WR) made full use of the money available under the 'Railway Modernisation Plan' of 1955 to modernise its passenger stock and motive power, and by 1960 it had a growing fleet of main-line diesel-hydraulic locomotives. 'Warship' Class No D833 *Panther* crosses the Royal Albert Bridge at Saltash with the down 'Cornish Riviera' express from Paddington 14 July 1960. The train comprises new BR Mark I coaches in the old GWR chocolate and cream livery, which had been reintroduced by BR(WR) for its crack expresses in June 1956. No D833 was the first of its class to be built by the North British Locomotive Co in 1960 and was withdrawn in October 1971. Note the Tamar road bridge under construction in the background *M. E. J. Deane collection, courtesy of Ian Bennett*

After the War Britain's railways were returned to civilian management, but in an exceedingly run-down condition. West Country lines once again came under the control of the GWR and SR, but nationalisation was to follow in 1948. Control of the railways was then vested in the British Transport Commission (BTC), and the actual running of British Railways was delegated to the Railways Executive. In the West Country this body in turn gave day-to-day responsibility for running the ex-GWR lines to the newly formed Western Region (BR(WR)) while the former SR lines became part of the Southern Region (BR(SR)). This situation only lasted until July 1950, when all BR(SR) lines west of Exeter were transferred to BR(WR). The Western Region was soon accused of neglecting them at the expense of the old GWR network, and in January 1958 they were transferred to BR(SR) once more. Five years later in January 1963 they were returned finally to BR(WR), together with all BR(SR) lines west of Wilton.

The 'Railway Modernisation Plan' of 1955 had for the first time made money available to update the country's rail network. Even so, during the first ten years after nationalisation travellers saw very few changes to the service provided. The rebuilding of Plymouth North Road station for instance, suspended at the outbreak of the Second World War, did not restart until 1958. BR(WR), however, soon began to make good use of the new money to replace its fleet of steam engines with diesel power.

In 1962 a new Transport Act became law. This abolished the British Transport Commission, replacing it with a new British Railways Board (BRB). The Board's first Chairman was Dr Richard Beeching.

The Network

BR(WR) had replaced steam on most of its branch lines by the end of 1961, and was already planning the closure of more uneconomic lines. Prior to dieselisation ex-GWR 'Small Prairie' tanks had dominated traffic on West Country branch lines for more than half a century. Here, viewed from the end of the platform at Helston in 1961, ex-GWR Class '4500' 'Small Prairie' No 4563 is waiting to depart with the daily pick-up goods as a classmate arrives with a train from Gwinear Road. The small engine shed, which was a sub-shed of Penzance, appears to contain a single mineral wagon. No 4563 was built at Swindon in 1924 and was withdrawn in October 1961. *M. E. J. Deane collection, courtesy of Ian Bennett*

Until nationalisation both the GWR and SR owned a main line from London to Plymouth with an extensive network of secondary and branch lines linked to it. The SR line ran from London Waterloo through Salisbury and Honiton to a station at Exeter Central (originally Queen Street), with a series of short branch lines to the coastal resorts on the Dorset and East Devon coast. The GWR trains took a more northerly route from London Paddington to Exeter St David's via Westbury and Taunton, where the line from London was joined by the main line from Bristol. The GWR and SR lines crossed at the GWR's Exeter St David's station. Here SR trains for Plymouth and North Devon and Cornwall arrived from the east down a steep incline from Exeter Central. They then shared the GWR main line for a few miles before branching north at Cowley Bridge Junction to climb around the northern flanks of Dartmoor to Okehampton. A further SR main line headed north to Barnstaple, Ilfracombe and Torrington, while at Okehampton a network of secondary lines covered the area between Bude and Padstow. The effect of this arrangement was that an SR train to Plymouth could be seen heading east away from Exeter St David's passing a westbound GWR Plymouth express as it approached St David's from the east. West of St David's the GWR initially had the much easier route along the coast to Newton Abbot before having to cope with the hill country of southern Dartmoor.

West of Plymouth the GWR's main line continued to Penzance, crossing the River Tamar by Brunel's famous Royal Albert Bridge. The SR main line from Waterloo entered Plymouth from the west and a passenger crossing the Royal Albert Bridge on a train to Cornwall might spot a Plymouth-bound train on the SR route along the banks of the Tamar far below. West of Exeter the GWR lines included a series of branches to the resorts on the south coast of Devon and Cornwall. The GWR also controlled north Cornwall from Newquay westwards.

At nationalisation the SR lost its lines west of Exeter to BR(WR), but these were returned to it in May 1958. The former ex-SR network west of Wilton finally became part of BR(WR) at the beginning of 1963.

The Locomotives and Coaching Stock

G. W. R.

EXETER

Since the start of the 20th century the GWR and LSWR had followed very different policies regarding motive power and coaching stock. Since 1902, when G. J. Churchward had become the Chief Mechanical Engineer (CME), the GWR had produced standard engines and stock for specific tasks, a policy that was followed by his successor C. B. Collett from 1922. The LSWR in contrast had had a policy of cascading its older engines and coaches from main line to secondary and branch-line use.

As a result, in 1947 BR(WR) inherited a series of tank engine classes for branch-line work, the most characteristic of which were the 'Prairie' tanks. These 2-6-2 tank engines (indicating that they had six driving wheels with a two-wheeled pony truck fore and aft) came in three sizes: the diminutive '4400' Class of 1905/06, Classes '4500' and '4575', known as 'Small Prairies', built from 1906 and 1927 respectively, and the '5100' and '4100' classes, the 'Large Prairies', built between 1929 and 1949. Although the '4400' Class became extinct in 1955 with the closure of the Princetown branch, many of the others were still at work in 1960. Also at work in 1960 were the '4800' Class (later renumbered '1400'), built between 1932 and 1936, with just four driving wheels and one trailing pair (0-4-2). These engines were push-pull-fitted, an arrangement that allowed the train to be driven from a cab at the front of the leading coach with the engine pushing from behind. This device avoided the need for the engine to run around its train at each end of the journey.

The first replacement DMUs arrived in Plymouth for crew training in April 1960. One of the 15 three-car units (Class 118), supplied by the Birmingham Railway Carriage & Wagon Co in 1960, stands in Falmouth station with the 11.20am for Truro on 7 September 1965. The line from Truro to Falmouth was notable as the only branch line in the West Country to escape unscathed from the Beeching Report. *Author*

These engines were complemented by a fleet of 0-6-0 pannier tanks. This basic 19th-century design, with slight modifications, was built throughout the first half of the 20th century. The design was standardised in the Class '5700' of 1929, many of which were still in use in 1960. The final '1600' Class was not introduced until 1949, the last being built in 1955. In addition, two further Classes ('5400' and '6400'), fitted for push-pull working, appeared in 1931 and 1932. Two classes of ex-GWR tender engine were also still in use on the longer cross-country lines such as that from Taunton to Barnstaple. These were the Class '4300' 'Mogul' 2-6-0s, built between 1916 and 1932, and the Class '2251' 0-6-0s, introduced between 1938 and 1948. On the main line, expresses were

In 1960 BR(SR) still
used many ex-LSWR
engines built in the late
19th century. Class 'T9'
'Greyhound' 4-4-0 No
30712 is seen on the
turntable at Padstow after
arrival from Okehampton
on 2 July 1958. No 30712
was built by Dubs & Co in
June 1899 and withdrawn
in November 1958. Other
ex-LSWR classes used
included the 'O2' and 'M7'
0-4-4 tanks built from 1889
and 1897 respectively.
Terry Gough

in the hands ex-GWR 4-6-0s (indicating that they had six driving wheels with a leading four-wheeled pony truck). These ranged in size from the mighty 'King' Class to the lightweight 'Manors'. Swindon Works had continued to build a number of these classes after nationalisation.

Throughout the interwar years the GWR built a series of more and more luxurious coaches for its crack expresses to the West Country, including the 'Cornish Riviera Limited'. Although former main-line coaches were often used on the branches, two-coach sets of non-corridor coaches (the 'B' sets) were introduced specifically for branch-line use in 1929. The design was subsequently updated with the last sets built by BR(WR) in 1954. In addition, from 1929 special 'auto-fitted' coaches were built for the push-pull services; the last updated versions were again built up to 1954.

In contrast BR(SR) found itself with many locos of LSWR vintage. A number of former express Class 'T9' 4-4-0s of 1899, known as 'Greyhounds', were still at work together with Class 'O2' and 'M7' 0-4-4 tank engines. These classes was built to the designs of W. Adams and D. Drummond (successive CMEs of the LSWR from 1889 and 1897 respectively) for the pre-electrification suburban services from Waterloo. Drummond had also designed the 'T9s'. In the 1920s a number of the 'M7s' had been push-pull-fitted and in 1960 were still at work on a number of West Country branch lines. In addition, the Lyme Regis branch was famously worked by Adams Class '0415' 4-4-2 tanks of 1882, while in North Cornwall Beattie Class '0298' 2-4-0 well tanks of 1874 were still occasionally used on local passenger trains around Wadebridge. W. G. Beattie had been CME of the LSWR between 1871 and 1878.

Prior to the Second World War the only relatively modern engines

As a precursor to the electrification of its line to Exeter, envisaged in the 'Railway Modernisation Plan' of 1955, BR(SR) continued to rely on its fleet of modern steam engines. This included many 'West Country' and 'Battle of Britain' Class 'Light Pacifics'. Built from 1945 with an 'air-smoothed' casing, many were subsequently rebuilt along conventional lines but, due to weight restrictions, were excluded from the lines to north Devon and Cornwall. In 1963 BR(WR), by then largely dieselised, inherited the West Country lines of BR(SR). This busy scene at its Exmouth Junction shed on 3 September 1963 shows the extent to which BR(SR) still relied on steam power. Facing the camera are three unrebuilt 'Light Pacifics', which will later work trains west of Exeter, as will the three visible Class 'N' 2-6-0s. Those 'Merchant Navy' 'Pacifics' and 'Light Pacifics' with their tenders facing the camera will later haul trains to Salisbury and Waterloo. *Author*

in the area were the 'N' Class 'Mogul' 2-6-0s, an SECR design of 1917 by R. E. L. Maunsell, who was soon to became CME of the Southern Railway. After the First World War 50 of these engines were built at the Woolwich Arsenal as a Government-sponsored job creation scheme and transferred to the West Country, where they remained for the next 40 years. The situation changed in 1945 when O. V. S. Bulleid, then SR's CME, introduced his 'West Country' and 'Battle of Britain' Class 4-6-2 'Light Pacifics'. One hundred and ten were eventually built, their relatively light weight allowing them to run on the secondary lines of the South West. The coal-hungry engines were, however, not economic on the more lightly patronised trains, which allowed the older classes to continue their bucolic existence into the 1960s.

In general the coaching stock used on the ex-SR lines was of similar vintage to the locomotives, especially on local services. BR(SR) continued to use coaching sets of LSWR vintage for push-pull working into the late 1950s, when they were at last replaced by 'new' two-car sets rebuilt from corridor coaches of the 1930s. Things were, however, better on the through trains to Waterloo, where new corridor coaches were built soon after the formation of the Southern Railway. In the late 1940s spacious new coaches were introduced to a design by Bulleid.

Since nationalisation the motive power policies of the two Regions had also been very different. In 1958 BR(WR) began its rapid dieselisation of main-line services in the South West with the introduction of a fleet of 'Warship' Class diesel-hydraulic locomotives. Members of the smaller Type 2 diesel-hydraulics, built by the North British Locomotive Co from 1959, were also soon appearing on some branch-line services. By 1961 these had been joined by Type 3 'Hymeks', built by Beyer Peacock, and the BR-built Type 4 'Westerns'. Ironically all had been withdrawn by February 1977, replaced by standard BR diesel-electrics.

By the late 1950s, however, BR(WR) had also acquired a fleet of modern diesel multiple units (DMUs). The first to make a significant impact on West Country services were built by the Birmingham Railway Carriage & Wagon Co. These three-car units, later classified Class 118, arrived in Plymouth for crew training in April 1960. In addition the

BR(SR) policy appeared to be one of maintaining its branch lines and replacing its Victorian engines with more modern steam power. Trains continued to run on the meandering line between Torrington and Halwill into the early 1960s. Here Ivatt Class 2 2-6-2 tank No 41298 approaches Halwill with a single Bulleid-designed coach forming the 4.00pm service from Torrington on 5 July 1961. Although No 41298 was a local engine, other 2-6-2 and 2-6-4 tanks used in the West Country at this time had been replaced by the electrification of lines in Kent and elsewhere in south and east England. *Terry Gough*

Gloucester Railway Carriage & Wagon Co had built 20 single-unit railcars from 1958 (Class 122), specifically for branch-line work. A further 16 similar units were produced by the Pressed Steel Co from 1960 (Class 121). Dieselisation by BR(WR) of its branch lines in Cornwall and in most of Devon and Somerset was virtually complete by the beginning of the winter timetable of 1961. BR(WR) also rapidly introduced the new BR-designed 'Mark 1' coaches to its main-line trains. In 1956 these had been formed into sets and painted in the old GWR livery of chocolate and cream to work the Region's crack expresses, including the 'Cornish Riviera', 'Cornishman' and 'Torbay Express'.

In contrast, BR(SR) services remained steam-worked, although the 1950s did see some modernisation of branch-line motive power. In 1952 a fleet of newly built BR Standard Class 3 2-6-2 tanks was allocated to Exmouth Junction, the main locomotive depot of the area, but it was 1956 before new non-corridor stock appeared. Other tank engines, which made their appearance at about the same time, were the smaller Class 2 2-6-2 tanks designed by H. G. Ivatt, CME of the LMS, in 1946. They became in effect a BR standard design, appearing on both the former GWR and SR lines. They finally replaced the '0415' tanks on the Lyme Regis branch in 1962. From that year the larger BR Standard Class 4 2-6-4 tanks of 1951, displaced from services in the South East by electrification, arrived at Exmouth Junction and were soon sharing traffic

It was not until BR(WR) took control of the ex-SR lines in January 1963 that dieselisation and branch-line closures occurred. The DMUs had become available due to the run-down and closure of services elsewhere on BR(WR). Here a BR(WR) three-car Class 116 DMU enters Sidmouth station forming the 8.32am service from Sidmouth Junction on 6 September 1965. Dieselisation did not save these branch lines and passenger services to Sidmouth were withdrawn from 6 March 1967. *Author*

with the 'N' Class 2-6-0s on ex-SR lines in North Devon and Cornwall. A number of BR-built standard 4-6-0 tender engines also worked in the South West during this period, but never made a significant impact on the motive power scene.

Sixty of O. V. S. Bulleid's 'Light Pacifics' were rebuilt from 1957 and became extremely successful steam locomotives. Their weight was, however, increased by 4 tons, which excluded them from all but the Plymouth line west of Exeter. The unrebuilt examples continued to work trains to Ilfracombe and Padstow until the end of steam. East of Exeter Central the expresses to Waterloo were hauled by both unrebuilt and rebuilt types of 'Light Pacific', together with Bulleid's slightly larger 'Merchant Navy' Class, all of which were rebuilt from 1956.

Although BR(SR) used some Mark I stock on its London trains, they were not required in large numbers because of the fleet of relatively new Bulleid-designed coaches. From the mid-1950s all BR(SR) stock had reverted to SR green livery in place of the BR standard colour of carmine and cream. Apart from the Western Region's chocolate and cream coaches, all other BR coaching stock at this time was painted in maroon livery.

It should, however, be borne in mind that one reason that BR(SR) did not hurry to replace its ageing steam engines was that it favoured electrification over dieselisation. In fact, the electrification of its main line to Exeter Central was identified as a priority in the Modernisation Plan. In 1960 its Kent Coast electrification scheme was well advanced, and no doubt the Region hoped that in due course its lines west of Exeter would also be electrified. As we now know, this plan was never implemented and the future of the lines concerned was to be rather different.

Once under BR(WR) control, modernisation of motive power on the BR(SR) system soon commenced in earnest. At first, because of a shortage of diesel units, the old Class 'M7' tanks were replaced by push-pull-fitted ex-GWR pannier tanks with suitably fitted auto-coaches. However, the early closure of BR(WR) branches released more DMUs for use on the former BR(SR) lines, and all had been effectively dieselised by the end of 1964.

Closures prior to the Beeching Report

G.W.R.

West Bay

A significant pre-war closure was that of the 1ft 11½in-gauge Lynton & Barnstaple Railway. The railway had opened in May 1898 and became part of the Southern Railway in 1923; it closed in September 1935. After lying derelict for decades, a short section from the original Woody Bay station was reopened by the Lynton & Barnstaple Railway Association in 2004. Further sections are to follow. Here one of its trains, worked by 0-4-0 tank *Axe* (Kerr Stuart, 1915), hauling three replica L&B coaches, approaches Woody Bay station on 20 August 2016. *Author*

The withdrawal of little-used passenger services had occurred for many years prior to nationalisation. For instance, the Southern Railway closed the narrow-gauge line from Lynton to Barnstaple in September 1935, a line that is currently experiencing a renaissance, at least in part. After nationalisation, however, dealing with unprofitable railway services was high on the agenda, so much so that in March 1949 the British Transport Commission set up a Branch Line Committee specifically to seek out loss-making branch lines. As a result the rate of withdrawal proposals increased markedly. The title of the committee was later changed to the Unremunerative Railway Committee, thus widening its scope beyond just branch lines.

One early closure proposal of the Committee became the cause of much controversy, that of the 10½-mile branch line from Yelverton to Princetown. Situated high up on Dartmoor and serving as home to the notorious prison, the line was attracting few passengers. It still required 19 staff to run it and was said to be losing £11,000 a year. Nevertheless opponents to the scheme included a number of local worthies and the newly formed Railway Development Association with its Chairman John Betjeman. At the enquiry set up by the South Western Transport Users' Consultative Committee in 1955 they argued forcefully that economies could be made in the operation of the line and that no attempt had been made to attract tourist traffic to this scenic route. The roads in the area were poor and, it was claimed, frequently closed by snow. As a result, the national press took up the cause. Taken aback, the Committee at first postponed its decision, then recommended that, because of the special circumstances, the service should be retained. However, echoing similar situations in the Beeching era, central authority overruled the local committee and services ceased in March 1956. Only six years later the junction station at Yelverton on the line from Plymouth to

Table 1.0 West Country passenger services withdrawn between 1956 and 1960			
Ref	Railway line	Date implemented	Other information
1.01	Yelverton - Princetown	Mar-56	
1.02	Exeter - Heathfield	Jun-58	
1.03	Newton Abbot - Moretonhampstead	Feb-59	Retained for china clay traffic and then mothballed. Reopened from newton Abbot to Teignbridge for timber traffic in 2010.
1.04	Totnes - Ashburton	Nov-58	The section between Buckfastleigh and Totnes is now operated by the heritage South Devon Railway

Table 1.1. Lines listed in Appendix 2, Section 6 of the Beeching Report as "Already under consideration for withdrawal			
Ref	Railway Line	Date Implimented	Other Information
1.1	Taunton - Chard Junction	Sep-62	Closure implemented before publication of the Report
1.2	Helston - Gwinear Road	Oct-62	Proposal implemented before publication of the Report. The
1.3	Launceston - Plymouth	Dec-62	Closure implemented before publication of the Report. The section from Lydford to Launceston remained open to freight until Feb-66
1.4	Truro - Chacewater - Perranporth -	Feb-63	Closure implemented before publication of the Report. A
1.5	Churston - Brixham	May-63	
1.6	Brent - Kingsbridge	Sep-63	
1.7	Tiverton - Hemyock	Sep-63	Remained open for milk traffic to Hemyock until Oct-1975
1.8	Exeter St David's - Dulverton	Oct-63	Cadleigh station is now the home of the Devon Railway Centre

Launceston itself closed when passenger services were withdrawn from 31 December 1962. Two years later Devon was to lose three further passenger services: Exeter to Newton Abbot via Heathfield (23¾ miles), Heathfield to Moretonhampstead (8¾ miles), and Totnes to Ashburton (7¼ miles) (see Table 1.0).

The start of the 1960s saw a marked increase in the rate of closures.

A replica of one of the line's original engines, 2-4-2 tank *Lyn* (Baldwin [USA], 1898), was built by Alan Keef Ltd in 2017. The engine is seen here at Woody Bay on 17 June 2018. *Author*

Line 1.04 Totnes to Ashburton. Among the West Country branches to close prior to the Beeching Report was the 9½-mile line between Totnes and Ashburton, which closed to passengers from 3 November 1958 and to goods from 10 September 1962. Here ex-GWR 0-4-2 tank No 1427 stands under Ashburton station's overall roof on the last day of passenger traffic, Saturday 1 November 1958. The coach to the right of the engine is No W6276W, the first of ten new 'B' set non-corridor coaches built at Swindon for BR(WR) in 1954. These were the last GWR-designed coaches to be built, and three of them were used on the last day of passenger traffic. *M. E. J. Deane collection, courtesy of Ian Bennett*

Two ex-GWR 0-4-2 tanks, Nos 1470 and 1466, approach Ashburton station with their train of three non-corridor coaches from Totnes on the last day of service, 1 November 1958. Both engines are still painted in early BR black livery, both were later used on the Exe Valley line (see page 30), and survived at Exeter St David's shed until October 1962 and December 1963 respectively. No 1466 was then purchased by the Great Western Society and remains at the Didcot Railway Centre. The last ever BR 'passenger' train on the Ashburton branch was a Plymouth Railway Circle special on 8 September 1962, which comprised ex-GWR 'Small Prairie' No 4576 and 13 brake vans. *M. E. J. Deane collection, courtesy of Ian Bennett*

Soon after Dr Beeching became Chairman of the BTC in 1961, proposals were in place to withdraw a further eight passenger services: Truro to Newquay via Chacewater (23¾ miles), Plymouth to Launceston (34¾ miles), Taunton to Chard Junction (18¼ miles), Gwinear Road to Helston (9 miles), Churston to Brixham (2 miles), Brent to Kingsbridge (12½ miles), Tiverton Junction to Hemyock (7¼ miles), and Dulverton to Exeter St David's (24¾ miles). These were listed in Appendix 2, Section 1 of the Report 'Passenger services already under consideration for closure before formulation of the Report' (see Table 1.1).

It is interesting that all of these lines were managed by BR(WR). Proposals to close lines in the West Country on the former Southern Railway network did not start until after BR(WR) has assumed control of them on 1 January 1963.

In 1969 the line was taken over by the Dart Valley Light Railway (DVR). In a scene that is very different today, ex-GWR Class '4500' 'Small Prairie' tank No 4555 is seen taking water at Buckfastleigh in June 1970. The engine was built in 1924 and was the last of its class to remain active at Plymouth Laira shed, being withdrawn in November 1963. The DVR was thwarted in its ambition of reopening the whole line due to the construction of the A38 dual carriageway, which crosses it just north of Buckfastleigh station. The last passenger train to Ashburton, a special train from Paddington, was on 2 October 1971. Since then services have only operated between Buckfastleigh and Totnes. No 4555 is now based on the Paignton & Dartmouth Steam Railway but is little used. *Author*

In 1992 the DVLR was taken over by the South Devon Railway Trust, since when many guest locos and other motive power have appeared on the line. An example is rebuilt ex-GWR railmotor No 93, which is seen approaching Buckfastleigh forming a service from Totnes on 24 February 2013. Although railmotors first appeared on the Ashburton branch in October 1903, No 93 started life ferrying passengers to the White City Stadium for the 1908 Olympic Games. In 1936 the coach body was rebuilt as a conventional auto-coach, No 212. This was withdrawn in 1956 but survived in Swindon's Engineers Department until acquired by the GWS in 1970. No 93's vertical boiler was built new, and the unit re-entered service in March 2011. *Author*

Line 1.1 Services between Taunton and Chard Junction were withdrawn from 10 September 1962.
Ilminster station was situated 11¼ miles from Taunton, and here Standard Class 3 2-6-2 tank No 82044 arrives with a train from Chard Central during 1960. Prior to nationalisation the service from Chard Central was operated by the GWR, while the SR operated that from Chard Central to Chard Junction on its West of England main line; even in 1962 there were no through trains between Taunton and Chard Junction. No 82044 ended her days at Bath Green Park in November 1965, while Chard Junction station survived until 7 March 1966. *M. E. J. Deane collection, courtesy of Ian Bennett*

Line 1.2 The Helston branch to Gwinear Road lost its passenger service on 5 November 1962. Like many other ex-GWR branch lines, the service to Helston was dominated by Class '4500' and '4575' 'Small Prairie' tanks. Here one of the class, No 4559, is seen leaving Helston with a train for Gwinear Road in May 1960. No 4559 was built at Swindon in 1924 and withdrawn in October 1960. The Helston Railway Preservation Society is currently restoring part of the line. *M. E. J. Deane collection, courtesy of Ian Bennett*

Gwinear Road station on the ex-GWR Penzance main line was 8¾ miles from Helston. Here ex-GWR Class '4575' 'Small Prairie' No 5541 arrives with a train from Helston in May 1960. No 5541 was one of a later batch of 'Small Prairies' built from 1927. The engine was withdrawn in July 1962 after DMUs had replaced steam on the branch; after ten years at Barry scrapyard, it was purchased and restored by the Dean Forest Railway Preservation Society. *M. E. J. Deane collection, courtesy of Ian Bennett*

Line 1.3 The broad-gauge line between Launceston and Plymouth had become part of the GWR in February 1876. By this time an LSWR-sponsored line from Okehampton had reached Lydford and for a time its trains used the branch to reach Plymouth, running on mixed-gauge track. The line via Tavistock and Bere Alston became available in June 1890 (see Chapter 3.16). Following nationalisation all trains used the ex-LSWR station (see Chapter 3.9), where ex-GWR Class '4575' 'Small Prairie' No 4583 with a train for Plymouth is pictured on 13 July 1956. The passenger service was withdrawn from 31 December 1962; the last train, together with its passengers, became stranded in deep snowdrifts for three days. No 4583 was built at Swindon in February 1927 and was withdrawn in January 1958. *Frank Hornby*

Goods traffic continued to use the ex-GWR line from Lydford to Launceston until February 1966. On 5 September 1965 the Great Western Society's Launceston Branch ran a 'Centenary Rail Tour' over the line using Ivatt Class 2 2-6-2T No 41283 from Templecombe shed. The train is pictured at the former GWR station at Lydford, where a lower-quadrant signal and water tower were still in use. Here the engine ran round its train prior to traversing the line to Launceston, where it arrived at the long closed ex-GWR station. After shunting its train into the ex-LSWR station, it set out once more for Halwill. No 41283 was withdrawn in March 1966 on closure of the Somerset & Dorset line. *Author*

Line 1.4 Truro, Chacewater, Perranporth and Newquay lost is passenger service from 4 February 1963. Here ex-GWR Class '4575' 'Small Prairie' No 5526 leaves Perranporth with a train for Newquay on 14 September 1958. At that time there was a through train to and from Paddington on summer Saturdays, which ran via Truro where a portion for Falmouth was attached. The last of these left Perranporth at 9.05am on 8 September 1962. No 5526 was built at Swindon in 1928 and withdrawn in June 1962. After more than 20 years in Barry scrapyard it was purchased for preservation and now works on the South Devon Railway. *Trevor Owen, Colour-Rail*

Some 1¼ miles of the former line south of Newquay is now used by the trains of the 15in-gauge Lappa Valley Railway, which runs between newly built halts at Benny Hill and St Newlyn East Golf Course. The engine in use on 18 May 2009 is *Zebedee*, an 0-6-4 tank built/rebuilt by Severn Lamb in 1974/90. *Author*

1.5 Churston to Brixham Ex-GWR 0-4-2 tank No 1427 waits at Brixham with a single auto-coach before departure for Churston in August 1955. Despite its antiquated appearance No 1427 was built at Swindon in November 1933, and withdrawn in June 1960. Single-unit railcars replaced steam on the branch line shortly before closure. *N. L. Browne, Frank Hornby collection*

Churston on the line from Paignton to Kingswear opened in March 1861 as Brixham Road with the branch to Brixham opening in February 1868. The neat track layout at the junction station is seen here on a wet day in September 1960. Ex-GWR 0-4-2 tank No. 1466, then shedded at Newton Abbot, stands in the Brixham bay with its single auto-coach while passengers wait for a connection to Kingswear on the main down platform. No 1466 was built at Swindon in 1936 and was withdrawn in December 1963. *Colour Rail*

Line 1.6 Brent to Kingsbridge. The branch ran for 12½ miles from Brent station, on the BR(WR) West of England main line, and its passenger service was withdrawn from 16 September 1963. Ex-GWR Class '4575' 'Small Prairie' No 5558 stands in Kingsbridge station with a train for Brent in the 1960s. Note the station's gas lamps and the coal being unloaded from a wagon in the goods yard. No 5558 was built at Swindon in 1928 and withdrawn in October 1960. It went to Barry scrapyard but was broken up before it could be preserved. *M. E. J. Deane collection, courtesy of Ian Bennett*

'Small Prairie' No 5558 is seen again approaching Kingsbridge with a train from Brent in the summer of 1960. Single-unit railcars replaced steam on the branch line before closure. *M. E. J. Deane collection, courtesy of Ian Bennett*

Line 1.7 Tiverton Junction to Hemyock The branch from Tiverton Junction lost is passenger service from 9 September 1963. Ex-GWR 0-4-2 tank No 1466 is seen approaching Uffculme, one of the four intermediate stations, in the early 1960s. The coach is one of two ex-Barry Railway vehicles allocated to the branch, which were still gas-lit. The train is heading for Hemyock to collect loaded milk tankers from the creamery there; the journey took almost an hour for the 7½ miles. No 1466 is now preserved by the GWS at Didcot. *M. E. J. Deane collection, courtesy of Ian Bennett*

Ex-GWR 0-4-2 tank No 1450 collects milk tankers from the yard at Hemyock to add to the single coach that will form the 6.00pm service to Tiverton Junction on 29 August 1963. By this time the ex-Barry Railway coaches had been replaced by ex-LNER vehicles. No 1450 remained in use until May 1965 when it was purchased for preservation. It is now based at the Severn Valley Railway and regularly appears at preserved railway galas around the country. The Hemyock branch remained open for milk traffic until September 1965. *Author*

Line 1.8 Exeter St David's to Dulverton Passenger trains on The Exe Valley line were worked by mainly auto-fitted Class '1400' tanks until closure from 7 October 1963. An exception was ex-GWR Class '4575' 'Small Prairie' No 4589, one of the 15 engines converted for auto-working by BR(WR) in the 1950s, which is pictured at Bampton in 1961 with a train for Dulverton. No 4589 was built at Swindon in 1927 and withdrawn in July 1962. *M. E. J. Deane collection, courtesy of Ian Bennett*

Exe Valley trains terminated at Dulverton, situated on the edge of Exmoor and 24¾ miles from Exeter. Here they connected with trains between Taunton and Barnstaple (see also Chapter 3.11). Ex-GWR 0–4–2 tank No. 1466, now shedded at Exeter, is seen at Dulverton on a summer's day in the early 1960s with a train for Exeter St. David's. The engine is pictured twice more in this book on trains to and from Tiverton Junction (see pages 29 and 78). Note the small turntable in the foreground. No. 1466 and is now preserved at the GWS's Didcot Railway Centre. *M.E.J.Deane collection, courtesy of Ian Bennett.*

2 ○ Passenger services listed for modification ○

Although much attention is rightly focussed on the withdrawal of passenger services on branch and secondary lines, the Beeching Report also proposed significant changes to the remaining network. That part of the Report that gave 'more detailed consideration of the main groups of traffic' included the issue of stopping trains. This concluded that 'although a high proportion of passenger services operate over lines of low total traffic density, there is also a considerable number of similar services operating over more densely loaded routes. In most cases, these services are just as unsound, financially, as those operating over branch lines.' The Report went on to say that such services did not pay their way if they attracted fewer than 17,000 passengers per week when all overheads are taken into consideration. The Report concluded that such services should also be withdrawn or radically modified.

Eight lines in the West Country were subsequently listed in Appendix 2, Section of the Report as requiring such modification. With three exceptions, these included all passenger-carrying lines in the West Country not proposed for closure in the Report. Two of the three excluded lines were the sections of the ex-GWR main line from Paddington to Plymouth between Castle Cary and Taunton, and from Newton Abbot to Plymouth. Local passenger services between Castle Cary and Taunton were, however, withdrawn in 1962, while local passenger services between Newton Abbot and Plymouth had gone in 1959. Of the two intermediate stations to survive, Totnes and Brent, the latter closed in September 1963 together with the branch to Kingsbridge, while Totnes was not listed for closure. In short, there was nothing left to 'modify' on either route and the whole main line survives today. Ivybridge, one of the stations closed in 1959, was reopened in July 1994, and in 2009 was marketed as a 'park and ride' station with services operated by First Great Western.

The absence of the third line, from Truro to Falmouth, is more surprising, as it is a branch line. Admittedly it was shown to carry up to 10,000 passengers a week, but both the Exmouth and Minehead branches had been listed for closure despite carrying up to 50,000 and 10,000 passengers a week respectively. Nevertheless, it was not listed for either closure or modification and neither were any of the four intermediate stations. Perhaps it was just forgotten! It remains today, operated by Great Western Railway. In recent years this and several other of the lines listed for closure have been subsidised and promoted by the Devon & Cornwall Rail Partnership; this is based at Plymouth University and includes Devon and Cornwall County Councils, Plymouth City Council and the train operator. The Falmouth line is promoted as the 'Maritime Line'.

Since publication of the first edition there have been a number of changes to the Train Operating Companies (TOCs) involved. Two of the three are part of the First Group; these are First Great Western, which now trades as Great Western Railway, while former South West

Trains services are operated by South Western Railway. At present CrossCountry retains the franchise for trains to the Midlands and the North, but this is currently being reviewed. In order to avoid confusion, the original Great Western Railway is shown in this book as GWR, while the name of its present-day successor is given in full.

The list of the eight lines where services were modified is shown in Table 2, while the stations on each line are shown in Appendix 2. Services on each line are described below.

Table 2. West Country passenger services listed for modification in Appendix 2, Section 2 of the Beeching Report

Ref	Railway line	Date implemented	Other information
2.1	Castle Cary - Weymouth	Apr-66	Intermediate stations closed and line singled
2.2	Taunton - Exeter St David's	Oct-64	Intermediate stations closed
2.3	Exeter St David's - Kingswear	Oct-72	Two stations closed in 1964. Paignton - Kingswear passenger service taken over by the Dart Valley Railway Co in November 1972. Now operates during holiday times only as the Dartmouth Steam Railway
2.4	Plymouth - Penzance	Oct-64	Intermediate stations closed
2.5	Par - Newquay (Cornwall)	1964 - 1987	Track rationalisation and shortening of platforms at Newquay
2.6	Yeovil Junction - Exeter Central	April-66/67	Intermediate stations closed and much of line singled.
2.7	Exeter Central - Barnstaple	Oct-71	Passing loops removed
2.8	Exeter Central - Okehampton	Jun-72	Yeoford - Okehampton passenger services withdrawn Line retained for traffic from Meldon Quarry, but Quarry mothballed in 2011. 'Dartmoor Ramblers' trains from St.James Park, Exeter intruduced for summer of 1984 which contuine to run on summer Sundays. The Dartmoor Railway operates heritage trains from Okehamton to Meldon Quarry

2.1 Castle Cary - Yeovil Pen Mill and Weymouth

The line between Castle Cary, Yeovil Pen Mill and Weymouth was built by the Wilts, Somerset & Weymouth Railway to Brunel's broad gauge. The railway reached Yeovil in September 1856 and was extended south to Weymouth in January 1857, by which time it had already been acquired by the GWR. The line provided a route to London via Westbury to the GWR's main line at Chippenham, and to Bristol via Bathampton, where it again joined the GWR main line. In 1880/81 the original single track was doubled and for many years the service comprised some four stopping trains between Westbury, Castle Cary, Yeovil Pen Mill and Weymouth.

Diesels replaced steam on most passenger trains on the Castle Cary to Weymouth line in 1959. After this steam working was confined to summer Saturdays. Here ex-GWR 4-6-0 No 6838 *Goodmoor Grange* has just emerged from Bincombe Tunnel north of Weymouth with the 11.05am service from Weymouth to Wolverhampton Low Level on 7 August 1965. No 6838 was built at Swindon in 1937 and withdrawn in November 1965. *Author*

The first of the 30 ex-GWR Hawksworth-designed 'County' Class 4-6-0s, No 1000 *County of Middlesex*, approaches Maiden Newton with a stopping train from Westbury to Weymouth on 26 May 1963. The line on the left is the branch line to Bridport, which closed in May 1975. No 1000 was built at Swindon in 1945 and withdrawn in July 1964. Note the weed free track bed even on the branch line. *Colour-Rail*

Through trains were also provided to and from Bristol and London Paddington, the latter initially running via Chippenham and, later, Devizes. The direct line from Paddington to Westbury via Lavington did not open until 1900. In 1906 the GWR completed its 'Somerton cut-off' and Castle Cary became a junction station on the main line from Paddington to the West Country.

Through trains from London Paddington to Weymouth, including the 'Channel Island Express' to and from Weymouth Quay, were largely withdrawn in 1960 when services from the capital were concentrated on the former Southern Railway route from Waterloo via Bournemouth. DMUs replaced steam on services between Bristol and Weymouth in June 1959, and the local service of auto-trains from Weymouth to Yeovil was dieselised at the same time. In the summer of 1963 seven local trains ran from Weymouth via Dorchester to Yeovil stopping at all 11 intermediate stations, while two continued to Westbury with two additional stops before Castle Cary. Eight trains ran to Bristol, all but one stopping only at the principal stations, while a further train ran direct to Chippenham. On summer Saturdays two trains ran to Weymouth from Birmingham and Wolverhampton, which remained steam-hauled until 1965. The BR(WR) timetable for the winter of 1962/63 is shown on pages 36 and 37.

In September 1964 BR(WR) published proposals to close most intermediate stations on the line between Bath Spa and Dorchester West from 5 January 1965. These included all 12 on the 34¼-mile section south of Castle Cary. Dr Beeching clearly saw little future for the line as Yeovil Pen Mill, Maiden Newton, the junction for the threatened branch line to Bridport (see Chapter 3.19), and Dorchester West were all listed for closure in his Report. Notices were published in September 1964 proposing the closure of all stations between Yeovil Pen Mill and Dorchester West, including the latter. After a Public Inquiry in November 1965, the Minister, Barbara Castle, refused BR(WR) permission to close Thornford Bridge Halt, Yetminster, Chetnole Halt, Maiden Newton and Dorchester West, which remain open today. The six intermediate

G.W.R.

Weymouth

Cardiff based Metropolitan-Cammell Class 101 three-car DMU Set No CF820 comprising Nos W51512, W59093 and W51500 leaves Yeovil Pen Mill past a BR(WR) lower-quadrant signal forming the 12.00 service from Swindon to Weymouth on 4 August 1987. On leaving Yeovil the train will travel over single track to Maiden Newton. *Author*

stations at Sparkford, Marston Magna, Evershot, Cattistock, Grimstone & Frampton and Bradford Peverell & Stratton Halt were closed from 3 October 1966.

The BR(WR) nevertheless appeared eager to run down services. At the start of the winter timetable of 1964 the number of trains from Weymouth to Yeovil was reduced to five, while the Bristol semi-fast trains were reduced to six. In addition, Sunday services were reduced to just one train each way between Weymouth and Westbury. In 1966 the former double track was singled between Castle Cary and Dorchester with just two passing places at Yeovil Pen Mill and Maiden Newton.

After closure of the intermediate stations the winter timetable for 1970/71 shows that only three trains ran from Weymouth to Bristol throughout the year. Other trains terminated at Westbury, where passengers for Bristol had to change to a connecting train from Salisbury. Since then the service has slowly improved. In 1994/95, the last year of BR operation, seven trains a day ran from Weymouth to Bristol, stopping at all stations. A number of trains were locomotive-hauled at this time. The line is now promoted as part of the 'Heart of Wessex Line', a partnership involving the local authorities, voluntary groups and the train operator, Great Western Railway. In the autumn of 2019 there were eight arrivals at Weymouth from Westbury each weekday. The first arrival at 08.24 was from Westbury; other were

The same DMU is seen again leaving Weymouth with the 14.58 to Swansea on the same day on the same day, this time past BR(SR) upper-quadrant signals. At the time Weymouth was still controlled by semaphore signals, provided by BR(SR). *Author*

Thornford Bridge Halt, on the line between Castle Cary and Weymouth, was one of the 12 stations between Yeovil Pen Mill and Dorchester West listed for closure in the Beeching Report. Six of them closed on 3 October 1966, but Thornford Bridge Halt survived and remains open today. After the retirement of the first-generation DMUs. services reverted to loco haulage for a while. Here Class 37 diesel-electric No 37412 leaves Thornford with the 19.38 Weymouth to Westbury train on 30 June 1995. *Terry Gough*

Extracts from BR(WR) Timetable 62, 10 September 1962-16 June 1963, showing trains between Castle Cary/Yeovil (Pen Mill) and Weymouth (Chapter 2.1), between 1.46pm and 7.45pm. The table also shows trains between Yeovil (Pen Mill) and Taunton via Martock (Chapter 3.1, see page 72). Also shown are stopping trains from Castle Cary and Taunton, although these were withdrawn from 10 September 1962.

Table 62 — WEEK DAYS—continued

Table 62—continued — LONDON, READING, NEWBURY, WESTBURY, FROME, YEOVIL, DORCHESTER WEST, WEYMOUTH and TAUNTON

Station	am	am	pm	am	pm	pm	am	pm	pm	pm	pm	pm	pm	pm	pm	pm	pm
PADDINGTON 50 dep		9 45		11 15		12 30	11 45			1230			2 30				
Reading General 61 dep		10 25		12 10		1 10	12 25			1 24							
Reading (West)				12 13						1 27							
Theale				12 20						1 34							
Aldermaston				12 26						1 40							
Midgham				12 30						1 44							
Thatcham				12 35						1 49							
Newbury arr				12 41						1 55							
Newbury dep				12 44						1 58							
Kintbury				12 52						2 6							
Hungerford				12 58						2 12							
Bedwyn				1 4						2 18							
Savernake (for Marlboro')																	
Wootton Rivers Halt																	
Pewsey																	
Manningford Halt																	
Woodborough																	
Patney and Chirton																	
Pans Lane Halt																	
Devizes arr																	
Devizes dep																	
Bromham & Rowde Halt																	
Seend Halt																	
Semington Halt																	
Lavington																	
61 Oxford dep		10 5				11H55	11H 5										
61 Didcot		10 47				12H12											
61 Swindon		11 19					1 15										
Chippenham dep		11 45					1 40										
Lacock Halt							1 47										
Melksham		11H57					1 52										
Holt Junction							1 57										
Staverton Halt							2 1										
Trowbridge arr							2J30	2 6									
72 Bristol (Tem. Mds.) dep	11&38				1 5					1657				3 5		3 20	
72 Bath Spa	12 4				1 22				2 20					3 22		3 57	
72 Bradford-on-Avon	12 20				1 40				2 37					3 40		4 18	
Trowbridge dep	12 30				1 52		2 8		2 49					3 52		4 27	
Westbury arr	12 37				2 0	2 8	2 15		2 56					4 0		4 34	
72 Salisbury arr	1 21								3 47								
Westbury dep			1 5		2 11				2 18					4 8			
Frome arr			1 14						2 29					4 17			
Frome dep			1 15						2 31		3 17			4 20			
Witham (Somerset)			1 23								3 25			4 27			
Bruton			1 31											4 34			
Castle Cary			1 39						2 46					4 40			
Sparkford			1 46						2 54					4 48			
Marston Magna			1 51											4 53			
Yeovil (Pen Mill) arr			1 57						3 4				4 04	4 59	5 17		
Yeovil (Pen Mill) dep			2 0			2 45		3 16	3 6				4 25	4 47	5 20		
Thornford Bridge Halt			2 10			2 52								4 55	5 25		
Yetminster			2 7			2 55								5 0	5 37		
Chetnole Halt			2 15			3 0											
Evershot			2 22			3 10											
Cattistock Halt			2 27			3 16		3 31					4 40	5 15	5 40		
Maiden Newton			2 32			3 21							4 46	5 17	5 46		
Grimstone & Frampton			2 38			3 21							4 50	5 21	5 49		
Bradford Peverell M			2 41			3 24							4 57				
Dorchester West			2 49			3 31		3v46					5 5	5 40	6 6		
Upwey and Broadwey			2 57			3 39							5 9	5 44	6 10		
Radipole Halt			3 1			3 43							5 12	5 47	6 13		
Weymouth Town arr			3 4			3 46		3 57					5 12				
Alford Halt dep																	
Keinton Mandeville																	
Charlton Mackrell																	
Somerton (Somerset)																	
Long Sutton and Pitney																	
Langport East														4&39			
Athelney														4 48			
Lyng Halt														4 50			
Durston														4 55			
Creech St. Michael Halt														5 1			
Taunton arr						3 0							4 47	5 7			
81 Exeter (St. David's) arr						3 35							5 22	5 56			
81 Torquay						4 22							6 19	7 0			
81 Paignton						4 33							6 28	7 10			
81 Plymouth						5 8							7 0	7 30			
81 Penzance						8 0							9 45	10 55			

For Notes, page 146

Maiden Newton remains the only passing place for trains between Yeovil Pen Mill and the junction with the line from Bournemouth to Weymouth. Here GWR 2-car Class 165/1 'Turbo' unit No. 165.131 arrives at the station with the 10.41 from Gloucester to Weymouth on 3 April 2019. Waiting for it is GWR 3-car Class 166 'Turbo Express' unit No. 166.221 *Reading Train Care Depot* with the 13.10 from Weymouth to Gloucester. The station buildings are no longer in railway use. The 'Turbo' units were among the last vehicles to be built at the BR's York works in 1992/1993. Since then they have worked suburban services from Paddington but are now being cascaded down to other services as the Paddington trains are electrified. *Author*

WEEK DAYS—continued   **Table 62**

Table 62— continued

LONDON, READING, NEWBURY, WESTBURY, FROME, YEOVIL, DORCHESTER WEST, WEYMOUTH and TAUNTON

	pm	pm	pm	pm	pm	pm	pm	pm	pm	pm	pm	pm	pm	pm	pm	pm	pm	pm	pm
PADDINGTON 50. dep	1 55							4 30			3 45			3 15	3 45				4 35
Reading General 61 dep	2 48							5 10			4 25			4 7	4 50				5 35
Reading (West).. .,	2 51														4 53				5 38
Theale	2 58														5 0				5 45
Aldermaston	3 3														5 6				5 51
Midgham	3 7													4 27	5 10				5 55
Thatcham	3 12													4 33	5 22				6 6
Newbury .... arr	3 18													4 36	5 36				6S10
Newbury .... dep	3 30													4 45	5 44				6S18
Kintbury	3 38													4 51	5 50				6S23
Hungerford	3 43													5 0	5 56				
Bedwyn														5 16					
Savernake (for Marlbro').														5 23					
Wootton Rivers Halt														5 27					
Pewsey														5 33					
Manningford Halt														5 39					
Woodborough																			
Patney and Chirton														5 47					
Pans Lane Halt														5 50					
Devizes { arr														6 27				**2**	6 45
Devizes { dep																			6 50
Bromham & Rowde Halt														6 34					6 54
Seend Halt																			7 0
Semington Halt																			
Lavington																			
61 Oxford ...... dep							3H45				2H39								
61 Didcot .... ,,							4H 3				2H49								
61 Swindon .... ,,											5 11								
Chippenham ... dep											5 47								
Lacock Halt											5 54								
Melksham					5 10				5 25	6 0									
Holt Junction					5 15					6 4			6 41					7 3	
Staverton Halt					5 18					6 8								7 6	
Trowbridge ..... arr					5 23					6 14			6 47					7 12	
72 Bristol (Tem. Mds.) dep		3 55					4 30	5 0			5 20		5638		5 55				
72 Bath Spa. .,		4 24					4 58	5 23			5 50		6 10		6 22				
72 Bradford-on-Avon . ,,		4 46								5†43	6 26								
Trowbridge .. dep		4 57			5 24		5 31	5 51			6 15	6 22	6 39		6 56			7 14	
Westbury .... arr		5 4			5 31		5 38	5 58	6 8		6 22	6 29	6 46		7 3			7 22	
72 Salisbury .... arr								6 41					7 31						
Westbury			5 15	5 35			6 1		6 18										
Frome .. { arr			5 24	5 44					6 27										
Frome .. { dep			5 26		6 0				6 29										
Witham (Somerset)						6 9			6 36										
Bruton									6 43										
Castle Cary	5 30		5 42						6 49	6 55									
Sparkford			5 50							6 57									
Marston Magna										7 2									
Yeovil (Pen Mill) { arr		5 45	6 0							7 9			7 45						
Yeovil (Pen Mill) { dep		5 45	6 2							7 11			7 52						
Thornford Bridge Halt.			6 12							7 19			7 55						
Yetminster										7 22			8 0						
Chetnole Halt										7 27			8 7						
Evershot .. .,										7 34			8 12						
Cattistock Halt										7 39			8 15						
Maiden Newton			6 25							7 43			8 21						
Grimstone & Frampton										7 49			8 26						
Bradford Peverell **M**..										7 53			8 31						
Dorchester West....			6 38							8 0			8 40						
Upwey and Broadwey..										8 8			8 43						
Radipole Halt										8 12			8 46						
Weymouth Town. arr			6 49							8 15									
Alford Halt .... dep	5 34										7 0								
Keinton Mandeville ..	5 40										7 6								
Charlton Mackrell ..	5 45										7 11								
Somerton (Somerset) ..	5 52										7 18								
Long Sutton and Pitney.	5 57										7 23								
Langport East .. .,	6 2	2	6 21								7 28								
Atheley ....,	6 11	6 31									7 37								
Lyng Halt ... ... ,,		6 33									7 39								
Durston .... ,,		6 38									7 43								
Creech St. Michael Halt. ,,		6 44									7 49								
Taunton .... arr	6 25	6 51							7 0		7 55								
81 Exeter (St. David's) arr									7 35										
81 Torquay .... ,,									8 28										
81 Paignton .... ,,									8 39										
81 Plymouth ... ... ,,									9 2										
81 Penzance. ... ... ,,																			

For Notes, page 146

Thornford Bridge Halt was typical of the rural stations that had no place in Dr Beeching's plans for British Railways. It was therefore listed for closure, but not only did it survive, it has also since prospered. In 2008 it won the first prize at the National 'ACoRP' (Association of Community Rail Partnerships) award for integrated transport schemes. The prize was awarded jointly to Dorset County Council and local resident and enthusiast Terry Gough. Here Class 150/2 'Sprinter' No 150253 arrives with the 11.10am service from Weymouth to Bristol Temple Meads on 12 December 2005. Note the newly installed nameboard which now reads 'Thornford alight here for Beer Hackett.
Terry Gough

from Cheltenham (2), Great Malvern (2) plus one each from Worcester Shrub Hill, Gloucester and Bristol Temple Meads. Two trains ran from Westbury to Yeovil Pen Mill arriving at 10.35 and 15.35. On Sundays there were four arrivals at Weymouth from Bristol Temple Meads with a fifth from Swindon at 15.54. The service is operated by Great Western Railway using Class 165/1 'Turbo' and Class 166 'Express Turbo' units.

2.2 Taunton – Exeter St David's

The 30¾ miles of railway from Taunton to Exeter St David's was opened by the Bristol & Exeter Railway in May 1844. Built by I. K. Brunel to his broad gauge, it joined the GWR at Bristol, creating the first through line from the capital to Exeter. Stations opened between Taunton and Exeter St David's included those at the market towns of Wellington and Cullompton, while Tiverton was initially served by Tiverton Road, some 4¾ miles from the town. The branch to Tiverton opened four years later when Tiverton Road became Tiverton Junction. A further branch to Hemyock opened in 1876. This was also the year that the B&E was taken over by the GWR.

Situated on the GWR's main line to the West Country, the stopping services on the line were often an inconvenience. This was especially true during the summer, when the capacity of the line was severely stretched by the number of holiday trains from London, the Midlands and the North of England. During the depression of the 1920s the Government made money available for capital schemes, which would ease unemployment. The GWR took advantage of this scheme to carry out work to relieve the congestion. In 1932 the track through Taunton was quadrupled as far west as Norton Fitzwarren. The intermediate stations at Wellington, Sampford Peverell, Tiverton Junction, Cullompton and Stoke Canon were all completely rebuilt to include four tracks: two at the platform faces for stopping trains and two central tracks for the expresses to pass.

Ex-GWR 'Large Prairie' tank No 4165 leaves Cullompton with the 6.15pm service from Taunton to Exeter on 19 March 1962. No 4165 was built at Swindon in 1948, after nationalisation, and was withdrawn in October 1965. The station at Cullompton was rebuilt in the 1930s with two additional through lines to allow expresses to pass stopping passenger trains. The station closed in September 1964. *Ron Lumber, David Mitchell collection*

By 1963 the stations at Norton Fitzwarren and Stoke Canon had already closed, in 1961 and 1960 respectively, while the remaining eight stations were all on the Beeching list for closure. In the summer there were four stopping trains on weekdays, supplemented by two semi-fast trains calling only at the principal stations, one of which was a through train from Paddington to Plymouth via Bristol. On Saturday, however, because of continuing heavy holiday traffic only two stopping trains ran, together with three semi-fast trains. At the time a number of trains were regularly steam-hauled, mainly by 'Hall' Class 4-6-0s. These were among

The station layout at Tiverton Junction was also enlarged in the 1930s. Here one of the GWR's large mixed-traffic 2-8-0s, No 4707, built at Swindon in 1923, stands in the station with the 3.00pm train from Exeter to Taunton on 29 August 1963. Only nine of these machines were built and by 1963 three had already been withdrawn, No 4707 going in May 1964. Despite being listed for closure, Tiverton Junction station survived until 1986, when it was replaced by Tiverton Parkway, which remains open today. *Author*

Ex-GWR 'Modified Hall' 4-6-0 No 6965 *Thirlestaine Hall* passes Wellington station with a West Country express during the summer of 1962. Like Cullompton and Tiverton Junction, the station was rebuilt with four tracks during the 1930s, and a banking engine was kept there to assist goods trains up the Wellington Bank to Whiteball Tunnel; at this time this engine was ex-GWR 'Large Prairie' No 4143. *M. E. J. Deane collection, courtesy of Ian Bennett*

the last steam turns on the BR(WR) main line west of Taunton. The BR(WR) timetable for the winter of 1962/63 is shown on pages 42 - 43.

Formal proposals to close all eight intermediate stations were published in the spring of 1964 and seven were subsequently closed in October. Wellington received the distinction of being the largest market town on the West of England main line to lose its rail service! Tiverton Junction, however, survived (although the branch to Tiverton was closed in November 1964), and remained in use until May 1986 when it was demolished to make way for the M5 motorway; at the same time a new station, Tiverton Parkway, was opened on the site of Sampford Peverell Halt some 2 miles to the north. It is served by a series of trains between London, the Midlands and the South West operated by Great Western Railway and CrossCountry.

All intermediate stations between Taunton and Exeter St David's apart from Tiverton Junction closed from 5 October 1964. While the up platform line at Wellington had been removed, that for the down platform was retained for the banking engine that was still based there, by this time a Type 3 'Hymek' diesel-hydraulic. One of the class No D7077 is pictured backing an engineer's train into the down platform line on Sunday 27 June 1965. The hymek was withdrawn in July 1972 *Author*

Although listed for closure, the station at Tiverton Junction survived after the closure of the six other stations between Taunton and Exeter St David's in September 1964. It finally closed in May 1986 to be replaced by a new station, Tiverton Parkway, near the site of the former Sampford Peverell Halt. With its passengers safely on board, the Great Western Railway 13.55 service from Plymouth to Paddington is seen leaving the station on Saturday 29 December 2018. The train is formed of two five-car Class 802 units, built by Hitachi earlier that year. Such is the popularity of the station that parking and drop-off facilities can be very congested. *Author*

BR(WR) Timetable 81, 10 September 1962-16 June 1963, showing trains between Taunton and Exeter St David's (Chapter 2.2), Exeter St David's and Kingswear (Chapter 2.3) and Plymouth and Penzance (Chapter 2.4) between 11.15am and 7.38pm. Note the departure from Paddington of the 'Cornish Riviera' and 'Torbay Express' at 10.30am and 12.30pm respectively, with through coaches to Kingswear and Penzance. In addition the 'Cornishman' and 'Devonian' ran from Sheffield and Bradford to Paignton.

Table 81				WEEK DAYS—continued												
Table 81—continued		LONDON, TAUNTON, EXETER, TORQUAY, PLYMOUTH and PENZANCE														
		pm	pm	am	am	pm	pm	pm	am	pm	pm	pm	am	pm	pm	pm
61 PADDINGTON 62dp		..	..	9 30	..	..	..	..	1030	..	..	..	11 30	..	..	..
61 Reading General 62 ,,		..	..	..	..	..	..	..		..	..	..		..	..	..
62 Newbury 62 ,,		..	..	..	..	..	..	..		..	..	..		..	..	..
62 Westbury ,,		..	..	..	..	..	..	..		..	..	..	12 5	..	..	..
61 Bristol (T. Meads). ,,		..	..	..	1120	..	..	..	1247	..	..	..	1 4	..	..	..
61 Taunton 62 .... arr		..	..	11 48	1217	..	..	..		..	..	..		..	..	..
		pm	pm	am	am	pm	pm	pm	am	pm	pm	pm	pm	pm	pm	pm
Taunton .... dep		11 15	11 52	1221				1250			1 8			2 30		
Norton Fitzwarren M..		..	..													
Wellington (Som.)		11 27														
Burlescombe		11 36														
Sampford Peverell Halt		11 41														
Tiverton Junction....		11 46														
Cullompton		11 52														
Hele and Bradninch ...		12 0														
Silverton		12 4														
Exeter (St. David's) { arr		12 15	12 25	1253			1 22		1 42							
Exeter (St. David's) { dep		12 31	1258	1 5	1 30		1 47						2 34			
Exeter (St. Thomas)....				1 8	1 35							2 44				
Exminster		..		1 18								2 49				
Starcross for Exmouth...		..		1 23				2 3				2 54				
Dawlish Warren......		..		1 28				2 11								
Dawlish............		..		1 35				2 20				3 1				
Teignmouth		12 55														
Newton Abbot .. arr		1 23	1 44				2 1									
Newton Abbot .. dep		1 10	1 35				2 4			2 30		2 50	3 1			
Kingskerswell																
Torre .... arr		1 20	1 46		2 15	2 43										
Torquay .... { arr		1 26	1 51		2 17	2 48			3 23							
Torquay .... { dep		1 29	1 53		2 25	2 51			3 27							
Paignton		1 35	2 0			2 57			3 29							
Goodrington Sands Halt													3 36			
Churston (for Brixham)..					2 36											
Kingswear .... arr					2 41				3 49							
Dartmouth W. ,,					2 59				3 58							
Newton Abbot .. dep		1 29			2 26		2 44						4 11			
Totnes		1 47	2 7										Stop			
Brent																
92 Kingsbridge .. arr		2 59			3 17	3 35										
Plymouth .... { arr		2 26														
Plymouth .... { dep		33 45	2 26		2 37	2 50	3 10	3 25			3 43	3 46				
Devonport, Albert Rd..		37 49			2 41		3 15					3 50				
Dockyard Halt.......		39 51			2 43											
Keyham		41 53			2 45		3 18					3 55				
St. Budeaux, Ferry Rd.,.		44 56			2 48		3 20					3 59				
Saltash............		48 2 0			2 52		3 25					4 4				
St. Germans							Stop					4 13				
Menheniot																
Liskeard					3 54					4 11	4 32					
96 Looe .. arr											5 65	6 ..				
Doublebois					4 11				4 30	4 40						
Bodmin Road 97										4 37	4 58					
Lostwithiel																
98 Fowey .. arr				4§22					4 55							
Par................				3 42	3 51	4 25			4 48	5 8						
99 Newquay .. arr				4 47		5 30			5 57							
St. Austell.........					4 14	4 37			5 0	5 20						
Grampound Road									5 31							
Truro............ arr				4 11		4 59			5 22	5 43						
101 Falmouth .. arr				5 0	pm	5B50			5 56	6 31						
Truro............ dep				4 15	4 20	5 3	5 15			5 51						
Chacewater					4 30		5 26			pm						
Scorrier					4 35		5 32			6 9						
Redruth...........					4 45	5 20	5 38			6 15	6 25					
Camborne				4 39	4 52	5 28	5 45			6 23						
Gwinear Road					4 58					6 30						
102 Helston .. arr				5 25	5 25											
Hayle				5 5		5 56			6 37							
St. Erth...........				4 51	5 11	5 42	6 3			6 43						
103 St. Ives .. arr				5 37					6 59							
Marazion						5 51			6 51							
Penzance .... arr				5 5	5 27	5 55	6 19			6 59						

(Notes running vertically in columns of table:) Saturdays only · Except Saturdays · Runs 15th, 22nd, 29th September, 1962 and from 25th May, 1963 · TC Paddington to Paignton · RB and TC Paddington to Paignton · Western National Omnibus — Heavy luggage not conveyed · MB and TC Cardiff to Paignton · TC Cardiff to Plymouth · CORNISH RIVIERA EXPRESS · RC and TC Paddington to Penzance · TC Paddington to Kingswear · THE CORNISHMAN · TC Sheffield to Penzance (Table 16) · Stop · RB and TC Sheffield to Penzance · RC & TC Paddington to Plymouth · TC Paddington to Paignton · Also conveys TC to Falmouth (Plymouth dep 3 43 pm) on Saturdays only from 25th May, 1963 · Runs until 29th September, 20th, 21st and 22nd December, 1962, 8th to 11th and 15th to 20th April, 1963, and Sats. from 25th May · Saturdays only and commences 25th May, 1963 TC Paddington dep 11 30 am to Falmouth · Stop · Western National Omnibus — Heavy luggage not conveyed

WEEK DAYS—continued   **Table 81**

Table 81—continued   LONDON, TAUNTON, EXETER, TORQUAY, PLYMOUTH and PENZANCE

	pm	pm	pm	pm	pm	pm	pm	pm	pm	pm	pm	pm	pm	pm	pm	pm	pm	pm
61 PADDINGTON 62 dp	..	..	..	12 30	..	..	..	..	..	..	..	..	2 30	..	..	..	..	..
61 Reading General 62 "	..	..	..	1 10	..	..	..	..	..	..	..	..	..	..	..	..	..	..
62 Newbury .. "	..	..	..	..	..	..	..	..	..	..	..	..	..	..	..	..	..	..
62 Westbury .. "	..	..	..	2 11	..	..	..	..	..	..	..	..	..	..	..	..	..	..
61 Bristol (T. Meads). "	..	..	..	3 0	..	2 10	..	3 20	..	..	..	..	..	..	..	4 5	..	..
61 Taunton 62 .. arr	..	..	..	..	..	3 5	..	4 11	..	..	..	..	4 47	..	..	5 13	..	..

	pm	pm	pm	pm	pm	pm	pm	pm	pm	pm	pm	pm	pm	pm	pm	pm	pm	pm
Taunton .. .. dep	..	..	..	3 3	..	3 12	..	4 14	..	..	..	4 20	4 50	..	..	5 19	..	..
Norton Fitzwarren M ..	..	..	..	..	..	..	..	..	..	..	..	..	..	..	..	..	..	..
Wellington (Som.) ..	..	..	..	..	..	..	..	..	..	..	..	4 34	..	..	..	..	..	..
Burlescombe ..	..	..	..	..	..	..	..	..	..	..	..	4 43	..	..	..	..	..	..
Sampford Peverell Halt .	..	..	..	..	..	..	..	..	..	..	..	4 48	..	..	..	..	..	..
Tiverton Junction ..	..	..	..	..	..	..	..	..	..	..	..	5 0	..	..	5 14	..	..	..
Cullompton ..	..	..	..	..	..	..	..	..	..	..	..	5 4	..	..	5 22	..	..	..
Hele and Bradninch ..	..	..	..	..	..	..	..	..	..	..	..	..	..	..	5 26	..	..	..
Silverton	..	..	..	..	..	..	..	..	..	..	..	..	..	..	5 37	..	..	..
Exeter (St. David's) { arr	..	..	..	3 35	..	3 47	..	4 48	..	..	..	..	5 22	..	..	5 56	..	..
dep	..	..	..	3 40	..	3 52	..	4 25 4 52	5 8	..	..	5 27	5 35 5 47	6 3	..	..	..	..
Exeter (St. Thomas) ..	..	..	..	..	..	..	..	4 28	5 11	..	..	..	5 38 5 52	..	..	..	..	..
Exminster ..	..	..	..	..	..	..	..	4 38	5 21	..	..	..	..	..	..	..	..	..
Starcross for Exmouth ..	..	..	..	..	..	..	..	4 43	5 26	..	..	..	5 48 6 2	..	..	..	..	..
Dawlish Warren ..	..	..	..	..	..	4 9	..	4 48	5 37	..	..	..	5 53 6 7	..	..	..	..	..
Dawlish ..	..	..	..	..	..	4 17	..	4 55	..	..	..	..	5 58 6 12 6 21	..	..	..	..	..
Teignmouth ..	..	..	..	..	..	4 26	..	5 4 5 18	5 46	..	..	..	6 6 56 19 6 29	..	..	..	..	..
Newton Abbot .. arr	..	..	..	4 5	..	..	..	..	..	..	..	5 52	6 14 6 28 6 38	..	..	..	..	..

	pm	pm	pm	pm	pm	pm	pm	pm	pm	pm	pm	pm	pm	pm	pm
Newton Abbot .. dep	..	4 9	..	4 32	..	5 7	5 30	..	..	..	6 26 6 20	..	6 44	..	..
Kingskerswell ..	..	..	..	..	..	5 12	5 36	..	..	..	6 24	..	..	..	..
Torre .. arr	..	4 22	..	4 42	..	5 18	5 45	..	..	..	6 14 6 31	..	6 55	..	..
Torquay { arr	..	4 25	..	4 47	..	5 22	5 50	..	..	..	6 19 6 35	..	7 0	..	..
dep	..	4 33	..	4 50	..	5 24	5 52	..	..	..	6 21 6 36	..	7 4	..	..
Paignton ..	..	..	..	4 58	..	5 30	5 58	..	..	..	6 28 6 41	..	7 10	..	..
Goodrington Sands Halt ..	..	..	..	..	..	..	..	..	..	..	6 39	..	..	..	..
Churston (for Brixham) ..	..	4 53	..	5 11	..	5 40	..	..	..	..	6 48	..	..	..	..
Kingswear .. arr	..	5 11	..	5 20	..	5 49	..	..	..	..	6 59	..	..	..	..
Dartmouth W. ..	..	..	..	5 35	..	5 59	..	..	..	..	..	..	..	..	..

	pm	pm	pm	pm	pm	pm	pm	pm	pm	pm	pm	pm	pm	pm
Newton Abbot .. dep	4 15	..	4 15	..	4 40	..	5 24	..	..	..	5 58	..	..	6 45
Totnes ..	4 15	..	..	..	4 58	..	5 42	..	..	..	6 16	..	..	..
Brent	4 30	..	..	..	5 17	..	6 1	..	..	..	6 35	..	..	..
92 Kingsbridge .. arr	..	..	..	..	5 52	..	..	..	..	..	7 10	..	..	..
Plymouth { arr	..	..	5 8	..	5 42	..	6 26	..	..	..	7 0	..	..	7 30
dep	4 29 4 40	..	5 16 5 23	..	5 50	..	..	6 44	..	7 9	..	..	7 38
Devonport, Albert Rd. ..	4 34 4 45	..	5 27	..	5 54	..	..	6 47	..	..	..	..	7 42
Dockyard Halt ..	..	..	..	..	..	..	..	6 49	..	..	..	..	7 44
Keyham ..	4 38 4 50	..	5 30	..	5 57	..	..	6 52	..	..	..	..	7 46
St. Budeaux, Ferry Rd. ..	4 41 4 54	..	5 33	..	6 0	..	..	6 55	..	..	..	..	7 49
Saltash ..	4 47 4 59	..	5 38	..	6 4	..	..	7 1	7 18	..	..	7 53
St. Germans ..	4 55 7	..	5 46	..	6 12	..	..	7 10	..	..	..	8 1
Menheniot ..	5 45 16	..	5 56	..	6 22	..	..	..	..	..	..	8 11
Liskeard ..	5 11 5 23	..	5 46 6 4	..	6 30	..	..	7 39	..	..	8 18
96 Looe .. .. arr	..	..	6 25	..	..	..	..	..	8 15	..	..	..
Doublebois ..	5 18 5 30	..	6 11	..	..	..	..	..	..	..	..	..
Bodmin Road 97 ..	5 28 5 40	..	6 5	..	6 46	..	..	7 55	..	..	..
Lostwithiel ..	5 34 5 46	..	6 12	..	6 52	..	..	8 2	..	..	..
98 Fowey .. .. arr	6 10 6 10	..	6 51	..	7§49	..	..	8§54	..	..	..
Par ..	5 43 5 55	..	6 23	..	7 2	..	..	8 13	..	..	..
99 Newquay .. arr	..	..	7 22	..	8L48	..	..	10 t 4	..	..	..
St. Austell ..	5 53 6 5	..	6 35	..	7 13	..	..	8 25	..	..	..
Grampound Road ..	..	..	..	..	7 24	..	..	..	..	..	..
Truro .. arr	..	..	6 57	..	7 34	..	..	8 47	..	..	..
101 Falmouth .. arr	..	..	7 32	..	8 21	..	..	9 31	..	..	..
Truro .. dep	..	..	7 1	..	7 36	..	..	8 50	..	..	..
Chacewater ..	..	..	7 12	..	..	..	..	..	..	..	..
Scorrier ..	..	..	..	..	..	..	..	..	..	..	..
Redruth ..	..	..	7 22	..	7 50	..	..	9 6	..	..	..
Camborne ..	..	..	7 29	..	7 58	..	..	9 13	..	..	..
Gwinear Road ..	..	..	7 35	..	..	..	..	9 19	..	..	..
102 Helston .. arr	..	..	8 10	..	..	..	..	9 50	..	..	..
Hayle ..	..	..	7 42	..	8 7	..	..	9 26	..	..	..
St. Erth ..	..	..	7 47	..	8 12	..	..	9 32	..	..	..
103 St. Ives .. arr	..	..	8 5	..	9Z12	..	..	10G 8	..	..	..
Marazion ..	..	..	..	..	..	..	..	..	..	..	..
Penzance .. arr	..	..	8 0	..	8 25	..	..	9 45	..	..	..

For Notes see page 177

Column headings (vertical): TC Paddington to Kingswear · Except Fridays and Saturdays · Fridays only · TORBAY EXPRESS · RC and TC Paddington to Kingswear · TC Paddington to Penzance · TC Liverpool to Kingswear (Table 168) · RC and TC Liverpool to Plymouth · MB Bristol to Plymouth · TC Cardiff to Plymouth · TC Cardiff to Paignton · To Newton Abbot Cullompton dep 5 14 pm · RB Paddington to Plymouth · TC Paddington to Penzance · 4 20 pm from Taunton · THE DEVONIAN · TC Paddington to Kingswear · RB, RC and TC Bradford to Paignton (Table 17)

G. W. R.

TORQUAY

G. W. R.

Torre

2.3 Exeter St David's – Kingswear

The line between Exeter St David's and Kingswear was the next section of the main line to Plymouth and Penzance. It was again engineered by I. K. Brunel, this time working for the South Devon Railway (SDR). The line is famous for the stretch along the coast between Dawlish and Teignmouth and for the unsuccessful use by Brunel of the atmospheric system. The latter involved the propulsion of trains by a vacuum created in a continuous pipe laid in the centre of the broad-gauge track. One of the old pumping stations still exists at Starcross. The line opened with steam haulage in 1846 and the atmospheric system was completed two years later, but only lasted six months before it was abandoned because of overwhelming technical problems.

At Newton (later Newton Abbot), 20 miles from Exeter, the South Devon Railway main line continued to Plymouth, while a branch to Torquay was constructed, opening in December 1848. A number of proposals were made to extend the line to Kingswear, convenient for the Royal Naval College across the River Dart at Dartmouth. Little happened until the Dartmouth & Torbay Railway (D&TR) started work in the 1850s. The line opened to Brixham Road (later Churston, junction for the Brixham branch) in 1861, but a further three years were to elapse before passenger trains reached Kingswear, 19¼ miles from Newton Abbot. Here passengers were transported across the Dart by ferry to a floating pontoon at Dartmouth. In 1872 the D&TR was amalgamated with the SDR, then in 1876 the SDR was itself absorbed by the GWR.

The railway line between Exeter and Newton Abbot is famous for its views across the estuaries of the Rivers Exe and Teign, together with those over the English Channel. The line and its wayside stations saw heavy holiday traffic and although five were listed for closure, only two, Exminster and Kingskerswell, did so from 30 March and 5 October 1964 respectively. Here an ex-GWR 'Hall' Class 4-6-0 leaves Dawlish station with a stopping train from Exeter St David's during May 1960. *M. E. J. Deane collection, courtesy of Ian Bennett*

The line was renowned for its holiday destinations. The five stations between Exeter St David's and Newton Abbot included Dawlish Warren, Dawlish and Teignmouth. Among the further six stations between Newton Abbot and Kingswear were the resorts of Torquay and Paignton. Newton Abbot station was substantially enlarged in 1927, while in 1930 the platforms at Paignton station were lengthened and extra carriage sidings constructed at Goodrington. The line also benefited from the Government job creation scheme of the 1930s, when four tracks were

The line is still much used by holidaymakers today. Dawlish Warren station retains its through lines, which allow expresses to overtake stopping trains. First Great Western 'Pacer' unit No 143620 approaches the station as the 12.35 service from Paignton to Exeter Central while an HST set passes with a westbound express from Paddington on 10 December 2009. The eight camping coaches visible in the old station yard were completely refurbished during 2017/2018. During 2019 the 'Brunel Boutique Camping Coach Park' was promoted by Blue Chip Holidays. *Author*

provided through Exminster and Dawlish Warren stations to allow the many expresses to pass the local passenger trains. Although the passenger services on the line were only listed for 'modification', the stations at Exeter St Thomas, Exminster, Starcross, Kingskerswell and Churston were listed for closure. Exminster and Kingskerswell stations subsequently closed in March and October 1964 respectively, although Exeter St Thomas and Starcross remain open. Churston also remained open at least for the time being. The BR(WR) timetable for the winter of 1962/63 is shown on pages 42 and 43.

Despite these closures the future of the line as a whole seemed to be secure. At the start of the 1960s the 6¾-mile line from Paignton to Kingswear still saw regular through coaches to and from London Paddington. In addition, the 'Devonian' ran from Bradford to Paignton with through coaches from Kingswear on summer Saturdays. After 1964 BR(WR) appeared to deliberately run down the service, and by the summer of 1966 just two through trains ran from London to Kingswear on Saturdays only, one of which was still named the 'Torbay Express'. All other services terminated at Paignton. All Sunday trains between Paignton and Kingswear were withdrawn after the summer of 1968.

Although only single track, the Kingswear line was available to all ex-GWR steam engines including the powerful 'King' Class 4-6-0s. Dieselisation of main-line services began in 1958 and steam was finally extinguished at the end of the summer of 1963. The line is rather an anomaly in that it was never officially closed by BR(WR). In December 1971 the Board of the Dart Valley Railway (DVR), which had recently taken over the Totnes to Buckfastleigh line, resolved to acquire responsibility for the Paignton to Kingswear line and to run it as both a tourist attraction and a year-round public service. In May 1972 it was reported that the purchase of the line from BR had been agreed for

Historically services on the line west of Dawlish Warren have frequently been disrupted by flooding from the sea; in February 2014 a substantial length of line was washed out and services were suspended for eight weeks. Network Rail has subsequently implemented a costly series of flood prevention measures, but the line was once again breached in March 2018. Even on a relatively quiet day waves still wet the coastal footpath between Dawlish Warren and Dawlish as a four-Car 'CrossCountry' Class 220 'Voyager' unit passes on 10 December 2009 forming the 14.25 service from Plymouth to Edinburgh. *Author*

£250,000 and that a Light Railway Order was being applied for. BR(WR) relinquished responsibility for the line from Saturday 28 October 1972. However after failing to get agreements from the railway unions, BR ran a DMU service, subsidised by Devon County Council until the DVR's steam operation started on Monday 1 January 1973. The winter service ran mainly for school children using restored ex-Barry 'Small Prairie' No. 4588. This engine was soon joined by 4-6-0 No 7827 *Lydham Manor*. Both ex-GWR engines had been rescued from Barry scrapyard and restored at

Kingswear station is pictured on 30 March 1964. On the left a BR(WR) three-car 'Cross Country' Class 120 DMU waits to form a service to Exeter St David's. These units were built at Swindon Works from 1957. *Author*

In this general view of Kingswear on 15 September 1966, although the dockside sidings are long gone the station remains much the same today thanks to its acquisition by the heritage Torbay & Dartmouth Railway in September 1972. A Class 118 DMU is standing in the right-hand platform under the station canopy. The engine servicing facilities, including a turntable, which were situated behind the camera, were removed by BR(WR), but a new turntable was subsequently installed at Churston. J. M. Tolson, Frank Hornby collection

The Class 118 DMU seen in the previous photograph standing under the station canopy at Kingswear is seen again on the same day, forming a service for Newton Abbot. J. M. Tolson, Frank Hornby collection

Swindon Works and at Buckfastleigh respectively. After 1973 the subsidies were withdrawn and the railway operated during the summer months only. The line is now operated by the Paignton & Dartmouth Steam Railway using mainly ex-GWR steam engines.

The line from Exeter to Paignton remains open today and is served mainly by local trains to and from Exmouth operated by Great Western Railway with 'Sprinter' and 'Pacer' units. In the autumn of 2019 there was one through train a day from London, which ran as the 'Torbay Express' on weekdays. Great Western Railway also ran a through train from Cardiff which arrived at Paignton at 11.20. In addition through trains from York and Manchester Piccadilly were operated by CrossCountry (CC). On Sundays Paignton saw one arrival from Paddington and one from Manchester Piccadilly. On Saturdays until 6 September There were two Great Western Railway arrivals from Paddington, the second of which was the Torbay Express. CC ran through trains from Birmingham New Street,

The final view of the same DMU sees it after arrival at Paignton with its service from Kingswear to Newton Abbot. J. M. Tolson, Frank Hornby collection

Leeds, Manchester Piccadilly and Glasgow Central. Only the Manchester train ran throughout the year.

Although not part of the Devon & Cornwall Rail Partnership, the line is promoted as the 'Riviera Line'. The steam-hauled 'Torbay Express' has also seen a renaissance in the form of the steam-hauled charter trains between Bristol and Kingswear operated by Torbay Express Ltd during the summer months and at Christmas. These have been scaled back in recent years with just five trains were advertised between July and September 2019. These were due to run alternately via Weston-super-Mare and Bath/Westbury. In the event several of these were afflicted by engine failures and restrictions due to the fire risk.

A year after the line's transfer to the Torbay & Dartmouth Railway ex-GWR steam power had reappeared on the Kingswear branch. Here Class '6400' pannier tank No 6412 climbs away from Goodrington with a train from Paignton to Kingswear in September 1973. No 6412 was built in 1934 and withdrawn in November 1964. It was purchased from BR for use on the embryo DVR at Buckfastleigh, but was then transferred to the Torbay & Dartmouth Railway. It later spent some years on the West Somerset Railway, but has returned to the DVR, now operating as the South Devon Railway. The Kingswear line is now known as the Dartmouth Steam Railway. Author

The Paignton & Dartmouth Steam Railway is frequently the host to steam-hauled specials from the main line. Here unrebuilt 'Battle of Britain' 'Pacific' No 34067 *Tangmere* propels the stock of the 'Torbay Express' from Bristol Temple Meads out of Kingswear station on 13 July 2008. No 34067 will then run light engine to Churston where it will turn on the railway's turntable. The engine was withdrawn in November 1963 and spent 16 years at Barry scrapyard before being purchased for preservation. *Author*

2.4 Plymouth to Penzance

The 79½ miles of broad-gauge railway from Plymouth to Penzance presented many difficulties for its engineer I. K. Brunel. The greatest involved crossing the 1,100-foot-wide River Tamar, just 4 miles from Plymouth, at a height that would not interfere with navigation by high-masted naval vessels. Brunel's solution was the spectacular Royal Albert Bridge at Saltash, opened by the Prince Consort on 2 May 1859, and still carrying trains today. In addition, because of the many valleys running down to the sea on the Cornish coast, numerous viaducts were also required – between Plymouth and Truro alone there were 34. To meet this challenge Brunel produced a brilliant design using standard lengths of yellow pine from the Baltic coast. Each length was designed to be easily replaced without disrupting traffic. The pine had a life expectancy of between 30 and 60 years and the viaducts remained a feature of the line for many years, the last only being replaced in 1931, when Baltic pine was no longer available.

The interior of Penzance station is seen here on 12 July 1955, with ex-GWR 'Modified Hall' No 7916 *Mobberley Hall* having arrived with a stopping train from Newton Abbot. No 7916 was built for BR(WR) in 1950 and withdrawn in December 1964. Many of the intermediate stations between Plymouth and Penzance closed on 5 October 1964. *Frank Hornby*

St Erth station, the junction
for St Ives, is seen in
May 1960 with ex-GWR
'Grange' Class 4-6-0
No 6825 *Llanvair Grange*
standing in the up platform
with a single luggage van.
St Erth was not one of the
stations listed for closure,
although the branch from
there to St Ives was.
Despite this, the branch
survives today. *M. E. J.
Deane collection, courtesy of
Ian Bennett*

The line between Plymouth
and Penzance abounds
with bridges and viaducts.
Many of these were
originally built in timber to
the design of I. K. Brunel
when the line opened in
1850s. The most iconic
structure was, however,
the Royal Albert Bridge,
Brunel's masterpiece over
the River Tamar east of
Saltash, which opened in
April 1859 shortly before
Brunel's death. Here an
ex-GWR 'County' Class
4-6-0 comes off the single
line over the bridge with
an up BR(WR) express
during 1959. The train
comprises new BR Mark 1
coaches in chocolate and
cream livery; it is therefore
either the 'Cornish Riviera'
or 'Cornishman' express.
*M. E. J. Deane collection,
courtesy of Ian Bennett*

The line was built in two sections. The first to open, in April 1852, was the West Cornwall Railway's line from Penzance to Redruth. In May 1857, following the opening of the Royal Albert Bridge, it was joined by the Cornwall Railway's line from Plymouth. The line served many of the more important towns in Cornwall, with a series of branch lines to the holiday resorts on the Cornish coast. In North Cornwall the resorts of Padstow and St Ives were reached by branch lines from Bodmin Road and St Erth respectively, while Newquay could be reached by branch lines from both Par and Chacewater. To the south branch lines to Looe, Fowey and Falmouth left the main line at Liskeard, Lostwithiel and Truro respectively. A further

branch ran from Gwinear Road on the main line to Helston. For a hundred years the line was among the most popular in the country with holidaymakers.

By 1876 the whole area was under the control of the GWR, which began actively promoting its potential for holiday traffic. By the early 20th century posters, books and even jigsaws appeared, including in 1908 a poster that compared the outline of Cornwall with that of Italy. It read 'There is a great similarity between Cornwall and Italy in shape, climate and natural beauty'! Until 1906 all GWR trains from Paddington to Plymouth had to run via Bristol, leading critics to dub the company 'the Great Way Round'. In that year a shorter route

Gwinear Road was one of the nine stations between Plymouth and Penzance listed for closure in the Beeching Report. It was also the junction for the Helston branch. The passenger service to Helston was withdrawn in November 1962, while Gwinear Road station closed on 5 October 1964, together with five others on the line. Here a 'Warship' diesel-hydraulic and a rake of chocolate and cream coaches approach the station with the down 'Cornish Riviera Express' in May 1960. *M. E. J. Deane collection, courtesy of Ian Bennett*

via Newbury, Westbury and Somerton was opened, giving a journey time to Penzance of less than 7 hours. At the same time the 10.30am from Paddington was officially named the 'Cornish Riviera Limited'. Its departure time was to remain the same until 1972. The BR(WR) timetable for the winter of 1962/63 is shown on page pages 42 and 43.

Over the years the number of intermediate stations varied, but by 1963 twenty two still remained between Penzance and Plymouth. Four of these were situated on the outskirts of Plymouth itself and enjoyed a frequent service of stopping trains between the city and Saltash on the Cornish side of the Tamar. For many years the service had been worked by push-pull-fitted ex-GWR 0-4-2 and 0-6-0 pannier tanks, but DMUs took over the service in 1960. The Cornish peninsula was the first to be dieselised by BR(WR) and the 'Cornish Riviera' was diesel-hauled from August 1958. Steam was eliminated from the branch lines by September 1961 and from all other trains a year later. The last BR steam engine to cross the Royal Albert Bridge was 'West Country' 'Pacific' No 34002 *Salisbury*, which hauled an enthusiasts' special from Plymouth to Penzance on 3 May 1964.

West of Saltash the service in the summer of 1963 comprised a number of trains between Plymouth and Penzance stopping at virtually all stations, while a further local service ran from Truro to Penzance. Seven through trains arrived from London Paddington, including an overnight sleeper and the 'Cornish Riviera'. In addition the 'Mayflower' express ran as far as Truro. Other long-distance trains included the 'Cornishman' from Sheffield and a service from Glasgow and Manchester. Many additional trains ran on summer Saturdays, including two overnight trains from Newcastle to Penzance and Newquay. In addition the 'Cornish Riviera' carried through coaches to St Ives. By this time,

BR Class 47 diesel-electric No 47565 (formerly No D1620) enters Par with the 1.00pm train from Plymouth to Penzance on 29 March 1989. These Sulzer-powered engines were built by Brush from 1962, and replaced the Western Region fleet of 'Warship' and 'Western' diesel-hydraulic locos in the 1970s. 'Super Sprinter' DMUs were introduced to the service shortly after the photo was taken. Par was the junction for the Newquay branch, which, like the main line, was also subject to Dr Beeching's 'Modification' proposals (see Chapter 2.5). *Author*

however, the branches to Helston and Newquay via Chacewater had already closed.

The Beeching Report proposed the closure of nine intermediate stations and all of the remaining branch lines apart from those to Newquay and Falmouth. In the event six of these stations were closed in 1964 but three, at Menheniot, Lostwithiel and Hayle, survived and remain open today. In addition, as will be described in Chapter 3, BR(WR) failed to obtain approval for the closure of the branch lines to Looe and St Ives (Chapters 3.21 and 3.22).

The rail map of Cornwall today therefore looks very different from that envisaged by Dr Beeching in 1963. Even the 7½-mile section between Burngullow near St Austell and Probus near Truro, which was singled in the 1960s, was restored to double track in August 2004. Today local and London trains are operated by Great Western Railway, while those to the Midlands and North are part of the CrossCountry franchise. The daily (Sundays excepted) overnight sleeper service between Paddington and Penzance is now the last to run between two English termini.

Soon to be replaced by new Hitachi-built Class 802 units, an HST unit, headed by power car No 43170 with No 43194 at the rear, leaves Lostwithiel with Great Western Railway's 09.26 service from Exeter St David's to Penzance on Friday 28 December 2018. Despite being listed for closure, the station has survived, together with one of its two distinctive palm trees. Five other stations between Plymouth and Penzance closed in October 1964. The remaining semaphore signals on the line are also now due for replacement. *Author*

St Columb Road station, 6½ miles from Newquay, was one of those listed for closure in the Beeching Report, but survives today. Ex-GWR 'Small Prairie' No 4587 calls there during the spring of 1960. No 4587 was built at Swindon in 1927 and withdrawn in August 1960. *M. E. J. Deane collection, courtesy of Ian Bennett*

2.5 Par to Newquay

The spacious station at Newquay, well able to cope with heavy summer traffic, is visible in this view of ex-GWR 'Large Prairie' No 5193 standing in Platform 1 with a train for Par in the spring of 1960. The train comprises an ex-GWR 'B' set of two non-corridor coaches. No 5193 was built at Swindon in 1934 and withdrawn in June 1962. After 17 years at Barry scrapyard it was purchased for preservation by the '5193 Fund' and went to the now defunct Steamport Transport Museum at Southport. In 2003 it went to the West Somerset Railway, where it was restored and converted into a 2-6-0 tender engine, No 9351. *M. E. J. Deane collection, courtesy of Ian Bennett*

The branch line from Par to Newquay was opened by the Cornwall Minerals Railway in June 1876. The line incorporated sections of horse-worked mineral lines first opened in 1846. From October 1877 trains were operated by the GWR, which purchased the line in 1896. Newquay rapidly gained popularity as a holiday destination and through coaches from Paddington were introduced in 1907. The platforms at Newquay station were lengthened in 1928 and again in 1935 and 1938.

The BR(WR) timetable for the winter of 1962/63 (reproduced on page 42 and 43) shows that the 20¾-mile line had five intermediate stations with a stopping service of nine up and eight down trains each weekday. Additional trains ran on weekdays during the summer, when the service increased further to 17 up and 16 down trains on Saturdays.

A Class 118 three-car DMU heads away from St Dennis Junction near St Columb Road on 18 August 1969 forming the 09.48 service from Newquay to Bodmin Road via Par. The track of the former branch to St Dennis and Burngullow can be seen to the right. The section from St Dennis Junction to just south of St Dennis closed in 1960.
David Mitchell

Two of these were through trains to and from Paddington and one to and from Birmingham Snow Hill and Wolverhampton Low Level. By then all services had been dieselised. Local trains were operated by DMUs while diesel-hydraulics hauled the through trains. It is interesting to note that none of these through trains is shown in Table 99 of the 1963 Summer timetable, which shows only local trains to Par. The through services are only shown in the small print on Table 81, which included all services between Taunton and Penzance.

Dr Beeching envisaged a radical reduction of service on the branch. It is perhaps surprising that he did not propose its complete closure, as all five intermediate stations were so listed. The proposal to withdraw the stopping services was dropped and all five stations are open today,

Another Class 118 three-car DMU stands in Newquay's Platform 1 as the 2.20pm service to Par on 7 September 1965.
Author

Class 121 single-unit railcar No W55026 arrives at Newquay as the 10.25 service from Par on 29 April 1989. This was one of the Pressed Steel Co units built from 1960. Although the proposals to close all intermediate stations on the branch had been refused, by this time track rationalisation had taken place. Only one of the once lengthy platforms remains in use for just part of its length. The line is now promoted as the 'Atlantic Coast Line' by the Devon & Cornwall Rail Partnership. The station was substantially rebuilt in 2012 but still retains just one platform. *Author*

although facilities at Newquay station have been slowly run down. The platform roofs were removed in 1964 and the platforms themselves progressively shortened and reduced until by October 1987 only one remained. In addition, the number of passing loops was reduced to two, at Goonbarrow and St Dennis Junction. However, since then the line has seen a slow but steady renaissance. The line is promoted by the Devon & Cornwall Rail Partnership as the 'Atlantic Coast Line' (although it was never one of the destinations of the old Southern Railway's 'Atlantic Coast Express'). Since 2007 First Great Western/Great Western Railway has run a daily train to and from Paddington, which on Saturdays runs as the 'Atlantic Coast Express', while CrossCountry has run through trains from Dundee and Manchester. Other summer Saturday trains in 2019 came from Plymouth (two) and Exeter (one), while only one, which left Par at 20.23, called at all stations. In the autumn of 2019 there were six trains between Par and Newquay each weekday with seven on Saturdays and three on Sundays.

On its return journey to Par, No W55026 pauses at Quintrell Downs station, just 2¼ miles from Newquay. Like all other intermediate stations on the branch, this station was listed for closure but remains open today despite its rather basic facilities. *Author*

5
4/5
HST
2+4
PR
5

The extensive track formation around Par station on the former GWR Plymouth to Penzance main line was still controlled by semaphore signals in this view from Friday 28 December 2018. Class 150 DMU No 150244 leaves the station as Great Western Railway's 12.11 service to Newquay. *Author*

BRITISH RAILWAYS
THE RAILWAY EXECUTIVE
B.R. 21716/586
NEWQUAY

BR(WR) Timetable 99, 10 September 1962-16 June 1963, showing trains between Par and Newquay.

Table 99

PAR and NEWQUAY

Miles		Week Days am	am	am	pm	pm	pm	pm	pm G	pm	pm W	Sundays am H	am H	pm H
	Par dep	**6 35**	**7 20**	**1020**	**1248**	**2 43**	**3 50**	**4 35**	**4 58**	**6 27**	**8 15**	**9 0**	**1115**	**4 55**
4¼	Luxulyan	6 48	7 33	1035	1 1	2 58	4 5	4 48	5 13	6 40	8 30	9 13	1128	5 8
6¼	Bugle	6 54	7 39	1040	1 7	3 5	4 11	4 54	5 20	6 46	8 36	9 19	1134	5 14
8¾	Roche	7 0	7 45	1046	1 13	3 11	4 17	5 0	5 27	6 53	8 43	9 25	1140	5 20
14¼	St. Columb Road	7 14	7 58	11 2	1 27	3 25	4 31	5 14	5 41	7 7	8 57	9 39	1154	5 34
18½	Quintrel Downs	7 22	8 6	1110	1 35	3 33	4 39	5 22	5 49	7 15	..	9 47	12 2	5 42
20¾	**Newquay** arr	**7 29**	**8 13**	**1117**	**1 42**	**3 40**	**4 47**	**5 30**	**5 57**	**7 22**	**9 12**	**9 55**	**1210**	**5 50**

Miles		Week Days am	am	am T	am X	am	pm	pm	pm	pm	pm G	pm	pm	Sundays am H	pm H	pm H
	Newquay dep	**7 30**	**8 12**	**9 25**	**9 50**	**1045**	**1250**	**2 15**	**4 45**	**5 55**	**7 0**	**8 10**	**9 20**	**10 0**	**1 45**	**6 50**
2¼	Quintrel Downs	7 37	8 19	..	..	1052	1257	2 22	4 52	6 3	7 8	8 17	9 27	10 7	1 52	6 57
6½	St. Columb Road	7 46	8 28	9 40	10 5	11 1	1 7	2 30	5 0	6 12	7 17	8 26	9 36	1015	2 0	7 5
12	Roche	8 1	8 43	L	K	1116	1 24	2 46	5 14	6 27	7 32	8 43	9 50	1029	2 14	7 19
14½	Bugle	8 7	8 48	10 0	1025	1123	1 29	2 52	5 20	6 33	7 38	8 49	9 56	1035	2 20	7 25
16½	Luxulyan	8 14	8 54	10 6	1035	1129	1 35	2 57	5 26	6 40	7 44	8 55	10 2	1041	2 26	7 31
20¾	**Par** arr	**8 27**	**9 6**	**1018**	**1047**	**1141**	**1 47**	**3 9**	**5 39**	**6 56**	**7 58**	**9 8**	**1014**	**1054**	**2 39**	**7 44**

G Saturdays only and commences 25th May, 1963. Second class only

H Runs 16th and 23rd September, 1962 and from 2nd June, 1963

K Calls at 10 18 am to pick up passengers for London only on notice being given at the station by 9 30 am

L Calls at 9 53 am to take up passengers for London only on notice being given at the station by 9 0 am

T Saturdays only and commences 25th May, 1963

W Runs until 22nd September inclusive also on 20th, 21st, 22nd and 24th December, 1962 Monday 15th April and from 6th May 1963, Second class only

X Not on Saturdays commencing 25th May, 1963

2.6 Yeovil Junction - Exeter Central

The first standard-gauge railway to reach Yeovil was the Salisbury & Yeovil Railway in 1853. Three years later the London & South Western Railway (LSWR) started work on a 49-mile extension to Exeter. The single line opened in July 1860 and completed the LSWR main line from London Waterloo to Exeter Queen Street (renamed Exeter Central in 1933). Because of engineering constraints neither line reached the centre of Yeovil. Instead, a joint station was built at Yeovil Junction to the south, with a 1½-mile branch line into the town. The location of Yeovil Junction has caused problems to passengers trying to visit the town, or change to a connecting service at Yeovil Town or Pen Mill stations, ever since. The whole line between Salisbury and Exeter was doubled throughout by July 1870. In due course the LSWR extended its control to North Devon and, via the northern flanks of Dartmoor, to Plymouth and North Cornwall.

Ex-SR Class 'S15' No 30842 arrives at Seaton Junction with a Bulleid-designed three-coach set forming an up stopping train from Exeter Central to Salisbury on 2 July 1956. No 30842 was built by the SR in 1936 to an improved ex-LSWR design. A number of the class were shedded at Exmouth Junction until 1964, but did not usually work west of Exeter. No 30842 survived until withdrawal in 1965. Seaton Junction station was closed to passengers in March 1966 following closure of the branch line to Seaton, and the four tracks through the station were reduced to just one in 1967.
Frank Hornby

The line was to provide a fast service between London and the West Country for almost 90 years. Ten intermediate stations were eventually opened between Yeovil Junction and Exeter Central, including junctions at Chard, Seaton and Sidmouth, where branch lines diverged to their respective towns. In addition, the branch to Lyme Regis left the main line at Axminster. In 1923 the line passed to the Southern Railway and, as described in Chapter 1, on nationalisation to BR(SR). BR(WR) gained control of the lines from 1 January 1963.

The expresses from Waterloo were notable for the number of through coaches they included for the various destinations on the Devon and Cornwall coasts. On summer Saturdays in August 1962, the last year before BR(WR) took control of the line, 17 trains left Waterloo

Another sight never to be repeated at Yeovil Junction was the arrival of unrebuilt Bulleid 'West Country' 'Light Pacific' No 34099 *Lynmouth* on Saturday 5 September 1964 with the 1.10pm stopping train from Exeter Central to Yeovil Town. This train arrived at Chard Junction at 2.17pm and left again at 2.56pm. The two-coach train includes one Bulleid Brake, while the other coach is of LNER origin. From the following Monday all local trains west of Salisbury were worked by DMUs. No 34099 survived for just two more months, being withdrawn in November. *Author*

Saturday 5 September 1964 was the last day of the Summer timetable and the last before 'Modification' of the service by BR(WR). From the following Monday virtually all trains from Waterloo would terminate at Exeter St David's. Here 'Battle of Britain' Class No 34087 *145 Squadron* stands in the down platform at Yeovil Junction with the 11.15am train from Waterloo, which included through coaches to Plymouth, Padstow and Bude. Meanwhile 'Merchant Navy' Class No 35009 *Shaw Savill* heads through the up centre road with the up 'Atlantic Coast Express', the 10.30am service from Ilfracombe to Waterloo. *Author*

What is thought to be the only regular use of steam on a local train west of Salisbury in the summer of 1965 was the 9.20am from Salisbury to Exeter Central. Rebuilt 'Battle of Britain' 'Light Pacific' No 34052 *Lord Dowding* approaches Seaton Junction with the train on 29 August 1965. The return train left Exeter Central at 7.36pm *Author*

The track layout at
Yeovil Junction was much
simplified from 1967.
The down platform was
no longer used and the
footbridge across the
main lines demolished.
The up platform became
an island platform on
the 46-mile single-track
section from Pinhoe. Here
BR Class 50 No 50032
Courageous (formerly
No D432), running in
Network SouthEast livery,
approaches with the
12.25pm train from Exeter
St David's to Waterloo
on 12 October 1986. No
50032 was withdrawn in
October 1990 and broken
up at Old Oak Common
shortly afterwards. *Author*

with through coaches to destinations on the coastlines of both South
and North Devon and north Cornwall. Among them was the famous
'Atlantic Coast Express', which had first run in July 1926. In the winter
of 1962/63 the service was reduced to seven trains, which still included
through coaches to Plymouth, North Devon and Cornwall. The summer
through trains ran until September 1964, although both Lyme Regis and
Seaton (see Chapters 3.6 and 3.7) had lost their through coaches. In
1965 the number of additional through trains was reduced to just three,
with through coaches for Sidmouth and Exmouth (see Chapters 3.14 and
3.15). There were no additional summer trains from Waterloo in 1975.
Details of these trains are given in Appendices 3.1 to 3.3. The BR(SR)
timetable for the winter of 1962/63 is shown on pages 62 and 63.

The line attracted the attention of Dr Beeching, as Exeter was also
served by the BR(WR) route from Paddington, on which fast diesel-
hauled trains had already been introduced. The former BR(SR) route
was initially considered for complete closure, but because of the outcry
this caused it was decided to 'modify' the service instead. Six of the
intermediate stations, Chard Junction, Seaton Junction, Sidmouth Junction,
Whimple, Broad Clyst and Pinhoe, were listed for closure in the Report.

From September 1964 the through expresses were replaced by a
semi-fast service of five trains a day from Waterloo to Exeter using the
WR's Swindon-built 'Warship' Type 4 diesel-hydraulics. The only trains to
run west of Exeter via Okehampton were the 1.10am newspaper train
from Waterloo to Plymouth and the long-established through train from
Brighton, which joined the route at Salisbury. The local stations remained
open for the time being and a revised service of five stopping trains each
weekday from Salisbury to Exeter was introduced, operated by DMUs.
Two of these continued via the old SR route to Plymouth, while two
more went to Ilfracombe. The last stopping train of the day, the 5.25pm
from Salisbury, terminated at Barnstaple Junction. Stopping trains also ran

Since modification of the Waterloo to Exeter service in 1964, the track layout at Exeter Central has been much simplified. The two centre tracks, previously used for freight and light engine movements, have been removed together with the up bay platform. Here two three-car Class 159/0 'Sprinter' units, Nos 159001 and 159009, leave as the 12.10 service from Exeter St David's to Waterloo on 10 December 2009. On the following Monday South West Trains increased the service from two-hourly to hourly throughout the day. The service is now operated by South Western Railway *Author*

to Exeter from Yeovil Town and from Axminster, one of which left Lyme Regis at 5.27pm.

The new timetable experienced many problems due to failure of both diesel locomotives and multiple units, leading to the occasional reappearance of steam on trains west of Salisbury. Late running inevitably became commonplace. Further delays occurred as the DMUs provided lacked toilets, on journeys that could last several hours, and passengers were forced to use the facilities at the wayside stations. As a result the timetable was soon revised and the units replaced. Summer Saturdays in 1965 saw the reappearance of steam on one of the three through trains from Waterloo to Sidmouth and Exmouth and on enthusiasts' specials. In 1966 two BR Eastern Region 'Pacifics', Class 'A4' No 60024 *Kingfisher* and Class 'A2' No 60532 *Blue Peter*, had also appeared on specials from Waterloo to Exeter. The last run by BR steam from Exeter St David's to Yeovil Junction was by 'West Country' 'Pacific' No 34019 *Bideford* on 13 November 1966. The train was taken forward to Waterloo by 'Merchant Navy' No 35023 *Holland-Afrika Line*.

The singling of much of the former SR route between Salisbury and Exeter in 1967 caused operational problems from the start. In 2009, to increase capacity on the line, work started on a three-mile passing loop which included Axminster station where the second platform was reinstated. South Western Railway's 09.20 from Waterloo to Exeter St. David's arrives at the station on 4 April 2019. Heading the train, still in South West Railway livery, is 3-car Class 159/1 unit No. 159.108. Class 159 unit No. 159.013, is at the rear. *Author*

The closure of six intermediate stations was announced in September 1964, which would leave just Crewkerne, Axminster and Honiton open, together with the halt at St James' Park. The closure of Yeovil Junction had also been considered on the basis that, due to its remoteness from the town, intending passengers could travel some 5 miles to the east to Sherborne where the station was to remain open. A further public outcry ensued and this plan was dropped. Following a public inquiry BR(WR) was refused permission to close the station at Whimple, but four of the remaining five stations succumbed in April 1966. These included Seaton Junction, together with the branch to Seaton, as described in Chapter 3.7. The fifth station, at Sidmouth Junction, closed a year later, together with

BR(SR) Timetable 35, 10 September 1962–16 June 1963, showing trains between Yeovil Junction and Exeter Central (Chapter 2.6), from Exeter Central to Barnstaple (Chapter 2.7), and from Exeter Central to Okehampton (Chapter 2.8) between 11.53am and 4.29pm. Also shown are trains from Barnstaple to Torrington and Ilfracombe (Chapters 3.5 and 3.17), and from Okehampton to Plymouth, Padstow and Bude (Chapters 3.9 and 3.10). Note the departure of the 'ACE' at 11.00am with through coaches from Waterloo to Padstow, Bude, Plymouth, Ilfracombe, Torrington, Exmouth and Sidmouth.

Table 35 — Week Days — From LONDON to THE WEST OF ENGLAND — Week Days — continued. Trains include the ATLANTIC COAST EXPRESS (Restaurant Car Waterloo to Exeter; Through Carriages to Padstow, Bude, Plymouth, Ilfracombe, Torrington, Exmouth and Sidmouth), Buffet Car services Waterloo to Exeter, and the Buffet Car Train Brighton (dep 11 30 am) to Plymouth. Stations listed include London Waterloo, Surbiton, Woking, Basingstoke, Oakley, Overton, Whitchurch North, Hurstbourne, Andover Junction, Grateley, Idmiston Halt, Porton, Salisbury, Wilton South, Dinton, Tisbury, Semley, Gillingham, Templecombe, Milborne Port Halt, Sherborne, Yeovil Junction, Yeovil Town, Sutton Bingham Halt, Crewkerne, Chard Junction, Chard Central, Axminster, Seaton Junction, Seaton, Lyme Regis, Seaton Junction, Honiton, Sidmouth Junction, Budleigh Salterton, Exmouth, Sidmouth, Whimple, Broad Clyst, Pinhoe, St James' Park Halt, Exeter Central, Exeter St David's, Newton St Cyres, Crediton.

the branches to Sidmouth and Exmouth (Chapters 3.14 and 3.15).

During the summer of 1967 the line was singled from Sherborne to Pinhoe, with passing places at Chard Junction and Honiton but not initially at Yeovil Junction. This caused further problems, and in October the double track between Sherborne and Yeovil Junction was reinstated. Yeovil Junction nevertheless saw one of its two island platforms decommissioned and the footbridge between the two demolished.

Despite its unpromising start, the line has prospered. The station at Sidmouth Junction was reopened in May 1971, when it reverted to its original name of Feniton. This followed intensive lobbying by the

Week Days   Table 35

from Portsmouth and Southsea (dep 12 15 pm) (Tables 28 and 54)

ATLANTIC COAST EXPRESS

ATLANTIC COAST EXPRESS

Saturdays only

Yeoford
Bow
North Tawton
Sampford Courtenay
Okehampton

Okehampton
Bridestowe
Lydford
Brentor
Tavistock North
Bere Alston
Bere Ferrers
Tamerton Foliot Halt
St. Budeaux, Victoria Road
Ford
Devonport, King's Road
Plymouth

Copplestone
Morchard Road
Lapford
Eggesford
King's Nympton
Portsmouth Arms
Umberleigh
Chapelton

Barnstaple Junction
Barnstaple Town
Wrafton
Braunton
Mortehoe & Woolacombe
Ilfracombe
Instow
Bideford
Torrington
Fremington

Okehampton
Maddaford Moor Halt
Ashbury
Halwill

Halwill
Dunsland Cross
Holsworthy
Whitstone & Bridgerule
Budd

Halwill
Ashwater
Tower Hill
Launceston
Egloskerry
Tresmeer
Otterham
Camelford
Delabole
Port Isaac Road
St. Kew Highway
Wadebridge
Padstow

local residents to serve a new housing development in the village. Pinhoe station also reopened, in May 1983. To increase capacity on the line, work started in 2009 on a 3-mile passing loop to include Axminster station. As a result an hourly service of 14 through trains from Waterloo to Exeter St David's now runs each weekday, operated by South Western Railway. In the autumn of 2019 the first arrival from Waterloo was at 10.43. Earlier arrivals originated from Axminster, Gillingham and Salisbury respectively. In addition, a local train from Honiton arrived at Exeter St Davids at 17.33.

2.7 Exeter Central - Barnstaple

Once the LSWR had opened its main line between Yeovil and Exeter Queen Street in 1860 it looked to extend its empire into North Devon and Cornwall, where the broad-gauge South Devon Railway (SDR) had so far failed to penetrate. The first step was the completion in February 1862 of a line down from Exeter Queen Street (now Exeter Central) to the SDR's station at St David's, where mixed-gauge track had to be laid (the SDR was amalgamated with the GWR in 1876). From there the LSWR set its sights on the Exeter & Crediton Railway (E&CR), which had opened a 6¼-mile broad-gauge line from Exeter St David's to Crediton in May 1851. This was extended to Barnstaple by the North Devon Railway (NDR) in 1854 and to Bideford a year later. As broad-gauge lines their

The up 'Atlantic Coast Express' from Ilfracombe to Waterloo arrives at Copplestone behind unrebuilt 'West Country' No 34002 *Salisbury* on 5 May 1964. A restaurant car will be added at Exeter Central and the 'West Country' replaced by a 'Merchant Navy' Class 'Pacific'. At the time double track was in place from Cowley Bridge Junction, Exeter, as far west as Copplestone. This was singled in 1971 while the only passing loop to survive on the single-track section to Barnstaple was at Eggesford. R. A. Lumber, *David Mitchell collection*

natural ally should have been the SDR. However, in a political sleight of hand the LSWR leased the E&CR and NDR in 1862 and 1863 respectively and laid a third rail for its standard-gauge trains. The line was soon doubled as far as Copplestone, 6¾ miles north of Crediton, beyond which the line was to remain single, although passing loops were provided at Morchard Road, Lapford, Eggesford, Kings Nympton and Portsmouth Arms. The track from the next station at Umberleigh to Barnstaple was doubled in 1890.

By 1891 line from Barnstaple to Ilfracombe, opened in 1874, had been upgraded, permitting a significant increase in holiday traffic (Chapter 3.17). For many years through trains ran from Waterloo to Ilfracombe

Crediton was the only town of any size west of Exeter on the lines to both Okehampton and Barnstaple. Ex-SR 'N' Class 'Mogul' No 31853 approaches the station on a train from Padstow to Waterloo during 1964. At Exeter Central the 'Mogul' would be replaced by a Bulleid 'Pacific', while coaches from Plymouth would be added to the train together with a restaurant car. No 31853 was an Exmouth Junction engine, built at Ashford in 1925 and withdrawn in September 1964. *R. A. Lumber, David Mitchell collection*

Some 20 years later a two-car Class 116 DMU approaches the station as a service for Barnstaple on 9 August 1988. By this time regular passenger services on the Okehampton line had been withdrawn and the whole of the Barnstaple line singled. West of Crediton the former double track to Yeoford had become separate lines to Okehampton (for the remaining stone traffic from Meldon Quarry) and Barnstaple. *Terry Gough*

In the 1960s Yeoford had four platform faces and was an interchange station for passengers from the Barnstaple line with trains to Plymouth and North Cornwall. After track rationalisation in 1971 only the up platform remained in use for trains between Barnstaple and Exeter. Class 150/2 'Sprinter' No 150219, operated by Wessex Trains, is pictured arriving at Yeoford forming a service for Barnstaple on 13 July 2005. The track on the right runs to Okehampton and Meldon Quarry. *Author*

Barnstaple Junction station, now just known as Barnstaple, is seen during 1979. A Class 25 diesel-electric loco, one of the classes that replaced BR(WR)'s diesel-hydraulics, appears to be adding a luggage van to a three-car DMU for Exeter. At the time the line to Torrington was still in use for freight traffic (see Chapter 3.5). *M. E. J. Deane collection, courtesy of Ian Bennett*

via Crediton. The end of the Second World War saw a further rapid increase in the demand for holiday traffic. On summer Saturdays in 1962 ten through trains from Waterloo to Ilfracombe used the route, eight of which included through coaches to Torrington and one to Bideford. In winter, however, the number of through trains was reduced to two. Details of the summer trains are given in Appendix 3.1. The BR(SR) timetable for the winter of 1962/63 is shown on page 62 and 63.

The survey of passengers carried out for the Beeching Report in April 1961 showed that a maximum of only 5,000 per week were using the line, reflecting the difference in usage of the line between holiday and non-holiday seasons. Nevertheless, the line to Barnstaple was not included in the list of closures, while the alternative former GWR route from London to Barnstaple via Taunton (Chapter 3.11), which showed a similar level of patronage, closed in October 1966. Instead the Report proposed the closure of all 11 intermediate stations apart from Crediton, Lapford and Eggesford. Although BR(WR) was subsequently refused permission to close any of these, the rundown of the line began from 1964 onwards.

Although the green station sign appears to be of 1960s BR(SR) origin there was never a station of that name at Barnstaple. In those days the station was named Barnstaple Junction as it was the junction for the lines to Torrington and Ilfracombe. Only one platform face had been in use for many years when Class 142 'Pacer' unit No. 142.068 was pictured there on 13 October 2010 with a train for Exmouth. The Class 142 'Skipper' units first introduced in the 1980s, made an unwelcome reappearance in December 2007. Now known as 'Pacers' the last of the unpopular Class 142 units were returned to Northern Rail in November 2011, although the similar Class 143 units remain in use. *Author*

Although eight stations between Exeter St David's and Barnstaple survived their listing for closure in the Beeching Report, many see only an infrequent service. Among them is the station at King's Nympton, which saw only five departures for Exeter each weekday, compared with 14 from Barnstaple. The station building, which is now a private house, can be seen in the distance as Great Western Railway's 11.53 service from Exmouth, worked by 'Pacer' units Nos 143620 and 621, passes en route for Barnstaple. *Author*

In the interim BR(WR) replaced steam on local trains with DMUs in the autumn of 1963, while a number of the through trains were turned over to diesel-hydraulic haulage. Steam was not, however, finally eliminated until the through trains to and from London Waterloo disappeared from September 1964. Although the replacement DMU service included through trains from Salisbury, they stopped at all stations and took 3hr 55min to reach Barnstaple. As noted above, this service was soon revised and the through trains withdrawn. The last steam-hauled train over the route was the 'Exeter Flyer' from Waterloo on 3 October 1965, a special train hauled from Exeter to Barnstaple Junction by BR Standard Class 4 2-6-4 tanks Nos 80043 and 80039.

Cowley Bridge Junction, where the line left the BR(WR) main line, was singled in 1967, although double track survived from there to Crediton until 1984. North of Crediton all passing places were removed in 1971 apart from that at Eggesford, while the track was singled again from Umberleigh. Despite this, three through trains ran from London Paddington in 1965 (see Appendix 3.2). One of the trains, which included coaches for Bude, travelled from Paddington to Exeter St David's via Castle Cary and Yeovil Junction, where it joined the former SR route to Exeter Central. This route avoided the need for the train to reverse at Exeter St David's in order to reach Barnstaple via Crediton. In subsequent years the trains travelled via Taunton and Exeter St David's, where they had to reverse. After the closure of the Ilfracombe line in October 1970 the remaining summer train from Paddington terminated at Barnstaple.

Today the service is promoted by the Devon & Cornwall Rail Partnership as the 'Tarka Line'. The service now comprises only local trains operated by Great Western Railway, which run approximately hourly throughout the day. The first arrival at Barnstaple from Exeter St David's in the autumn of 2019 was at 06.59. All later trains came from Exmouth, most of them stopping at only the principal stations, while other stations, including Newton St Cyres, had a rather limited service.

2.8
Exeter Central
– Okehampton

Rebuilt Bulleid 'Battle of Britain' 'Pacific' No 34060 *25 Squadron* calls at Exeter St David's with the Plymouth to Brighton through train on 3 September 1963; it has travelled via Okehampton. After climbing to Exeter Central, the train ran non-stop to Salisbury, then via Fareham, where coaches for Portsmouth & Southsea were detached. This train continued to use the ex-SR route via Okehampton after other through trains had been withdrawn in September 1964. After closure of the line west of Okehampton it ran for several years via Newton Abbot, Exeter Central and Salisbury. *Author*

The double track of the old SR main line from Exeter to Plymouth still survives in this view of North Tawton on 4 April 1968. Here a three-car Class 119 DMU arrives forming a service for Exeter. Services west of Okehampton were withdrawn from 6 May 1968, while passenger services to Exeter succumbed from 5 June 1972. The track was singled in 1971, but remained in use for ballast trains from Meldon Quarry until 2011. *David Mitchell*

Rebuilt 'Bulleid' 'Pacific' No 34034 *Honiton* arrives at Yeoford with a train to Plymouth on 12 August 1961. The two platforms used by trains between Exeter Central, Barnstaple and Ilfracombe are behind the station buildings on the left. Only one of these, the former up platform, now remains in use today. *AFH, Colour-Rail*

By 1863 the LSWR had consolidated its position between Exeter and Barnstaple and looked again to expand its empire. A new line, which left the Barnstaple line north of Crediton at Coleford Junction, opened as far as Sampford Courtenay (then called Okehampton Road) in January 1867. The difficult terrain encountered on the northern slopes of Dartmoor delayed opening to Okehampton, 14½ miles from Sampford, until October 1871. By 1876 LSWR trains were able to run through to Plymouth via the GWR's branch from Lydford

Despite its closure to passenger trains in 1972, the station at Okehampton remained remarkably intact. Thanks to the intervention of Devon County Council, trains from Exeter, the 'Dartmoor Rambler', were reintroduced on summer Saturdays in 1984, while the heritage Dartmoor Railway commenced a summer service to Meldon Quarry. More recently the trains have run on summer Sundays, and here Class 150/2 'Sprinter' No 150246 has arrived at the station with the Wessex Trains 11.18 service from Exeter Central on 10 July 2005. To the right preserved Class 205 'Hampshire Unit' DEMU No 205032 waits to depart with a 'Dartmoor Railway' train for the Quarry; these units were built at Eastleigh Works in 1957. Today the trains are operated by Great Western Railway between St James' Park (Exeter) and Okehampton. *Author*

and, from 1890, by the Plymouth, Devonport & South Western Junction Railway's line via Bere Alston. In addition, branches ran from Meldon Junction west of Okehampton to Bude and Padstow in North Cornwall.

The Beeching Report included major changes for the line to Plymouth, which it saw as duplicating the BR(WR) route via Newton Abbot. The whole of the former BR(SR) network west of Okehampton was listed for closure (Chapter 3.16), while the service from Exeter to Okehampton was to be 'modified'. The BR(SR) timetable for the winter 1962/63 is shown on page 62 and 63. BR(WR) replaced steam with DMUs on local trains between Exeter and Plymouth in the autumn of 1963, while a number of the through trains were turned over to diesel-hydraulic haulage. Trains to Bude and Padstow, however, remained largely steam-worked until the end of 1964, despite other services on ex-BR(SR) lines being revised and dieselised from that September. The only through services to survive into 1965 were the overnight newspaper train from Waterloo and the Brighton to Plymouth train (Appendix 3.2). Both ceased to use the route in March 1967, and the line between Bere Alston and Okehampton was closed in May 1968. As described in Chapters 3.9 and 3.10, services to Padstow and Bude had already been withdrawn in October 1966. The track rationalisation, which affected the Barnstaple line, was also extended to Okehampton. From October 1971 the former double-track line from Crediton to Coleford Junction was operated as two single lines and the junction abandoned. The line to Okehampton was singled throughout.

Steam was not entirely eliminated in 1964 as ballast trains from and to Meldon Quarry, situated a couple of miles west of

Reliving the days when a 'USA' Class 0-6-0 tank was based at BR(SR)'s Meldon Quarry, one of the Class, No 30075, enters Okehampton station with a 'Dartmoor Railway' train from the Quarry to Sampford Peverell on 28 August 2010. The train comprises Class 117 DMU carriage No 59520 and an ex-LMS goods brake van. Sampford Peverell station closed on 5 October 1964, but has since been used both by Dartmoor Railway trains and the Sunday trains from Exeter. The 'USA' is not one of those purchased by the Southern Railway after the Second World War, but was built new in Yugoslavia by Duro Dakovic in 1960. The engine is based at the Shillingstone Station Project in Dorset. *Author*

Okehampton, remained steam-worked for some time. The local shunting engine there, a 'USA' 0-6-0 tank, was not replaced by a diesel until the autumn of 1966. The last steam passenger train from Okehampton was the Great Western Society's 'Launceston Branch Centenary Special', hauled by Ivatt Class 2 2-6-2 tank No 41283, which ran on 5 September 1965.

The DMU-operated service at the start of 1972 comprised seven return workings from Exeter St David's. In this case 'modification' involved withdrawal of the passenger service, which was due to occur from 12 May 1972. The trains, however, had a ten-day reprieve due to problems with the replacement bus service, the closure occurring from 22 May. The line to Meldon Quarry remained in place and a campaign was launched to restore passenger services to Okehampton. This has achieved limited success with the introduction on four summer Saturdays in 1984 of 'Dartmoor Rambler' trains subsidised by Devon County Council. Okehampton station was restored, while Sampford Courtenay station reopened in 2006. The heritage Dartmoor Railway was then operating a service during holiday times between Sampford Courtenay, Okehampton and Meldon Quarry. The line has also seen the brief reappearance of steam: in October 2003 'Battle of Britain' Class No 34067 *Tangmere* worked over the line with a special charter train, while in 2010 a Yugoslavian-built 'USA' Class 0-6-0 tank, renumbered 30075, worked Dartmoor Railway trains between Sampford Peverell and the Quarry.

In 2008 the line was acquired by Iowa Pacific Holdings, which, in addition to running the stone trains from Meldon Quarry, stated that its aim was to extend the tourist operation to Yeoford to connect with 'Tarka Line' trains between Exeter and Barnstaple. These aims have sadly not been realised as the quarry operator, Bardon Aggregates, closed it in 2011, while the heritage operation no longer runs south of Okehampton. In 2018 the Dartmoor Railway still ran its diesel-worked 'Heritage Shuttle' to Meldon Quarry during the summer and its 'Train to Christmas Town' in December. On a more optimistic note, in 2019 Great Western Railway ran four 'Dartmoor Rambler' trains between St James' Park Halt, Exeter Central and Okehampton each Sunday during the summer.

SOUTHERN RAILWAY.
(9/84)
Stock
787
TO
OKEHAMPTON

3 ○ Passenger services listed for withdrawal ○

Figures presented in the Beeching Report showed that virtually all the branch lines in the West Country were carrying fewer than 5,000 passengers per week, 2,000 less than the figure considered to be financially viable. The list of 'Passenger Services to be Withdrawn' for the West Country, contained in the Report, was needless to say a long one; in all, 22 branch-line services were listed for withdrawal as shown in Table 3.

In the event, objections were received to all of the formal notices proposing the withdrawal of passenger services, forcing the local Transport Users' Consultative Committee to hold public meetings. The case against each closure was typically led by the local authority, usually with support from the local newspaper. The arguments put forward were often well thought out and caused BR a few headaches. Objectors made much of the fact that the survey of passenger numbers had been carried out over a week in April 1961, outside the holiday season. However, in most cases the objections were quickly overruled and the passenger service withdrawn from the line concerned within a matter of months.

It often seemed that the railway management did its best to deter people from travelling on the threatened lines. Examples can be seen in the BR(WR) passenger timetables of the period, which often failed to mention that on summer Saturdays through trains ran from termini to destinations beyond the branch line. In addition, the timetable covering the period from April 1966 to March 1967 showed only a bus service on two separate sections of the former Taunton to Barnstaple line, and between Okehampton and Bude and Wadebridge respectively, when in fact trains continued to run on all three lines until October 1966.

Even after the Transport Act of 1968, which allowed social need to be taken into consideration, the only branch lines in the West Country to be retained on this basis were those to Looe and St Ives, together with the branch from Plymouth across the Tamar to Gunnislake. The Exmouth branch was the only line listed in the Report that BR itself decided not to close. In 1970 the future of rail services in Cornwall came under review again when a two-part cost benefit analysis of rail services was carried out. No further line or station closures in the county resulted, then or since.

G. W. R.
_____

BARNSTAPLE

(ʳ/ₓ) SOUTHERN RAILWAY. Stock (39 F)

FRAGILE

WITH CARE.

Table 3. West Country passenger services to be withdrawn as listed in Appendix 2, Section 1 of the Beeching Report

Ref	Railway line	Date implemented	Other information
3.1	Taunton to Yeovil Pen Mill	Jun-64	
3.2	Tiverton - Tiverton Junction	Nov-64	
3.3	Lostwithiel - Fowey	Jan-65	Remains open for China Clay traffic
3.4	Halwill - Torrington	Mar-65	Remained open for China Clay traffic from Meeth and Petrostock via Torrington until 1982
3.5	Barnstaple Junction - Torrington	Oct-65	Temporarily reopened to passengers Jan-68. Milk and ferilizer traffic from Torrington was withdrawn in 1978 & 1980 respectively. Closed completely Mar-83
3.6	Axminster - Lyme Regis	Nov-65	
3.7	Seaton Junction - Seaton	Mar-66	2½ mile section from Colyton to a new terminus at Seaton now operated as the 2ft 9ins gauge Seaton Tramway. The tramway opened between 19'70 & 1980
3.8	Yeovil Junction - Yeovil Town	Oct-66	Trains diverted to Yeovil Pen Mill but withdrawn in May 68. The track remains in use between Junction and Penn Mill stations
3.9	Okehampton - Padstow	Oct-66	Wadebridge - Padstow remained open until Jan 67*. Section west of Launceston used by the 1ft 11½ ins gauge Launceston Steam Railway from Dec-83
3.10	Halwill - Bude	Oct-66	
3.11	Taunton - Barnstable Junction	Oct-66	
3.12	Bere Alston - Callington	Nov-66	Gunnislake - Callington only. Bere Alston - Gunnislake remains open
3.13	Bodmin Road/Bodmin North - Wadebridge - Padstow	Jan-67*	China clay traffic from Wenford ran through Bodmin until Oct-68. The heritage Bodmin & Wenford Railway opened from 1990.
3.14	Sidmouth Junction - Sidmouth	Mar-67	
3.15	Tipton St. John's - Exmouth	Mar-67	
3.16	Okehampton - Plymouth	May-68	Okehampton to Bere Alston only (ex-SR line via Devonport Kings Road closed Sept 1964).
3.17	Barnstaple Junction - Ilfracombe	Oct-70	
3.18	Taunton - Minehead	Jan-71	The heritage West Somerset Railway opened from 1976. Now runs from Bishop's Lydeard to Minehead, with physical connection to Network Rail lines at Norton Fitzwarren
3.19	Maiden Newton - Bridport	May-75	
3.20	Exeter Central - Exmouth	Open	Closure proposal withdrawn
3.21	Liskeard - Looe	Open	Closure proposal refused
3.22	St Erth - St Ives	Open	Closure proposal refused

3.1 Taunton - Yeovil Pen Mill (June 1964)

The line from Taunton was the first railway to reach Yeovil in October 1853, and took the form of a branch off the broad-gauge main line of the Bristol & Exeter Railway (B&E) at Durston, 5¾ miles east of Taunton. At first trains terminated at Hendford station to the west of the town. Three years later in September 1856 the Wilts, Somerset & Weymouth Railway opened its station at Pen Mill to the east of the town. A line linking the two stations opened in February 1857. The Taunton line was single throughout with passing loops at each of the four original stations at Athelney, Langport, Martock and Montacute. The broad-gauge monopoly of services in the town was soon broken by the arrival of the standard-gauge Salisbury & Yeovil and Yeovil & Exeter railways in July 1860. Although through trains called at Yeovil Junction to the south of the town, the companies also built a station at Yeovil Town, situated between Hendford and Pen Mill, which was also used by the B&E trains from Durston. Hendford station was closed to passengers in 1861. In 1876 the B&E was taken over by the GWR, which operated the line until nationalisation.

In 1906 the GWR completed its 'Somerton cut-off' between Castle Cary and Cogload Junction, thereby creating a new direct main line from Paddington to the West Country. The new line ran just south of Durston and a short stretch of the Yeovil branch was incorporated within it. The

BR Standard Class 3 2-6-2 tank No 82001 leaves Yeovil Town with a train of BR Mark 1 coaches for Taunton in the spring of 1964. No 82001 was built at Swindon in 1952 and was allocated to Taunton shed for six months between December 1963 and June 1964. Passenger services between Yeovil and Taunton were withdrawn from 15 June 1964. No 82001 was then transferred to Bristol Barrow Road depot, where it lasted until December 1965. *Owen Mogg*

A number of trains on the single-track line were scheduled to pass at Martock station. The fireman of an ex-GWR '5700' Class pannier tank can be seen shovelling forward coal in the engine's bunker while sister engine No 4656 of Yeovil Town shed arrives with a Taunton to Yeovil Pen Mill train; the trains are thought to be the 12.40pm and 12.50pm departures (Saturdays only) from Taunton and Yeovil respectively. The first coach of the Yeovil train is ex-GWR No W7073W; this was originally built at Swindon as a slip coach in 1938 and was one of the few ex-GWR vehicles repainted in chocolate and cream livery by BR(WR) in 1956. *M. E. J. Deane collection, courtesy of Ian Bennett*

line through Athelney was doubled and two new junctions with the branch constructed, one just to the west of the station, the other 3 miles to the east at Curry Rivel Junction. A new station was opened on the main line at Langport East, while the old branch-line station was renamed Langport West.

Prior to the Second World War new halts were provided at Lyng (1928), on the remaining single track between Durston and Athelney, at Thorney & Kingsbury east of Langport (1927), and at Hendford in 1932. A halt at Creech St Michael on the main line between Durston and Taunton had opened in 1928.

Soon after nationalisation, in 1950, the line east of Langport West became part of BR(SR). The old GWR loco shed at Yeovil Pen Mill closed in 1959 and its Taunton branch engines transferred to the ex-SR depot at Yeovil Town. The situation changed again from 1 January 1963 when BR(WR) took control of all lines in and around Yeovil, together with the responsibility for motive power.

At the start of 1964 four up and five down trains ran over the 26-mile

Langport station opened with the line in October 1853, and became Langport West in July 1902 when the GWR opened its 'Westbury cut-off', enabling its trains from Paddington to the West Country to avoid Bristol. A second station, Langport East was provided on the new line. This station closed in September 1962, while Langport West closed with the branch in June 1964. Here ex-GWR 'Small Prairie' No 5521 of Taunton shed arrives at Langport West with a train for Yeovil Pen Mill in the early 1960s. No 5521 was built at Swindon in 1927 and was withdrawn, from Plymouth Laira shed, in April 1964. After spending time at Barry scrapyard it is now preserved, and in recent years has run in unauthentic London Transport lined red livery.
M. E. J. Deane collection, courtesy of Ian Bennett

route between Taunton and Yeovil Pen Mill via Durston each weekday. A further train ran in each direction on Saturdays. On leaving Durston most up trains called at Lyng Halt before joining the 1906 Paddington main line at Athelney, while down trains had to climb the embankment, built in the 1930s, which would take them over the London main line to join the four-track section to Taunton. Two up trains and one down train a day ran direct from Taunton to Yeovil via Athelney, avoiding Durston and Lyng Halt. Services on the line remained largely steam-hauled by ex-GWR 'Prairie' and BR Standard Class 3 2-6-2 tanks until closure. In the last month of services NB Type 2 diesel-hydraulic No D6331 also appeared.

The Beeching Report had revealed that the branch carried fewer than 5,000 passengers a week and that only Yeovil Town and Pen Mill stations had annual passenger receipts above £5,000. Proposals to close the line were therefore published towards the end of 1963 and, despite much local opposition, services between Taunton and Yeovil were withdrawn from 15 June. The final trains ran on the previous Saturday, the 13th. The last up train, the 8.20pm from Taunton, was hauled by 'Small Prairie' No 4593, while the 7.50pm train from Yeovil Pen Mill was in the hands of

Ex-GWR 'Small Prairie' No 4593 is seen again, this time approaching Yeovil Town with the 11.21am train from Yeovil Pen Mill to Taunton on 12 February 1964. The line from Yeovil Pen Mill remained open until October 1966 following withdrawal of the service to Taunton. The Yeovil to Taunton trains were the last in the West County to be hauled by these engines, which had dominated such workings for almost 60 years. No 4593 was built at Swindon in 1927 and was among the last of its class to be withdrawn, in September 1964. In 1959 the engine was allocated to Pontypool Road shed in South Wales before moving to Truro and finally Taunton). *Author*

'Large Prairie' No 4131. The two trains passed at Athelney where crowds witnessed the last rites on the line; it was the last line in the West Country to be worked by ex-GWR 'Small Prairie' tanks, ending an association that had lasted for almost 60 years.

Creech St Michael and Durston both remained open until the stopping service between Bristol and Taunton was modified in October 1964. A passenger service of four trains a day was also maintained between Yeovil Town and Yeovil Pen Mill, but these were withdrawn in November 1965, while Yeovil Town station itself closed a year later.

Western Region Timetable 9 September 1963 - 14 June 1964 (Table 80)

Table 80

TAUNTON, DURSTON and YEOVIL

WEEK DAYS ONLY

Miles		am	am	am	am	pm	pm	pm S	pm	pm	pm	pm	pm
	Taunton dep	6 45	..	9 45	..	1258	..	2 10	..	4 25	5 55	8 20	..
2¾	Creech St. Michael Halt	6 50									6 2		
5¾	Durston	6 57	..	..	..	..	..	2 20	..	4 34	6 9	8 29	..
7½	Lyng Halt	7 2						2 24		4 38	6 13		
8	Athelney	7 5	..	9 57	..	1 10	..	2 28	..	4 40	6 17	8 34	..
13	Langport West	7 18		10 7		1 20		2 42		4 51	6 26	8 43	
15¼	Thorney & Kingsbury Halt	7 23	..	1012	..	1 25	..	2 49	..	4 57	6 31	3 48	..
18	Martock	7 29		1022		1 31		2 58		5 4	6 37	8 54	
20¾	Montacute	7 37	..	1029	..	1 37	..	3 6	..	5 13	6 44	9 0	..
24½	Hendford Halt	7 45		1037		1 45		3 14		5 21	6 52	9 8	
25½	**Yeovil** **Town** arr	7 48	..	1040	..	1 48	..	3 17	..	5 24	6 54	9 11	..
	Yeovil **Town** dep	7 50	8 42	1042	1131	1 51	2 39	3 20	4 28	5 33	6 56	9 13	9 50
26	**Yeovil** **Pen Mill** arr	7 54	8 46	1045	1133	1 55	2 41	3 24	4 30	5 37	6 59	9 16	9 52

Miles		am	am	am	am	am	pm S	pm	pm	pm	pm	pm
	Yeovil **Pen Mill** dep	7 5	8 50	9 56	1052	1121	1237	2 25	4 0	5 45	7 50	9 58
	Yeovil **Town** arr	7 7	8 52	9 58	1054	1123	1239	2 27	4 2	5 47	7 52	10 0
½	**Yeovil** **Town** dep	7 10	..	10 0	..	1124	1241	..	4 8	5 50	7 54	..
1½	Hendford Halt	7 15		10 3		1127	1244		4 12	5 54	7 58	
5¼	Montacute	7 24	..	1012	..	1136	1253	..	4 21	6 4	8 7	..
8	Martock	7 32		1019		1142	1259		4 28	6 10	8 13	
10¾	Thorney & Kingsbury Halt	7 39	..	1025	..	1148	1 5	..	4 34	6 16	8 19	..
13	Langport West	7 45		1030		1157	1 11		4 39	6 21	8 25	
18	Athelney	7 54	..	1039	..	12 6	1 21	..	4 48	6 31	8 35	..
18½	Lyng Halt	7 57				12 8	1 23		4 50	6 33	8 37	
20¼	Durston	8 2	..	..	..	1213	1 28	..	4 55	6 38	8 42	..
23¼	Creech St. Michael Halt	8 8				1219	1 34		5 1	6 44	8 48	
26	**Taunton** arr	8 14	..	1052	..	1225	1 40	..	5 7	6 51	8 55	..

S Saturdays only

No 4593 stands at Yeovil Town with the 11.21am train from Yeovil Pen Mill to Taunton on 12 February 1964. On this occasion the train comprised four BR Mark I coaches, two of which are in the old GWR livery of chocolate and cream introduced by BR(WR) for its named expresses in June 1956. By 1964 the sets had been broken up, resulting in the coaches appearing on a range of secondary services. *Author*

3.2 Tiverton - Tiverton Junction (October 1964)

The first railway to serve the historic Devon town of Tiverton was the broad-gauge Bristol & Exeter Railway, which opened in May 1844 with a station at Tiverton Road, some 4¾ miles from the town. The branch line, which was to link the town with the main line for almost 120 years, opened four years later. Tiverton Road was renamed Tiverton Junction in June 1848. The construction of this short line involved little in the way of engineering works. The main structure of note was the two-arched aqueduct that carried the Grand Western Canal (GWC) over the line west of the intermediate halt at Halberton. The GWC was a grandiose scheme to link the Bristol and English Channels via the Rivers Parrett and

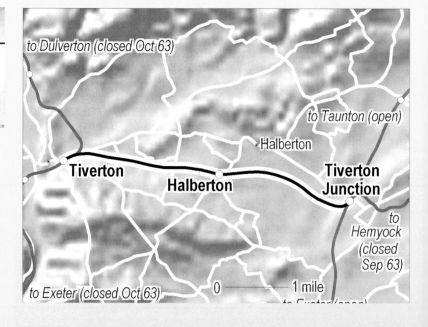

to Dulverton (closed Oct 63)

to Taunton (open)

Halberton

Tiverton

Halberton

Tiverton Junction

to Hemyock (closed Sep 63)

to Exeter (closed Oct 63)

0 ———— 1 mile

In this view of Tiverton Station in April 1961, an ex-GWR 0-4-2 tank and single auto-coach wait to depart from Tiverton with the 'Tivvy Bumper' to Tiverton Junction. *M. E. J. Deane collection, courtesy of Ian Bennett*

G. W. R.

Tiverton Junction

Exe, with a branch to Tiverton, which opened in 1814. Although the canal managed to reach Taunton in 1838, it soon succumbed to competition from the railways; in 1971 part of it was acquired and restored by Devon County Council.

Tiverton became a junction station in 1884 with the arrival of the Tiverton & North Devon Railway from Dulverton. This line was built to the standard gauge and the older broad-gauge branch from Tiverton Junction was converted to standard at the same time. A year later the Exe Valley Railway opened its direct line from Tiverton to Exeter, with most trains running through from Exeter to Dulverton on what became known as the Exe Valley line.

By this time Tiverton Junction had gained a second branch, to Hemyock, which was opened by the Culm Valley Light Railway Company in May 1876. Both the Culm and Exe Valley lines appeared on the last pre-Beeching Report list of closures. Passenger trains were withdrawn from 9 September and 7 October 1963 respectively (Chapter 1, lines 1.7 and 1.8).

Halberton Halt was situated about halfway along the 4¾-mile branch from Tiverton to Tiverton Junction. Ex-GWR 0-4-2 tank No 1470 calls briefly at the Halt while working the 'Tivvy Bumper' in May 1961. This loco was one of a fleet of Class '1400' tank engines based at Exeter St David's shed to work the lines through Tiverton; built at Swindon in 1936, it was withdrawn in October 1962. *M. E. J. Deane collection, courtesy of Ian Bennett*

Another ex-GWR 0-4-2 tank, No 1466, is seen at Tiverton Junction after arrival with the 3.15pm train from Tiverton on 29 August 1963. Built in 1936, No 1466 was withdrawn in December 1963 but was purchased by the Great Western Society and is now housed at the Didcot Railway Centre. *Author*

Western Region Timetable 15 June 1964 - 13 June 1965 (Table 65)

Table 65

Weekdays

NOT on Saturdays 20 June to 5 September

Tiverton Junction to Tiverton   (Second class only)

													C			
TIVERTON JUNCTION .. .. .. d	8 10	..	9 18	..	10 25	..	..	13 42	..	15 30	16 15	..	16 55	..	18 55	..	19 50	20 18	..	21 28	.. ..
HALBERTON HALT .... d	8 15	..	9 24	..	10 30	..	..	13 47	..	15 35	16 20	..	17 01	..	19 00	..	19 55	20 23	..	21 33	.. ..
TIVERTON .. .. a	8 22	..	9 30	..	10 37	..	..	13 54	..	15 42	16 27	..	17 08	..	19 07	..	20 02	20 30	..	21 40	.. ..

Saturdays

20 June to 5 September

Sundays

															D		
TIVERTON JUNCTION .. .. .. d	7 55	9 03	9 37	12 50	.. ..	13 22	..	17 35	..	18 55	..	20 10	..	21 28	..	21 55	..	19 55	.. ..
HALBERTON HALT .... d	8 00	9 08	9 42	12 55	.. ..	13 27	..	17 40	..	19 00	..	20 15	..	21 33	..	22 00	..	20 00	.. ..
TIVERTON .. .. a	8 07	9 15	9 49	13 02	.. ..	13 34	..	17 47	..	19 07	..	20 22	..	21 40	..	22 07	..	20 07	.. ..

Weekdays

NOT on Saturdays 20 June to 5 September

Tiverton to Tiverton Junction   (Second class only)

	SX																
TIVERTON .. .. d	7 10	..	7 40	..	8 58	..	10 05	..	..	13 25	..	15 11	16 00	..	16 35	..	18 33	..	19 35	..	20 50	..
HALBERTON HALT .... d	7 16	..	7 46	..	9 05	..	10 11	..	..	13 31	..	15 18	16 06	..	16 41	..	18 40	..	19 41	..	20 56	..
TIVERTON JUNCTION .. .. .. a	7 22	..	7 52	..	9 10	..	10 17	..	..	13 37	..	15 23	16 12	..	16 47	..	18 45	..	19 47	..	21 02	..

Saturdays

20 June to 5 September

Sundays

													B		
TIVERTON .. .. d	7 35	..	8 40	..	9 20	..	12 25	..	13 05	..	17 20	..	18 33	..	19 55	21 05	..	..	9 20	..	.. ..
HALBERTON HALT .... d	7 41	..	8 46	..	9 26	..	12 31	..	13 11	..	17 26	..	18 40	..	20 01	21 11	..	..	9 26	..	.. ..
TIVERTON JUNCTION .. .. .. a	7 47	..	8 52	..	9 32	..	12 37	..	13 17	..	17 32	..	18 45	..	20 07	21 17	..	..	9 33	..	.. ..

For general notes see page 49

B Until 6 September. Through train to Exmouth and Sidmouth
C Until 4 September
D Until 6 September

Ex-GWR 0-4-2 tank No 1470 sets out from Tiverton Junction for Tiverton in July 1961. A small sub-shed was provided at Tiverton Junction to service engines working the lines to Tiverton and Hemyock, and its open doors can been seen to the left of the train, together with an ex-GWR Class '5700' 0-6-0 pannier tank. *M. E. J. Deane collection, courtesy of Ian Bennett*

The short branch from Tiverton Junction to Tiverton was to survive for another two years. The Beeching Report had revealed that it carried fewer than 5,000 passengers a week and that only Tiverton station itself had annual passenger receipts above £5,000. At the time of the survey in April 1962 the Exe Valley line was still running, so this total included receipts from these trains. Proposals for the withdrawal of passenger services on the branch were therefore soon published.

It might seem surprising that passenger receipts from a town the size of Tiverton were so low, given that a 12-minute journey would give passengers access to trains to London on the West of England main line. During 1964 there were ten return trains each weekday with one extra down train in the summer. These still involved push-pull auto-coach working using ex-GWR Class '1400' 0-4-2 tanks. One train ran in each direction on summer Sundays. As has been noted for other lines scheduled for closure, the contemporary BR(WR) timetable was not helpful in planning a through journey. In fact, connections were

Tiverton station is seen on 5 August 1966, almost two years after its closure to passenger traffic on 5 October 1964. The station remained open for freight traffic until 1967. *Author*

The service between Tiverton and Tiverton Junction was the last ex-GWR branch in the West Country to see Class '1400' 0-4-2 tank engines and auto-coaches on push-pull working. As a result several of the engines were preserved, including No 1466 pictured previously. Two other Tiverton engines, Nos 1450 and 1442, were also preserved after working trains on ex-SR lines. No 1442 was purchased for the town by the late Viscount Amory, and for a time was mounted on a plinth on the outskirts, where it was pictured on 5 August 1966. It now resides in the town museum. *Author*

made with the stopping trains between Exeter and Taunton, allowing passengers to change at Taunton for Paddington. In addition, a connection was also made with the 6.20am from Newton Abbot, which arrived at Paddington at 10.30am. Rather surprisingly the down train was the 6.30pm from Paddington to Plymouth, 'The Mayflower', which called at Tiverton Junction at 9.21pm on Mondays to Saturdays. The connecting train reached Tiverton at 9.40pm. On summer Saturdays the first through connection from Tiverton Junction was the 8.35am to Cardiff, while the 9.37am arrived at Paddington at 12.45pm. There were no connections on Sundays.

The service was finally withdrawn from 5 October 1964. Tiverton Junction remained open until May 1986, when part of the site was required for the construction of the M5 motorway. A new station, Tiverton Parkway, was opened on the site of Sampford Peverell Halt some 2 miles to the east (Chapter 2.2). Today the new station sees a succession of trains throughout the day linking the West Country with both London and the Midlands.

At the time of closure the two branch-line engines, 0-4-2Ts Nos 1442 and 1450, were the last of their class at work in the West Country. They survived until May 1965, finding further work on the ex-BR(SR) branch lines at Seaton and Yeovil Town (Chapters 3.7 and 3.8). Both also survived the cutter's torch. No 1442 was purchased by the former Tiverton MP, the late Viscount Amory, and presented to the town; it was then cosmetically restored to GWR livery and displayed on a plinth by a main road on the outskirts of the town, but is now interned in Tiverton Museum. No 1450 was also preserved and in recent years has been seen back on auto-train working on heritage railways in the West Country.

3.3 Lostwithiel to Fowey (January 1965)

Despite their popularity with holidaymakers, the ex-GWR branch lines in Cornwall fared no better in the Beeching Report than those in other counties. The Helston branch had already closed in November 1962 (it was listed in the Report as one of the 'Passenger services already under consideration for withdrawal before formulation of the Report', (Chapter 1, line 1.2 and Table 1.1), while the branches to Fowey, Looe and St Ives (see also Chapters 3.21 and 3.22) were all listed for closure. In the event the short 5½-mile branch from Lostwithiel, on the BR(WR) main line to Penzance, to the coastal town of Fowey was the only one to lose its passenger service.

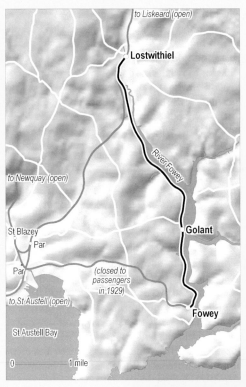

The history of railways in this part of Cornwall has always been closely linked to the production of china clay and the need to export it by sea. The development of the lines to Fowey was surprisingly complex. The broad-gauge line from Lostwithiel was built by the Lostwithiel & Fowey Railway (L&FR) and opened for china clay traffic in 1869. The line was built along the eastern bank of the River Fowey to a deep-water quay at Carne Point, north of the town of Fowey. However, in 1874 the Cornwall Minerals Railway (CMR) opened a rival route from Par. A passenger station was built at Fowey and in June 1876 a passenger service was introduced between there, St Blazey and Newquay.

The L&FR soon lost the resulting price war, and in January 1880 suspended all traffic. The line was subsequently leased to the CMR, which used it for storing disused stock. In 1892 the CMR, by then operated by the GWR, acquired the line and rebuilt it to the standard gauge. The quay at Carne Point was rebuilt and a spur built to link the old L&FR line with that of the CMR in Fowey. Passenger services between Fowey and Lostwithiel commenced for the first time in September 1895, while a year later a halt was opened at Golant, some 1¾ miles to the north. The CMR became part of the GWR on the same day.

Passenger services were maintained over the lines to both Newquay and Lostwithiel until July 1929, when regular services to Newquay were withdrawn, although china clay traffic continued to use the line until 1968. The passenger service to Lostwithiel continued and by the 1930s were worked by ex-GWR Class '1400' 0-4-2 tanks and one or two auto-coaches. For many years in the late 1950s and early 1960s the branch-line engine was No 1419; based at the former Cornwall Minerals Railway shed at St Blazey, it was withdrawn in April 1961. St Blazey depot itself closed to steam in April 1962. Single-unit railcars (BR Classes 121 and

Ex-GWR 0-4-2T No 1419 worked the branch from Lostwithiel to Fowey for many years, shedded at St Blazey depot, and is seen here at Lostwithiel on 14 April 1956. DMUs replaced steam on the branch in September 1961, but by then No 1419 had already been withdrawn in April of that year. *Terry Gough*

Ex-GWR 0-4-2T No 1419 is seen again at Fowey station after arrival with a train from Lostwithiel shortly before the engine was withdrawn. At this time the lines curving beyond the train remained in use for china clay traffic from St Blazey; passenger services on this line had been withdrawn in 1929. *M. E. J. Deane collection, courtesy of Ian Bennett*

Western Region Timetable 15 June 1964 - 13 June 1965 (Table 65)

Lostwithiel to Fowey   Second class only   Weekdays

NOT on Saturdays 20 June to 5 September

																SO
LOSTWITHIEL	d	7 10	8 25	10 07	11 30	13 30	14 35		16 40	18 00	18 45					
GOLANT HALT	d	7 19	8 34	10 16	11 39	13 39	14 44		16 49	17 09	18 54					
FOWEY	a	7 25	8 40	10 22	11 45	13 45	14 50	15h54	16 55	18 15	19 00	20c54	22f11		23g11	

Saturdays

20 June to 5 September

LOSTWITHIEL	d	7 10	8 20	9 20	10 35	12 05	12 55	14 00	15 32	17 13	18 00	20 30		
GOLANT HALT	d	7 19	8 29	9 29	10 44	12 14	13 04	14 09	15 41	17 22	18 09	18 54	20 39	
FOWEY	a	7 25	8 35	9 35	10 50	12 20	13 10	14 15	15 47	17 28	18 15	19 00	20 45	23b11

Fowey to Lostwithiel   Second class only   Weekdays

NOT on Saturdays 20 June to 5 September

FOWEY	d	6 50	7 50	9 40	10 27	12 50	14 10	16 15	17 35	18 20	21k00	22n00	22p25
GOLANT HALT	d	6 55	7 55	9 45	10 32	12 55	14 15	16 20	17 40	18 25			
LOSTWITHIEL	a	7 05	8 05	9 55	10 42	13 05	14 25	16 30	17 50	18 35			

Saturdays

20 June to 5 September

FOWEY	d	6 50	8 00	8 45	9 45	11 30	12 28	13 15	15 00	16 45	17 33	18 20	20 20	20 53	22n00 22p25
GOLANT HALT	d	6 55	8 05	8 50	9 50	11 35	12 33	13 20	15 05	16 50	17 38	18 25	20 58		
LOSTWITHIEL	a	7 05	8 15	9 00	10 00	11 45	12 43	13 30	15 15	17 00	17 48	18 35	20 21	21 08	

For general notes see page 49

b (Western National) from Par dep. 22.47 to Fowey Safe Harbour Hotel

c (Western National) from Par dep. 20.34 to Fowey Safe Harbour Hotel

f (Western National) from Par dep. 21.53 to Fowey Safe Harbour Hotel

g (Western National) from Par dep. 22.47 to Fowey Safe Harbour Hotel

h (Western National) from Par dep. 15.34 to Fowey Safe Harbour Hotel

k (Western National) from Fowey Safe Harbour Hotel to Par Station Approach arr. 21.20

n (Western National) from Fowey Safe Harbour Hotel to Par Station Approach arr. 22.20

p (Western National) from Fowey Safe Harbour Hotel to Par Station Approach arr. 22.43

One of the Gloucester RCW-built single-unit railcars, No W55016 (Class 122), which had replaced the Class '1400' tanks, stands at Fowey to form the 12.35pm service to Lostwithiel on 31 August 1963. Services on the branch were withdrawn from 4 January 1965. *Author*

122) replaced steam working in September 1961. Connections with main line trains, including the 'Cornish Riviera Express' during the winter of 1962/63, is given in BR(WR)'s Table 81 (see pp. 42 & 43).

In June 1964 there were nine return workings each weekday, with 13 up workings and 12 down on summer Saturdays, operated by single-unit railcars. Unlike the St Ives branch, the service only comprised local trains and no through coaches to London were ever provided. The Beeching Report had revealed that the branch carried fewer than 5,000 passengers a week and that apart from at Lostwithiel the station passenger receipts were less than £5,000 per year. Withdrawal of passenger services was soon proposed and implemented from 4 January 1965.

Prior to demolition, the station at Fowey saw a final railtour, organised by the Branch Line Society, when Class 121 single-unit railcar No 55029 visited the line on 8 June 1968. Today the station area has become a car park, but china clay traffic continues to run from Lostwithiel to Carne

Another view of Fowey station, taken in 19 June 1965, six months after closure to passenger services, shows a line of china clay wagons awaiting transfer to the port at Carne Point on the Fowey estuary. As noted above, the line to St Blazey, seen in the foreground, remained open for china clay traffic until 1968 when it was converted into a haul-road. The station has since been demolished and the site is a car park. China clay is still transported by rail between Lostwithiel and Carne Point. *Frank Hornby*

Lostwithiel station was noted for the palm trees growing on the down platform. Here one of the Pressed Steel Co single-unit railcars, No W55029 (Class 121), has called with a special service for the Fowey branch organised by the Branch Line Society on 8 June 1968. Trains for Fowey had traditionally departed from the south side of this platform. The station remains open today on the main line to Penzance despite being listed for closure in the Beeching Report. (See photo on page 53)
Frank Hornby

Point docks. The branch line is thus back where it started in 1869! The old Cornwall Minerals Railway route from St Blazey has become a haul-road. The station at Lostwithiel remains open on the main line, with services operated by Great Western Railway and CrossCountry.

3.4 Halwill - Torrington (March 1965)

The first station at Torrington was opened by the LSWR in 1872 as the terminus of its line from Barnstaple (Chapter 3.5). Nine years later in 1881 a 6-mile 3-foot-gauge tramway, the Torrington & Marland Railway, was built to transport ball clay from Petrockstow to the railhead at Torrington.

Although conversion of the tramway to a standard-gauge railway had been planned before the First World War, it was not until Colonel Stephens became involved in the 1920s that construction actually started. Col Stephens, the 'Light Railway King', had earlier in 1908 engineered the Plymouth, Devonport & South Western Junction Railway's branch line from Bere Alston to Callington. The Light Railways Acts of 1896 and 1912 had allowed lines to be built without the complex signalling and other safety features required elsewhere; they were, however, limited to a maximum weight of 12 tons per axle and a maximum speed of 25mph. Not content with converting just the 6-mile tramway to a standard gauge line, Col Stephens extended it for a further 14½ miles to Halwill, a hamlet situated deep in the North Devon countryside. The grandly titled 'North

7 September Supplement to the Western Region Timetable dated 15 June 1964 - 13 June 1965 (Table 65)

Halwill to Torrington

HALWILL	.. .. d	..	..	10 35	..	..	..	..	18 20	..
HOLE	.... d	....	....	10 44	....	....	....	....	18 30	..
HATHERLEIGH	.. .. d	..	..	11 00	..	..	..	..	18 46	..
MEETH HALT	.... d	....	....	11 08	....	....	....	....	18 54	..
PETROCKSTOW	.... d	7 55	..	11 17	....	..	..	..	19 04	..
DUNSBEAR HALT	.... d	8 04	....	11 25	....	....	....	....	19 12	..
YARDE HALT	.. .. d	8 10	..	11 30	..	..	..	..	19 17	..
WATERGATE HALT	.... d	8 24	....	11 42	....	....	....	....	19 29	..
TORRINGTON	.. .. a	8 32	..	11 49	..	..	..	..	19 36	..

Torrington to Halwill

TORRINGTON	.. .. d	6 25	..	8 55	..	15 55	..
WATERGATE HALT	.... d	6 32	..	9 02	..	16 02	..
YARDE HALT	.. .. d	6 47	..	9 16	..	16 15	..
DUNSBEAR HALT	.... d	6a52	..	9 20	..	16 19	..
PETROCKSTOW	.... d	..	..	9 30	..	16 29	..
MEETH HALT	.... d	..	..	9 40	..	16 39	..
HATHERLEIGH	.... d	..	..	9 48	..	16 49	..
HOLE	.... d	..	..	10 08	..	17 08	..
HALWILL	.. .. a	..	..	10 18	..	17 18	..

Heavy figures indicate through carriages
For general notes see page 49

Ivatt Class 2 2-6-2 tank No 41249 crosses the viaduct to the west of Torrington station with a train of mixed stock from Petrockstow on 31 August 1964. The Halwill line opened as a Light Railway in 1925, and overall earthworks on the line were kept to a minimum, but this handsome viaduct was required to cross the River Torridge. Today the viaduct can be crossed by cyclists and pedestrians as part of the 'Tarka Trail'. *Author*

Devon & Cornwall Junction Light Railway' (ND&CJLR) finally opened for both freight and passenger traffic in July 1925, at a time when many other light railways were already struggling financially. Halwill station had opened in 1879 together with the Devon & Cornwall Railway's line from Okehampton to Holsworthy (Chapters 3.9 and 3.10). It had first become a junction in 1886 when the LSWR line opened its line to Launceston.

The line from Torrington was single throughout with passing places at Petrockstow and Hatherleigh, the latter being the only village of any size on the route. A maximum speed of 20mph was enforced between Torrington and Dunsbear Halt, and 25mph beyond to Halwill. Due to its alignment with the former tramway, the line's sharp curves were almost continuous, together with gradients as steep as 1 in 45. The main structure on the line was the fine viaduct, situated just west of Torrington station, where the line crossed the River Torridge. Five stations and halts were initially provided, with two additional halts, at Watergate and Yarde, opened a year later.

Although the ND&CJLR remained an independent company until nationalisation, it was operated by the Southern Railway from the start. Services were few and very slow. After its opening the line seems to have entered a time warp, with its meagre service of trains taking up to 1hr 23min to travel the 20½ miles. It is remarkable that it survived until the Beeching cuts. The timetable of trains for 1964 looks very similar to that operated by the Southern Railway before the Second World War. Two trains traversed the whole line each weekday, while a further train left Torrington at 6.25am for Dunsbear Halt, returning from Petrockstow at 7.55am. A train for Torrington also left Petrockstow at 4.37pm, Saturdays excepted. There was no Sunday service.

Ivatt Class 2 2-6-2 tank No 41298 stands in Torrington station after arrival with its single coach from Halwill on 12 July 1957. No 41298 survived until July 1967, when it was sent to Barry scrapyard. It was subsequently purchased for preservation and was later acquired by the Isle of Wight Railway at Havenstreet, and has since been restored to working order. *Frank Hornby*

The line remained steam-worked until September 1964, when steam in the West Country was virtually eliminated. Trains usually comprised a single coach hauled by an Ivatt Class 2 2-6-2 tank. The trains to and from Petrockstow ran as mixed trains and included ball clay wagons. Trains were then worked by a single-unit railcar, although the service remained the same apart from the 4.37pm, which ceased to run.

Needless to say, the assessment of the line in the Beeching Report was bleak. The branch carried fewer than 5,000 passengers a week, while only Torrington station was generating annual passenger receipts of more than £5,000. Closure proposals were therefore soon published and approved, and passenger services were withdrawn from 1 March 1965. The line west of Meeth was then closed completely, while that between Torrington and Meeth continued in use for ball clay traffic from Marland Sidings until August 1982.

The whole line was reopened on 27 March 1965 for the Plymouth Railway Circle/RCTS 'Exmoor Ranger' railtour. This was steam-hauled by Ivatt Class 2 tanks Nos 41291 and 41206 from Exeter St David's

No 41298 is seen again approaching Halwill with the 4.00pm train from Torrington on 5 July 1961. The line to the left is from Bude, which was to close from 3 October 1966. *Terry Gough*

Ivatt Class 2 2-6-2 tank No 41248 has arrived in the bay platform at Halwill with the 3.55pm train from Torrington on 31 August 1964. Only two trains a day traversed the whole of the 20¼-mile line, taking about 1hr 15min minutes to do so. The junction of the Bude and Padstow lines can be seen in the background with a train from Padstow approaching. Passenger services on the branch were withdrawn from 1 March 1965. *Author*

to Halwill, and became the last train ever to travel the whole line to Torrington. The truncated line from Meeth also saw railtour traffic including the 'Devon Quarryman', which ran on 25 June 1975 with Class 33 diesel-electric locomotives Nos 33119 and 33103 at either end. The viaduct to the west of Torrington station still stands and has become part of the 'Tarka Trail' footpath and cycleway; this 30-mile trail starts at Braunton, north-west of Barnstaple, and follows former railway trackbeds as far as Meeth.

Ivatt Class 2 2-6-2 tanks Nos 41206 and 41291 prepare to leave Halwill with the 'Exmoor Ranger' railtour on 27 March 1965, almost a month after the line had officially closed. The tour, organised jointly by the Plymouth Railway Circle and RCTS, had earlier arrived from Exeter St David's. It later visited Ilfracombe and the ex-GWR line to Taunton via Dulverton. *Owen Mogg*

3.5 Barnstaple Junction – Torrington (October 1965)

The broad-gauge line of the Exeter & Crediton Railway (E&CR) from Exeter had reached Barnstaple in 1854. A year later the line was extended to Bideford by upgrading a standard-gauge tramway that had opened between Fremington Quay and Barnstaple in 1848. In February 1862 the LSWR had managed to secure a lease from the E&CR and by 1863 had laid a third rail for its standard-gauge trains as far as Bideford. The line was extended to Torrington, 14¼ miles from Barnstaple, in 1872. The 5 miles of new railway involved considerable bridgework and other engineering as its route crossed the River Torridge four times. A short section followed the route of the former Rolle Canal, which had opened in 1827 to carry ball clay to the port of Bideford, and was closed in 1871 and sold to the LSWR. Double track was provided as far as Fremington, 2¾ miles from Barnstaple. After that the line was single through Instow station to Bideford, where a passing loop was provided. The whole line was converted to standard gauge in July 1876 and purchased by the

LSWR three years later. By this time Barnstaple station had become Barnstaple Junction with the opening of the Ilfracombe line in 1874 (Chapter 3.17).

On weekdays during the summer of 1962 through coaches to Torrington were attached to the 1.00pm and 3.00pm departures from Waterloo in addition to the 'ACE' at 11.00am. This increased to eight on Saturdays with an additional through train to Bideford (Appendix 2.1). The weekday train service to Torrington during the winter of 1962/63, including the arrival of the 'ACE' at 3.49pm, is given in BR(SR)'s Table 35 (see pp. 63 & 64). It was to be the last winter that through coaches ran from Waterloo to Torrington. On summer Saturdays in 1964 just three through workings from Waterloo remained, including the 'Atlantic Coast Express'; passengers for Torrington had otherwise to change at Barnstaple Junction. These through coaches were not, however, shown in the branch line's timetable for the period (Table 72). As described in Chapter 2.6, all ex-BR(SR) services, including those on the main line from Waterloo to Exeter, were rationalised and dieselised from 7 September 1964. Through working beyond Exeter had become a thing of the past.

BR(WR) commenced trials on the line with one of its NB Type 2 diesel-hydraulics in May 1963, although the loco involved is reported to have failed at Torrington. The type's first passenger working over the line was not, however, reported until 31 March 1964, when No D6347 took over the 4.21pm service from Exeter Central to Torrington at Barnstaple Junction. Despite this some steam working, mainly by Ivatt Class 2 2-6-2 tanks, lasted to the end of the 1964 summer service on 6 September. After that date all trains were worked by diesel-hydraulics or DMUs.

The figures collected for the Beeching Report in April 1961 had revealed that the branch carried fewer than 5,000 passengers a week, although both Torrington and Bideford stations had annual passenger

Ivatt Class 2 2-6-2 tank No 41298, then allocated to Barnstaple Junction depot, is pictured at Fremington with the 5.46pm train from Torrington to Barnstaple Junction on 9 April 1956. These LMS-designed tanks, which were introduced in 1946, had replaced many older ex-LSWR engines in the area from the 1950s. Services on the branch were withdrawn from 4 October 1965, although an emergency shuttle service was introduced in January 1968 when the town bridge over the River Torridge was damaged by floodwater. *Terry Gough*

Ivatt Class 2 2-6-2 tank No 41214 takes water in Torrington station on 18 June 1963 as a train departs for Barnstaple Junction. Tanks with milk for the local creamery can be seen on the right. Until September 1964 Torrington received through coaches from Waterloo, including those attached to the 'Atlantic Coast Express'. *A. J. Pike, Frank Hornby collection*

receipts above £5,000. These figures seem at odds with the level of service provided in the summer of that year; it is clearly an example of the difference between holiday and out-of-season travel. In addition it is probable that most tickets had been issued in London rather than at Torrington or Bideford. After rationalisation of the timetable from 4 September 1965, ten trains ran each way on weekdays with three on Sundays, although the latter ceased after 26 September. The Sunday service in winter had shrunk from three trains a day in 1962 to none in 1965. All passenger services were withdrawn from 4 October 1965.

Steam returned to the branch on 27 March 1965 when Ivatt Class 2 tanks Nos 41291 and 41206 hauled the Plymouth Railway Circle/RCTS's 'Exmoor Ranger' railtour from Torrington to Barnstaple Junction. The last train passenger steam working to Torrington occurred on 3 October 1965 when the 'Exeter Flyer' from Waterloo worked over the branch behind Standard Class 4 2-6-4 tank No 80039. The train was split at Barnstaple Junction and sister engine No 80043 took the other half to Ilfracombe and back.

The railway remained open for ball clay traffic from Petrockstow on the truncated line from Torrington to Halwill until August 1982. The last passenger train to reach Torrington was the 15-coach 'Last Atlantic Coast Express' special on 6 November hauled by Class 31 diesel-electrics Nos 31174 and 31138. Torrington station remains intact as a restaurant and a small railway preservation centre has been established there. Much of the trackbed now forms part of the 'Tarka Trail' long-distance foot and cycle path from Braunton and Barnstaple.

Another busy scene at Torrington was captured by M. E. J. Deane in April 1961 from the same vantage point. It includes three Ivatt Class 2 2-6-2 tank engines; one is standing in the up platform with a three-coach train to Barnstaple Junction, while two more are seen in the background. A single coach is also standing in the up platform and may later form a train to Halwill worked by one of the other 2-6-2 tanks. *M. E. J. Deane collection, courtesy of Ian Bennett*

The Ivatt Class 2 2-6-2 tank seen in the previous photo is pictured leaving Torrington for Barnstaple Junction in April 1961 past one it its sister engines. The first coach of its train is of Bulleid design. Note also the fine ex-LSWR lower-quadrant signal. *M. E. J. Deane collection, courtesy of Ian Bennett*

On 31 August 1964 Ivatt Class 2 2-6-2 tank No 41290 is sharing duties with the North British Type 2 diesel-hydraulics, and is seen here arriving at Torrington station with the 3.15pm train from Barnstaple Junction. Passenger services on the branch were withdrawn from 4 May. The line remained open for milk and ball clay traffic, finally closing in August 1982. Its trackbed can now be walked as part of the 'Tarka Trail'. *Author*

By 1964 BR(WR) diesel-hydraulics were beginning to replace steam on the lines in North Devon. Here North British-built Type 2 diesel-hydraulic No D6321 stands in Torrington station after arrival with the 1.15pm train from Barnstaple Junction on 31 August 1964. No D6321 was withdrawn in August 1968. *Author*

Western Region Timetable 14 June 1965 - 17 April 1966
By the summer of 1965 only local trains ran between Barnstaple Junction and Torrington. This compares with eight through trains from Waterloo to Torrington on Saturdays in 1962 and nine to Bideford (Appendix 3)

1735 2nd- CHEAP DAY
Torrington to BARNSTAPLE JUNCTION
(S)
For conditions see ov

Table 51

Weekdays — NOT on Saturdays 19 June to 4 September   **Saturdays 19 June to 4 September**

Barnstaple Junction to Torrington

	Miles									B	A											
BARNSTAPLE JUNCTION	—	d	06 19	07 40	08 45	09 58			13 00	14 45	15 25	16 35	17 40	18 55	20 55			06 18		07 27	08 48		10 00	11 15	
FREMINGTON	2¼	d	06 25	07 46	08 51	10 04			13 06	14 51	15 31	16 41	17 46	19 01	21 01			06 23		07 32	03 53		10 05	11 20	
INSTOW	6½	d	06 33	07 53	08 58	10 13			13 14	14 58	15 38	16 48	17 53	19 08	21 08			06 30		07 39	09 00		10 12	11 27	
BIDEFORD	9¼	d	06b46	08c15	09 04	10 19			13 19	15 04	15 44	16 54	17 59	19 14	21 14			06 37		07 46	09 07		10 19	11 34	
TORRINGTON	14¼	a	06 56	08 25	09 14	10 29			13 29	15 14	15 54	17 04	18 09	19 24	21 24			06 47		07 56	09 17		10 29	11 44	

Saturdays 19 June to 4 September—continued   **Sundays Until 26 September only**

BARNSTAPLE JUNCTION	d	12 30	13 45		15 00	16 10	17 30	18 56	20 50				10 12	11 50		14 42	16 00	18 26	
FREMINGTON	d	12 35	13 50		15 05	16 17	35	19 01	20 55				10 18	11 55		14 48	16 06	18 32	
INSTOW	d	12 42	13 57		15 12	16 22	17 42	19 08	21 02				10 25	12 03		14 55	16 13	18 39	
BIDEFORD	d	12 49	14 04		15 19	16 29	17 49	19 15	21 09				10 31	12 09		15 01	16 19	18 45	
TORRINGTON	a	12 59	14 14		15 29	16 39	17 59	19 25	21 19				10 41	12 19		15 11	16 29	18 55	

Weekdays — NOT on Saturdays 19 June to 4 September   **Saturdays 19 June to 4 September**

Torrington to Barnstaple Junction

	Miles						C	D	A	B				C							
TORRINGTON	—	d	06 58	08 00	09 55	10c55	11 20	11 56	13 50	15 57	17 20	18 12	19 45			06 52	08e02	09 25		10e40	11 49
BIDEFORD	5	d	07 09	08 11	10 06	11 06	11 31	12 07	14 01	16 08	17 31	18 23	19 56			07 04	08e14	09 37		10e52	12 01
INSTOW	7½	d	07 15	08 17	10 12	11 12	11 37	12 13	14 07	16 14	17 37	18 29	20 02			07 09	08e19	09 42		10e57	12 06
FREMINGTON	11½	d	07 23	08 25	10 20	11 20	11 45	12 21	14 15	16 22	17 45	18 37	20 10			07 15	08e25	09 48		11e03	12 12
BARNSTAPLE JUNCTION	14½	a	07 28	08 30	10 25	11 25	11 50	12 26	14 20	16 27	17 52	18 42	20 15			07 20	08 30	09 53		11 08	12 17

Saturdays 19 June to 4 September—continued   **Sundays Until 26 September only**

TORRINGTON	d	13 05	14e20	15 35	16 52		18 04	19 45	21 25				11 03	14 15	15 20	17 18	19 40		
BIDEFORD	d	13 17	14e32	15 47	17 04		18 16	19 57	21 37				11 19	13 56	15 31	17 29	19 51		
INSTOW	d	13 22	14e37	15 52	17 09		18 21	20 02	21 42				11 25	14 02	15 37	17 35	19 57		
FREMINGTON	d	13 28	14e43	15 58	17 15		18 27	20 08	21 48				11 33	14 10	15 45	17 43	20 05		
BARNSTAPLE JUNCTION	a	13 33	14e48	16 03	17 20		18 32	20 13	21 53				11 38	14 15	15 50	17 48	20 10		

Heavy figures denote through carriages;
light figures denote connecting services
For general notes see page 3

A Until 25 September
B From 27 September
C To Taunton
D To Exeter Central

b Arr 06 38
> Arr 08 04
e Passengers travelling to London Paddington by this connection require Regulation tickets see page 33

Western Region Timetable: 14 June 1965 to 17 April 1966

By the summer of 1965 only local trains ran between Barnstaple Junction and Torrington. This compares with eight through trains from Waterloo to Torrington on Saturdays in 1962 and nine to Bideford (Box 4.2)

3.6 Axminster – Lyme Regis (November 1965)

Soon after the opening of its railway from Yeovil and Exeter in 1860, the LSWR saw the potential of a branch line from Axminster to the popular seaside spa of Lyme Regis. It was not, however, until 1871 that the Lyme Regis Railway Company (LRRC) obtained a Parliamentary Act to build the line. Although work started in 1874 the LSWR appeared to lose interest, and without its support the LRRC was soon in financial difficulties and work came to a halt.

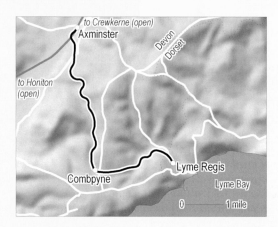

The line was rescued by the 1896 Light Railways Act as, following local pressure and with support from the LSWR, the LRRC obtained a Lyme Regis Light Railway Order in June 1899. Construction started in 1900, but although only the minimum of earthworks was required, the work was found to be more difficult than anticipated. The 600-foot viaduct across the Cannington Valley caused particular problems. It was among the first viaducts in the country to be constructed in concrete, but subsidence occurred and one of the arches had to be reinforced. Despite these problems, the 6¾-mile line opened in August 1903 with an intermediate station at Combpyne. The traffic

The Lyme Regis branch was famous for the continued use into the 1960s of ex-LSWR Class '0415' 4-4-2 tanks, a design first introduced in 1882. Here one of the three members of the class, then allocated to Exmouth Junction shed, No 30583, leaves Axminster with a train for Lyme Regis in the early 1960s. No 30583 was built by Neilson Reid & Co in 1885 and was to survive until July 1961. It is now preserved on the Bluebell Railway. *M. E. J. Deane collection, courtesy of Ian Bennett*

generated was, however, disappointing and in January 1907 the LRRC was absorbed by the LSWR. One of the line's problems was that the terminus at Lyme Regis was some three-quarters of a mile from the town and 250 feet above it.

The stiff gradients and sharp curves on the line immediately created a problem as far as suitable motive power was concerned. This needed to be powerful, light and with a wheelbase short enough to cope with

Another of the three '0415s', No 30582, also allocated to Exmouth Junction shed, leaves Axminster with the 1.06pm train to Lyme Regis on 16 August 1959. No 30582 was also built in 1885 and, like No 30583, survived until July 1961; sadly it was not preserved. *Terry Gough*

the curves. After several classes of tank engine were tried, the problem was finally solved when two ex-LSWR Class '0415' 4-4-2 tanks were allocated to the line. These engines, designed by W. Adams, had been introduced in 1882 to work suburban trains from Waterloo. By 1928 they were the last of their class at work on the SR and despite other attempts to replace them they soldiered on until the end of the Second World War. As summer holiday traffic increased, the need for a third engine to work the branch became imperative. The outcome was that in 1946 the SR purchased a third Class '0415' tank from the East Kent Railway, which had bought it from the LSWR in 1919. In 1947 the three became BR Nos 30582, 30583 and 30584. Despite further attempts to replace them the trio remained at work in the summer of 1960. In that year BR(SR) was forced to carry out some strengthening work on the line and conducted trials with an Ivatt Class 2 2-6-2 tank. Although the first Ivatt tank commenced work in March 1961, two of the Adams tanks remained at work through the summer of 1961 but were withdrawn in September. Connections with trains from Waterloo during the winter of 1962/63, are given in BR(SR) Table 35 (see pp. 63 & 64).

Unlike most other ex-SR branch lines, that to Lyme Regis only saw through coaches from Waterloo during the summer, and latterly only on Saturdays. It was then that two of the ancient Class '0415' tanks could be seen double-heading the through coaches up gradients as steep as 1 in 40 on their way to Lyme Regis. In the summer of 1962 coaches for Lyme Regis were attached to the 10.45am from Waterloo (Appendix 3.1), while two afternoon departures from Lyme Regis also included through

No 30583 is pictured again returning to Axminster over the Cannington Viaduct with a train from Lyme Regis. The viaduct was the most significant structure on the line and was among the first to be built in concrete. Still in existence today, it is more than 200 yards long, some 90 feet high and has ten arches. Slippage to its foundations during building resulted in the significant drop in its parapet, visible in this photo, as is the required strengthening to the third arch. *M. E. J. Deane collection, courtesy of Ian Bennett*

coaches for London. The Ivatt tanks' reign on the branch was, however, brief as, after working the last of the through coaches in the summer of 1963, they were replaced by single-unit railcars in November. In the spring of 1965, after problems with the railcars, the class made a brief reappearance with No 41291 hauling a BR(WR) auto-coach. During this period the branch saw a further steam working, as on 28 February 1965 part of an LCGB special from Waterloo traversed it hauled by Ivatt Class 2 2-6-2 tank No 41206. A second train ran on 7 March using No 41291.

The Beeching Report revealed that although the branch carried fewer than 5,000 passengers a week, both Lyme Regis and Axminster stations had annual passenger receipts above £5,000. Despite this closure was proposed and implemented on 29 November 1965. Until then the service comprised nine departures each weekday in 1965 and eleven on summer Saturdays. Nine trains ran each Sunday until 6 September.

Today the Cannington Viaduct remains but schemes to restore at least part of the old railway have so far failed. Class '0415' tank No 30583 survives on the Bluebell Railway, and Axminster station remains open on the main line with services provided by South West Trains.

No 30582 heads for Axminster with the 11.08am train from Lyme Regis on 13 August 1960. At the time through coaches for Lyme Regis were attached to the 'Atlantic Coast Express' from Waterloo throughout the year. In summer the heavy trains regularly required the use of two of the '0415' tanks. The through coaches lasted until September 1963. *Terry Gough*

No 30583 arrives at Lyme Regis with its train from Axminster in the early 1960s. The engine was sold to the Ministry of Munitions in 1917, which then sold it to the East Kent Railway in 1919. After the Second World War it was purchased by the SR for the Lyme Regis branch. At first numbered 3488, it became No 30583 on nationalisation. As mentioned above, it is now preserved on the Bluebell Railway. *M. E. J. Deane collection, courtesy of Ian Bennett*

Western Region Timetable 14 June 1965 - 17 April 1966
By the summer of 1965 only local trains ran between Axminster and Lyme Regis. This compares with one train from and two to Waterloo on Saturdays in 1962 (see Appendix 3)

Table 45 (Second class only)

Axminster to Lyme Regis — Weekdays — NOT on Saturdays 19 June to 4 September — Saturdays 19 June to 4 September

Lyme Regis to Axminster — Weekdays — NOT on Saturdays 19 June to 4 September — Saturdays 19 June to 4 September

(stations: AXMINSTER, COMBPYNE, LYME REGIS)

Sundays Until 26 September — Sundays From 3 October

Heavy figures denote through carriages;
light figures denote connecting services
For general notes see page 3

A Until 25 September
B From 27 September
C Through train to Exeter Central
D (Southern National) between Axminster and Lyme Regis (Langford's Shop)

Western Region Timetable: 14 June 1965 – 17 April 1966

By the summer of 1965 only local trains ran between Axminster and Lyme Regis. This compares with one train from and two to Waterloo on Saturdays in 1962 (Box 4.2)

Ivatt Class 2 2-6-2 tanks finally replaced the '0415' tanks in the summer of 1961, following the strengthening of bridges on the line. Here No 41309 stands at Lyme Regis with the 5.13pm train to Axminster on 2 September 1963. Single-unit railcars took over services in November 1963, then passenger services were withdrawn from 29 November 1965. *Author*

For a short period in the spring of 1965 a shortage of single-unit railcars saw a return of steam to the Lyme Regis branch in the form of Ivatt Class 2 2-6-2 tank No 41291 hauling an ex-GWR auto-coach. Then in April single-unit railcars became available, as seen here on the 22nd, with a unit entering Lyme Regis station forming the 3.05pm service from Axminster. By this time the track in the goods yard had been lifted, although the rusting run-round loop remains. *Author*

3.7 Seaton Junction - Seaton (March 1966)

The station at Seaton Junction first opened in July 1860 under the name 'Colyton for Seaton'. Axminster station, situated some 3¼ miles to the east, opened on the same day, together with the LSWR's line to Exeter.

At the time the seaside town of Seaton was becoming popular as a holiday resort and in March 1868 a branch was opened by the Seaton & Beer Railway. The 4¼-mile line followed the west side of the River Axe and involved few gradients or engineering works. Two intermediate stations were provided at Colyton and Colyford. The name of the junction station was changed first to Colyton

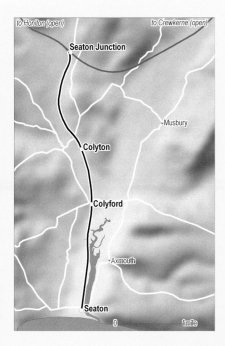

Junction in 1868 and finally to Seaton Junction in 1869. The short line was leased to the LSWR in January 1880 and absorbed by it eight years later.

Like other resorts along the East Devon coast, Seaton increased steadily in popularity to the benefit of the railway, particularly after the First World War. In 1927, four years after the Southern Railway had assumed responsibility for the line, the stations at both Seaton Junction and Seaton were rebuilt. At Seaton Junction four tracks were provided on the main line while a new branch-line platform was constructed on the south side of the station and at right angles to it. At Seaton a grand station building was erected, with one long island platform. The design followed the Art Deco style recently adopted by the SR and full use was made of prefabricated concrete components manufactured at the SR's own Exmouth Junction Concrete Works.

For many years the branch was the haunt of ex-LSWR 'M7' Class 0-4-4 tanks, an LSWR design of 1897. These machines had become redundant following the electrification of the LSWR's London suburban

Ex-LSWR Class 'M7' No 30021 stands at Seaton station with a train for Seaton Junction on 2 June 1953. As the first coach is an ex-SR main-line vehicle, it is probably a through coach to Waterloo. No 30021 was built at Nine Elms in 1904 and withdrawn in March 1964. Through coaches to Seaton ran from Waterloo during the summer until September 1963. *Frank Hornby*

A second ex-LSWR Class 'M7', No 30048, stands at Seaton station with a train for Seaton Junction in May 1961. No 30046 was built in 1905 and withdrawn in January 1964. The train comprises one of the two-coach push-pull sets converted from ex-SR Maunsell-built main-line coaches by BR(SR) in 1959/60. Note the handsome ex-LSWR water crane to the left of the engine. *M. E. J. Deane collection, courtesy of Ian Bennett*

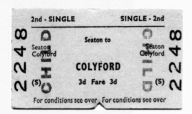

services during the First World War, and in 1925 the SR fitted a number for push-pull working on rural branch lines. A number of LSWR coaches were converted at the same time. This vintage combination was to work the branch for many years. The coaching stock, but not the motive power, was 'modernised' in 1959/60 by two-car sets rebuilt from Southern Railway corridor coaches of the 1930s.

When BR(WR) took over the line in January 1963 the 'M7s' and coaches were soon replaced, not by DMUs as might have been expected, but by ex-GWR auto-fitted pannier tanks and auto-coaches. These had recently been made redundant at Plymouth Laira by the closure of the branch line from Plymouth to Launceston in December 1962. Steam was then replaced by single-unit railcars at the end of October 1963. As at Lyme Regis, problems with these units saw the return of steam to the branch for a few weeks in the spring of 1965 in the form of ex-GWR 0-4-2 tanks Nos 1442 and 1450 and auto-coaches. Both are now preserved as described in the Tiverton to Tiverton Junction section. The LCGB specials from Waterloo also visited the branch using Ivatt 2-6-2 tanks Nos 41206 and 41291 on 28 February and 7 March respectively.

Like the other East Devon resorts adjacent to the ex-SR Waterloo to Exeter Central main line, by the 1930s Seaton had become very popular with holidaymakers. As a result for many years the push-pull-worked trains were supplemented by through coaches from Waterloo. Connections with trains from Waterloo during the winter of 1962/63, are given in BR(SR) Table 35 (see pp. 63 & 64).

On summer Saturdays in 1962 three departures from Waterloo included a Seaton coach, although only one, off the 'Atlantic Coast Express', ran throughout the year (Appendix 3.1). These trains ran for the last time during the summer timetable of 1963, although good connections were still provided at Seaton Junction. In 1965 services over the 4¼-mile branch still involved

'M7' No 30048 is seen again approaching Seaton Junction with the 8.03am train from Seaton on 20 August 1959. At the time ex-LSWR push-pull sets were still in use, prior to the introduction of the ex-Maunsell sets. *Terry Gough*

When BR(WR) took over the BR(SR) lines in January 1963 it quickly replaced the ancient LSWR engines. Because of a shortage of single-unit railcars, the service was handed over to ex-GWR Class '6400' 0-6-0 pannier tanks and auto-trailers. Here No 6400 stands at Seaton Junction with the 3.25pm train for Seaton on 2 September 1963. That was the last summer that through coaches ran between Seaton and Waterloo on Saturdays. *Author*

Another view of No 6400 as it stands in Seaton station with the 3.46pm service for Seaton Junction on 2 September 1963. No 6400 continued in use at Yeovil until withdrawn in March 1964. The single-road engine shed and water tower can be seen to the left; this concrete structure dated from when the station was rebuilt by the SR in 1937. *Author*

'M7' No 30021 pauses at Colyton, one of the two intermediate stations on the Seaton branch, in May 1961. Colyton is now the terminus of the Seaton Tramway from Seaton. *M. E. J. Deane collection, courtesy of Ian Bennett*

13 return workings with 16 on summer Saturdays. Eight trains ran on Sundays until 26 September.

Despite the heavy summer traffic the Beeching Report had revealed that the branch carried fewer than 5,000 passengers a week and that only Seaton station had annual passenger receipts above £5,000. The branch was closed from 7 March 1966, the track was soon lifted, and the station at Seaton demolished. In 1967 the main line through the site of Seaton Junction was reduced to a single track, although some of the station's structures can still be seen from passing trains. The trackbed between Colyton and Seaton was acquired by the Seaton & District Electric Tramway, which, after obtaining a Light Railway Order, opened its 2ft 9in-gauge line in August 1970. As Seaton station had been demolished the company acquired land to the west where a new terminus was established.

BR(WR)'s single-unit railcars took over services in November 1963, but were withdrawn from 7 March 1966. Here passengers prepare to board the 4.00pm from Seaton to Seaton Junction on 4 September 1965 while a porter loads a large parcel into the guard's van. *Author*

Seaton station was situated on the seafront and, after its rebuilding by the SR in 1937, had quite an imposing frontage. This view was taken on 13 September 1966, six months after closure. The site was subsequently cleared and the present-day Seaton trams use a terminus to the west. *J. M. Tolson, Frank Hornby collection*

Western Region Timetable 14 June 1965 - 17 April 1966

By the summer of 1965 only local trains ran between Seaton Junction and Seaton.
This compares with three trains from Waterloo on Saturdays in 1962 (see Appendix 3)

Table 46 (Second Class only)

Seaton Junction to Seaton

Weekdays
NOT on Saturdays 19 June to 4 September

Miles																							A	WSX L	WSO K
—	SEATON JUNCTION d	07 35	..	08 10	08 45	..	10 26	12 25	..	13 15	14 16	..	15 00	15 45	..	16 55	17 38	..	18 48	..	20<58	..	..
1½	COLYTON d	07 39	....	08 14	08 49	....	10 30	12 29	....	13 19	14 20	....	15 04	15 49	....	16 59	17 42	....	18 52	....	21<02	....	....
2½	COLYFORD d	07 42	..	08 17	08 52	..	10 33	12 32	..	13 22	14 23	..	15 07	15 52	..	17 02	17 45	..	18 55	..	21<05	..	..
4¼	SEATON a	07 45	....	08 20	08 55	....	10 36	12 35	....	13 25	14 26	....	15 10	15 55	....	17 05	17 48	....	18 58	....	21<08	22 40	23 47

Saturdays
19 June to 4 September

																							K
SEATON JUNCTION d	07 35	08 10	..	08 45	..	09 57	..	10 29	11 05	11 45	..	12 25	13 07	14 25	..	15 07	15 47	16 20	17 40	..	18 50	20 58	..
COLYTON d	07 39	08 14	....	08 49	....	10 01	....	10 33	11 09	11 49	....	12 29	13 11	14 29	....	15 11	15 51	16 24	17 44	....	18 54	21 02	....
COLYFORD d	07 42	08 17	..	08 52	..	10 04	..	10 36	11 12	11 52	..	12 32	13 14	14 32	..	15 14	15 54	16 27	17 47	..	18 57	21 05	..
SEATON a	07 45	08 20	....	08 55	....	10 07	....	10 39	11 15	11 55	....	12 35	13 17	14 35	....	15 17	15 57	16 30	17 50	....	19 00	21 08	23 47

Sundays Until 26 September | **Sundays** From 3 October (from Axminster)

										G		G	G	G	G	G	G	G	G	G	G	G	G
AXMINSTER STATION APP. d	..	..	..	..	..	..	..	..	..	21 45	..	11 42	13 32	14 30	14k55	15k44	17 03	17k34	18k20	19 40	19k50	21 45	22 10
SEATON JUNCTION d	10 25	11 12	12 20	14 08	15 05	16 35	19 13	20 23	....	....	....	....	....	....	....	....	....	....	....	....	....	....	....
COLYTON d	10 29	11 16	12 24	14 12	15 09	16 39	19 17	20 27	..	..	..	..	..	..	..	..	..	..	..	..	..	..	..
COLYFORD d	10 32	11 19	12 27	14 15	15 12	16 42	19 20	20 30	....	....	....	....	....	....	....	....	....	....	....	....	....	....	....
SEATON a	10 35	11 22	12 30	14 18	15 15	16 45	19 23	20 33	..	22b12	..	12b09	13b59	14b59	15b27	16b14	17b32	18b04	18b52	20b07	20b22	22b12	22b40

Seaton to Seaton Junction

Weekdays
NOT on Saturdays 19 June to 4 September

Miles		H	H				D SO	E	J	J		J									B	A	A
—	SEATON d	06 10	07 20	07 50	..	08 25	09<45	10<00	10 15	11 05	12 00	12 15	12 55	13 40	..	14 35	15 20	16 30	17 15	18 18	19<20	20<30	21<12
1¾	COLYFORD d	06 20	07 28	07 55	....	08 30	09<50	10<05	10 23	11 15	12 05	12 23	13 00	13 45	....	14 40	15 25	16 35	17 20	18 23	19<25	20<35	21<17
2¾	COLYTON d	06 24	07 32	07 59	..	08 34	09<54	10<09	10 27	11 19	12 09	12 27	13 04	13 49	..	14 44	15 29	16 39	17 24	18 27	19<29	20<39	21<21
4¼	SEATON JUNCTION a	....	....	08 03	....	08 38	09<58	10<13	....	....	12 13	....	13 08	13 53	....	14 48	15 33	16 43	17 28	18 31	19<33	20<43	21<25

Saturdays
19 June to 4 September

	H											J									C		
SEATON d	07 20	..	07 50	..	08 25	..	09 34	10 10	10 42	11 25	11 58	12 15	12 45	13 35	14 40	15 23	16 00	16 52	18 20	20 30	21 35	..	..
COLYFORD d	07 28	....	07 55	....	08 30	....	09 39	10 15	10 47	11 30	12 03	12 23	12 50	13 40	14 45	15 28	16 05	16 57	18 25	20 35	21 40	....	....
COLYTON d	07 32	..	07 59	..	08 34	..	09 43	10 19	10 51	11 34	12 07	12 27	12 54	13 44	14 49	15 32	16 09	17 01	18 29	20 39	21 44	..	..
SEATON JUNCTION a	....	....	08 03	....	08 38	....	09 47	10 23	10 55	11 38	12 11	....	12 58	13 48	14 53	15 36	16 13	17 05	18 33	20 43	21 48	....	....

Sundays Until 26 September | **Sundays** From 3 October (to Axminster)

			G				G			C	G	G	G	G	G	G	G	G	G	G	G	G	G
SEATON d	10 40	12 00	12b15	13 45	14 45	16 05	17b25	18 47	19 35	20 36	21b30	09b50	12b15	13b25	14b05	15b35	16b15	17b25	18b05	18b30	19b05	20b15	21b30
COLYFORD d	10 45	12 05	....	13 50	14 50	16 10	....	18 52	19 40	20 41	....	....	....	....	....	....	....	....	....	....	....	....	....
COLYTON d	10 49	12 09	..	13 54	14 54	16 14	..	18 56	19 44	20 45	..	..	..	..	..	..	..	..	..	..	..	..	..
SEATON JUNCTION a	10 53	12 13	....	13 58	14 58	16 18	....	19 00	19 48	20 49	....	....	....	....	....	....	....	....	....	....	....	....	....
AXMINSTER STATION APP. a	..	..	12 42	..	..	..	17 57	..	..	..	21 59	10 17	12 42	13 54	14 32	16 04	16 42	17k57	18 32	18 59	19 32	20 44	21 59

Heavy figures denote through carriages; light figures denote connecting services
For general notes see page 3

A Until 25 September
B From 27 September
C To Exeter Central
D 11, 18 and 25 September
E **Not** on Saturdays 11, 18 and 25 September
G (Southern or Western National)
H (Southern or Western National) from Seaton (Sea Front) to Axminster Station (journey time 30 minutes)
J (Southern or Western National) from Seaton (Sea Front) to Axminster Station Approach (journey time 30 minutes)
K (Southern or Western National) from Axminster Station Approach dep 23 18
L (Southern or Western National) from Axminster Station dep 22 10
b Seaton Sea Front
e (Southern or Western National) from Axminster Station Approach dep 23 15
k Axminster (Rail Station)

In 1971 some 3 miles of the Seaton branch opened as the 2ft 9in-gauge electrified Seaton Tramway, and Colyton station was restored as the line's northern terminus, seen here from the top of tram No 10 as it approaches the station on 10 April 2015. The original down station platform has been fenced off from the trams and is in use as part of the station buffet. *Author*

Passengers join open-topped double-decker tram No 10 at Colyton to return to Seaton on 10 April 2015, while single-deck No 19 waits to replace it on the departure line. No 10 was built for the line between 2002 and 2007 incorporating features of former Plymouth and Blackburn trams. No 19 was originally built for the 3ft 6in-gauge Exeter Corporation tramway in 1906, and was converted for use on the Seaton Tramway in the 1990s. *Author*

3.8 Yeovil Junction to Yeovil Town (October 1966) and Yeovil Junction to Yeovil Pen Mill (May 1968)

The development of railways around Yeovil was a complex process involving four different railway companies. While these were soon absorbed by either the GWR or LSWR, the two companies offered trains to London from Pen Mill and Yeovil Junction respectively. However, Yeovil Junction was inconveniently situated to the south of the town and a shuttle service was introduced in 1861 over the 1¾ miles between it and the centrally situated Yeovil Town station. Here passengers who wished to travel on to Bristol or Weymouth had to wait for a GWR train to Yeovil Pen Mill, where yet another connection would have to be made. This shuttle service continued into BR days and was operated for many years by push-pull-fitted ex-LSWR Class 'M7' 0-4-4 tanks.

In addition to the local trains a number ran daily from Yeovil Town to London Waterloo. The engines of the London trains had to run tender-first to Yeovil Junction where, after running round their train, they departed smokebox-first for London. The reverse process was necessary for down trains to Yeovil Town. These longstanding problems could have

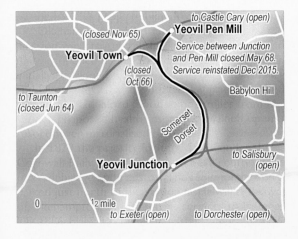

2nd - CHEAP DAY

Yeovil Town to

SALISBURY
via Yeovil Junction
(S)

...ditions see over

2891

been avoided had a joint station been built where the GWR line to Weymouth passed under the LSWR line just east of Yeovil Junction. In the event the two companies could not agree on the matter and the opportunity was lost. It was not until the Second World War that a new junction, Yeovil South Junction, was installed to allow trains to run direct from the SR's line, through Pen Mill station, to Castle Cary and Westbury. Since the war this junction had been used by engineering trains and for emergency diversions. Through trains from Waterloo during the winter of 1962/63, are given in BR(SR) Table 35 (see pp. 63 & 64)

As with the Seaton branch (Chapter 3.7), once BR(WR) had taken control of the line in January 1963 the vintage 'M7s' were soon replaced by ex-GWR auto-fitted pannier tanks and auto-coaches. Initially two Class '5400' locomotives, Nos 5410 and 5416, were used, but these were soon replaced by members of the very similar Class '6400'. After closure of the Tiverton branch in October 1964 (Chapter 3.2) ex-GWR 0-4-2Ts Nos 1442 and 1450 were transferred to Yeovil to work alongside the last remaining 0-6-0 pannier tank No 6419. Steam ended from 28 December 1964 when two AC railbuses, Nos W79975 and W79978, took over the service; these four-wheeled vehicles had once worked the Cirencester and Tetbury branches, which had closed the previous April. They were replaced by single-unit railcars at the end of 1965.

In 1966 there were still 15 return workings each way between Yeovil Junction and Town stations, increased to 19 on summer Saturdays.

The shuttle service provided between Yeovil Town and Yeovil Junction used ex-LSWR engines and push-pull sets. Here Class 'M7' 0-4-4 tank No 30131 approaches Yeovil Junction with the 7.35am shuttle from Yeovil Town on 16 August 1959. No 30131 was built in 1911 and withdrawn in November 1962 shortly before the class was replaced on the line by ex-GWR vehicles.
Terry Gough

At Yeovil BR(WR) initially replaced the ex-LSWR stock with two Class '5400' 0-6-0 pannier tanks, Nos 5410 and 5416, in March 1963. Here No 5410, missing its front number plate, stands in Yeovil Town station with a train for Yeovil Junction on 28 August 1963. Nos 5410 and 5416 were withdrawn in October and August 1963 respectively to be replaced by ex-GWR Class '6400' pannier tanks. *Author*

ORDINARY - 2nd
RETURN

Yeovil Town
to

YEOVIL
JUNCTION

Fare 1/0   (S)
For conditions see over

616685

Through trains to and from Waterloo continued until April 1966, hauled since September 1964 by BR(WR) 'Warship' Class diesel-hydraulics. From April 1966 the only through working from London was the newspaper train from Waterloo, which arrived at 4.55am. A Sunday service also operated during the summer months, including the London arrival at 5.37am. Rather strangely the only return working to Waterloo was the Sundays-only 7.10am from Yeovil Town, although this was not shown in the branch's timetable for the period (Table 36a).

Yeovil did not fare well in the Beeching Report. As discussed in Chapter 2, all three main stations were considered for closure. However, intense local pressure led to the retention of Pen Mill and Junction stations, but Yeovil Town closed from 3 October 1966. The shuttle service was to survive for another 18 months as it was diverted to Pen Mill. It was finally withdrawn from 5 May 1968, single-unit railcar No W55023 operating the last services.

Yeovil Town remained in use for engineering trains, but in 1970 Yeovil

One of the ex-GWR Class '6400' pannier tanks that had replaced the '5400s', No 6435, leaves Yeovil Junction with the 10.35am service for Yeovil Town on 12 February 1964. Two four-wheeled AC-built railbuses replaced steam working from 28 December 1964. The service to Yeovil Town was withdrawn on 3 October 1966 when that station was closed; trains were then diverted to Yeovil Pen Mill, but these ceased from 5 May 1968. *Author*

A second ex-GWR Class '6400' pannier tank, No 6430, is seen at Yeovil Town station after arrival with the 1.40pm train from Yeovil Junction on 5 September 1964. Both Nos 6430 and 6435 were withdrawn in October 1964 and were subsequently preserved by the fledgling Dart Valley Railway; No 6430 is now at Llangollen while No 6435 is at Bodmin. *Author*

Western Region Timetable 18 April 1966 - 5 March 1967

Table 36a (Second class only)

Yeovil Junction to Yeovil Town

Weekdays

Not on Saturdays 18 June to 3 September

		B																					
YEOVIL JUNCTION ... ... d		04 50	07 25	08 35	09 12	11 30	11 55	13 33	14 03	15 28	15 52	...	17 25	17 59	...	19 25	20 11	21 41	22 05	...	...	...
YEOVIL TOWN .... a		04 55	07 29	08 39	09 16	11 34	11 59	13 37	14 07	15 32	15 56	...	17 29	18 03	...	19 29	20 15	21 45	22 09	...	...	...

18 June to 3 September **Saturdays**

		B																					
YEOVIL JUNCTION ... ... d		04 50	07 25	08 35	09 12	10 00	11 30	11 55	12 30	13 33	14 03	14 50	15 28	15 52	16 45	17 25	17 59	19 25	20 11	21 41	22 05	...
YEOVIL TOWN .... a		04 55	07 29	08 39	09 16	10 04	11 34	11 59	12 34	13 37	14 07	14 54	15 32	15 56	16 49	17 29	18 03	19 29	20 15	21 45	22 09	...

Until 15 May and from 2 October		**Sundays**	From 22 May to 25 September	**Sundays**

		B	C						C		B										
YEOVIL JUNCTION ... ... d		05 32	09 10	11⟨42	12 10	13 27	13 55	17 49	18 30	18 54	19⟨50	20 54	05 32	09 10	11 55	12 45	13 27	13 55	17 49	18 30	18 54	19 50	20 54
YEOVIL TOWN .... a		05 37	09 14	11⟨46	12 14	13 31	13 59	17 53	18 34	18 58	19⟨54	20 58	05 37	09 14	11 59	12 49	13 31	13 59	17 53	18 34	18 58	19 54	20 58

Yeovil Town to Yeovil Junction

Weekdays

Not on Saturdays 18 June to 3 September

YEOVIL TOWN ... ... d		07 10	08 10	08 56	...	11 16	11 39	13 20	13 46	...	15 10	15 37	...	17 05	17 43	19 05	19 53	21 30	21 50
YEOVIL JUNCTION .... a		07 14	08 14	09 00	...	11 20	11 43	13 24	13 50	...	15 14	15 41	...	17 09	17 47	19 09	19 57	21 34	21 54

18 June to 3 September **Saturdays**

YEOVIL TOWN ... ... d		07 10	08 10	08 56	09 45	11 16	11 39	12 09	13 20	13 46	14 35	15 10	15 37	16 29	17 05	17 43	19 05	19 53	21 30	21 50
YEOVIL JUNCTION .... a		07 14	08 14	09 00	09 49	11 20	11 43	12 13	13 24	13 50	14 39	15 14	15 41	16 33	17 09	17 47	19 09	19 57	21 34	21 54

Until 15 May and from 2 October		**Sundays**	From 22 May to 25 September	**Sundays**

		B	C							C	B											
YEOVIL TOWN ... ... d		07 10	08 51	11⟨35	11 50	13 11	13 36	17 31	18 16	18 40	19⟨36	20 36	07 10	08 51	11 35	12 26	13 11	13 36	17 31	18 16	18 40	19 36	20 36
YEOVIL JUNCTION .... a		07 15	08 55	11⟨39	11 54	13 15	13 40	17 35	18 20	18 44	19⟨40	20 40	07 15	08 55	11 39	12 30	13 15	13 40	17 35	18 20	18 44	19 40	20 40

B From or to London Waterloo (Table 2)   C 1, 8 and 15 May only

The line between
Yeovil Town and Yeovil
Junction was also used
by through trains.
Here rebuilt 'West
Country' 'Pacific' No
34002 *Salisbury* arrives
at Yeovil Junction with
the 4.06pm service
from Yeovil Town to
Salisbury in September
1964. The engine will
run round its train
before departure,
smokebox first, for its
destination. The line
linking Yeovil Pen Mill
with Yeovil Junction
remains in use today.
Author

Services between Yeovil
Junction and Yeovil Pen
Mill were resumed on
a limited basis by South
West Trains in December
2015. Here 3-Car Class
159/1 unit No. 159.107,
still in its old SWT livery,
prepares to leave Yeovil
Pen Mill with the South
Western Railway's 15.44
to Yeovil Junction and
Waterloo on 4 April
2019. The train left
Waterloo at 12.50 and
had travelled via Salisbury
and Westbury, arriving
at Pen Mill at 15.35. The
train had had to reverse
its direction of travel at
Westbury and would
shortly do this again at
Yeovil Junction. Although
the ex-GWR signal box
still stands at the north
end of the station the
signals are now upper
quadrant. *Author*

Town Council purchased the site and the station was soon demolished to
make way for a car park. Today trains continue to serve Pen Mill and Junction
stations, operated by Great Western Railway and South Western Railway
respectively (Chapters 2.1 and 2.6). For many years a bus service has been
provided between the two stations, although connections were poor. Yeovil
South Junction remained in use and, in December 2015, South Western
Railway commenced a limited service between the two stations. In 2019
there were nine South Western Railway trains from Yeovil Junction to Pen
Mill with one on Saturdays while eight trains ran in the opposite direction,
three on Saturdays. Some of these trains ran to or from Waterloo.

Several of the ex-GWR tank engines that operated the shuttle service
in 1963/64 have since been active in preservation. Although both the Class
'5400' tanks were broken up, Nos 6412, 6430 and 6435 have all survived,
together with No 1450. In addition, No 1442 has for many years been
preserved in Tiverton Museum (Chapter 3.2).

3.9 and 3.10 Okehampton – Bude and – Padstow (October 1966)

The LSWR's projected line from Exeter to Plymouth reached Okehampton in 1871 and Lydford three years later. In 1879 a junction was created off this line at Meldon when the Devon & Cornwall Railway opened its line to Holsworthy. Three intermediate stations were initially provided on the single-track line at Ashbury, Halwill & Beaworthy and Dunsland Cross, all with passing places. In July 1926 a halt was opened at Maddaford Moor, some 2 miles from Meldon Junction; built to serve a proposed health resort, it remained open until 1966, although the resort never materialised.

In 1879 the priority for the LSWR, under the guise of the North Cornwall Railway (NCR), was to head south-west through Launceston to Wadebridge and Padstow. The Holsworthy and Launceston lines parted just north of the station at Halwill & Beaworthy, 17½ miles west of Okehampton, and passenger services to Launceston commenced in July 1886. Halwill & Beaworthy station became Halwill Junction in 1887. Although the NCR was to remain a legally independent company until the railway grouping of 1923, the line was worked by the LSWR from the start; Halwill Junction was renamed simply Halwill by the Southern Railway after the grouping.

Work did not start on the westward extension from Launceston until 1890, finally reaching Tresmeer, 8 miles away, in 1892. After this, progress was more rapid. Camelford was reached in August 1893 and Delabole, 19¾ miles from Launceston, two months later. The line finally reached Wadebridge in May 1895. The whole 44-mile line from Halwill was single track but passing places were provided at all ten intermediate stations. A mile east of Wadebridge the line joined the route of the old Bodmin & Wadebridge Railway; this line had been opened as long ago as 1834 but since 1847 had been owned by the LSWR. The two lines continued side by side into Wadebridge, where three platform faces were provided. The last 5¾ miles to Padstow finally opened in March 1899. Compared with Wadebridge the accommodation at Padstow was rather poor as only one platform face was ever built, despite its use both by LSWR trains from Waterloo and GWR branch-line trains from Bodmin Road on its main line to Penzance (Chapter 3.13). The LSWR's line in North Cornwall

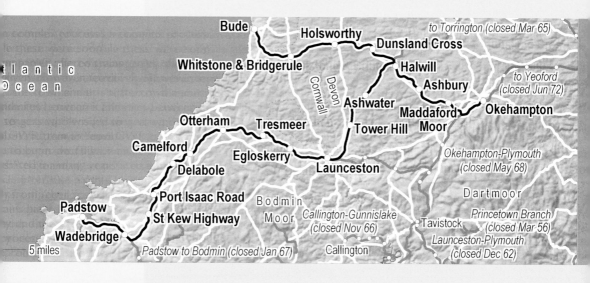

The ex-LSWR Class 'T9' 4-4-0s remained at work west of Exeter long after the arrival of more modern motive power. Here No 30717 stands at Halwill with a train from Okehampton to Padstow on 12 July 1957. The engine was built by Dubs & Co in 1899 and withdrawn in July 1961. *Frank Hornby*

The Class 'N' 2-6-0 was originally designed by R. E. L. Maunsell for the South Eastern & Chatham Railway in 1917. After the First World War a number were built at Woolwich Arsenal to alleviate unemployment, and the newly formed SR acquired 50 of these cheaply for use west of Exeter; as a result the class acquired the name 'Woolworths'. Here No 31837 approaches the girder bridge over Little Petherick Creek as it leaves Padstow with the 6.00pm departure to Okehampton on 2 July 1961. *Terry Gough*

from Halwill was for many years described as the 'Withered Arm', which was said to reflect its arching configuration when seen on the company's maps.

The LSWR had reached Holsworthy in January 1879, but the last 10½ miles to the seaside town of Bude did not open for almost 20 years, in August 1898. One intermediate station with a passing loop was built at Whitstone & Bridgerule, but did not open until the following November.

Now that the LSWR had established itself in the area it set about promoting its line for holiday traffic. The 'North Cornwall & Bude Express' was introduced in 1907, while in July 1926 the SR named its 11.00am departure from Waterloo to the West Country the 'Atlantic Coast Express'. As has already been described, this train became famous for the number of destinations covered by through coaches. The service of expresses was resumed after the Second World War and continued into nationalisation.

The weekday train service to Bude and Padstow during the winter of 1962/63, including the arrival of the 'Atlantic Coast Express' at 4.16 and 5.21pm respectively, is given in BR(SR) Table 35 (see pp. 63 & 64). On summer Saturdays in 1962 there were four

Western Region Timetable 14 June 1965 - 17 April 1966

Note that one train (shown as 'E' on the timetable) ran from Paddington to Bude on summer Saturdays in 1965. This compares with four trains from Waterloo to Bude and five to Padstow in 1962 (see Appendix 3)
This was the last nationally published timetable for the lines. They were omitted from the Western Region Timetable for the period 18 April 1966 to 5 March 1967. (see page 184) This indicates that buses have replaced the rail services although the lines did not actually close until October 1966

Table 50

Weekdays
NOT on Saturdays 19 June to 4 September

Saturdays
19 June to 4 September

Exeter St David's and Okehampton to Bude and Padstow

Miles	Station								B	B	B	A C	A	C			C		Saturdays 19 June to 4 September	Saturdays C	Saturdays D
—	40 EXETER ST DAVID'S	d	*05 20*			*09 05*		*10 57*	13 20			14 20		15 40			17 56		*05 20*	05 50	07 16
25	**OKEHAMPTON**	d	06 25			10 05		11 57	13 59			14 59		16 27	17 55		18 44		06 25	06 38	07 58
30	MADDAFORD MOOR HALT	d				10 17		12 10	14 10			15 10		16 38	18 06		18 55				
34	ASHBURY	d	06 41			10 25		12 18	14 17			15 17		16 44	18 12		19 01		06 41		
37½	HALWILL	a	06 47			10 31		12 25	14 23			15 23		16 51	18 19		19 08		06 47	07 02	08 29
—	HALWILL	d		06 53	08 30	10 41		12 26	14 26		15 26	15 26		16 58	18 26		19 09		06 50		08 30
41	DUNSLAND CROSS	d		06 59	08 36	10 47		12 32	14 32		15 32	15 32		17 04	18 32		19 15		06 56		08 36
45½	HOLSWORTHY	d		07 08	08 46	10 58		12 42	14 42		15 42	15 42		17 13	18 42		19 26		07 08		08 46
50½	WHITSTONE & BRIDGERULE	d		07 17	08 55	11 07		12 51	14 51		15 51	15 51		17 24	18 51		19 34		07 17		08 55
56	**BUDE**	a		07 26	09 04	11 16		13 00	15 00		16 00	16 00		17 33	19 00		19 43		07 26		09 04
—	HALWILL	d	07 00				10 40			14 35			15 35			18 30		19 22		07 04	
42½	ASHWATER	d	07 11				10 47			14 42			15 42			18 37		19 29		07 15	
46½	TOWER HILL	d	07 22				10 54			14 49			15 49			18 44		19 36		07 26	
51½	LAUNCESTON	d	07c45				11 02			14 57			15 57			18a51		19a43		07b45	
55¾	EGLOSKERRY	d	07 53				11 09			15 04			16 04							07 53	
59¼	TRESMEER	d	08 01				11 17			15 12			16 12							08 01	
64¼	OTTERHAM	d	08 11				11 26			15 21			16 21							08 11	
68¼	CAMELFORD	d	08 20				11 35			15 29			16 29							08 20	
71	DELABOLE	d	08 26				11 40			15 34			16 34							08 26	
75	PORT ISAAC ROAD	d	08 34				11 48			15 42			16 42							08 34	
77½	ST KEW HIGHWAY	d	08 39				11 52			15 46			16 46							08 39	
81½	WADEBRIDGE	a	08 46				11 59			15 54			16 54							08 46	
87¼	53 **PADSTOW**	a					*12 20*			16 18			17 21							09 26	

Saturdays
19 June to 4 September—continued

Sundays Until 26 September | **Sundays** From 3 October

Station		C		C		C	E	C			C		Sundays until 26 Sept. C	C	C	C		Sundays from 3 Oct. G
40 EXETER ST DAVID'S	d	09 25		11 23		13 41	14 32	15 48			17 53		08 50	10 22	15 12	17 15		*15 25*
OKEHAMPTON	d	10 05		12 00		14 25		16 34		17 55	18 44		09 33	11 07	16 01	18 02		16 50
MADDAFORD MOOR HALT	d	10 17		12 13				16 45		18 06	18 55		09 44	11 19	16 11	18 13		17 02
ASHBURY	d	10 25		12 25				16 52		18 12	19 01		09 52	11 28	16 19	18 21		17 11
HALWILL	a	10 31		12 31		14 51	15 32	16 58		18 19	19 08		09 58	11 34	16 25	18 27		17 21
HALWILL	d	10 41		12 32			15 34	17 00		18 26	19 09		10 03	11 38	16 27	18 30		17 21
DUNSLAND CROSS	d	10 47		12 39			15 41	17 06		18 32	19 15		10 09	11 44	16 34	18 36		17 30
HOLSWORTHY	d	10 57		12 49			15 51	17 17		18 42	19 26		10 18	11 53	16 43	18 45		17 43
WHITSTONE & BRIDGERULE	d	11 07		12 58			16 02	17 28		18 51	19 34		10 26	12 01	17 02	18 53		
BUDE	a	11 17		13 07			16 11	17 37		19 00	19 43		10 35	12 10	17 10	19 02		18 08
HALWILL	d		10 36		12 45	14 55			17 03			19 22	10 06				18 35	
ASHWATER	d		10 43			15 02						19 29	10 13				18 42	
TOWER HILL	d		10 50			15 09						19 36	10 20				18 49	
LAUNCESTON	d		11 00		13 07	15 18			17 23			19a43	10a27				18a56	
EGLOSKERRY	d		11 08		13 13	15 25			17 29									
TRESMEER	d		11 18		13 22	15 33			17 37									
OTTERHAM	d		11 28		13 33	15 43			17 47									
CAMELFORD	d		11 36		13 41	15 51			17 55									
DELABOLE	d		11 42		13 47	15 58			18 05									
PORT ISAAC ROAD	d		11 50		13 55	16 06			18 13									
ST KEW HIGHWAY	d		11 55		14 00	16 11			18 18									
WADEBRIDGE	a		12 05		14 07	16 18			18 25									
53 **PADSTOW**	a		*13 01*			16 29			*18 45*									

Heavy figures denote through carriages; light figures denote connecting services
For general notes see page 3

A Until 25 September
B From 27 September
C From Exeter Central
D From Newton Abbot
E From London Paddington
G 🚌 (Southern National) from Okehampton

b Arr 07 36
c Arr 07 32

departures from Waterloo for Bude and five for Padstow (Appendix 3.1). Some trains ran again in the summers of both 1963 and 1964, by which time the lines were managed by BR(WR). In the summer of 1964 the down 'Atlantic Coast Express' included coaches from Padstow only, which left there at 9.33am; its departure on Saturdays was at 11.00am. In addition, the 8.10am departure from Wadebridge was also a though train. Both included carriages from Bude, which left there at 9.00am

Another of the line's ex-LSWR Class 'T9', No 30715, is seen at Padstow during 1960. The engine was also built by Dubs & Co in 1899 and withdrawn in July 1961. The two white discs on either side of its smokebox indicate that its next working will be to Exeter Central, although the engine will probably work only as far as Okehampton. *M. E. J. Deane collection, courtesy of Ian Bennett*

and 11.45am respectively. None of these trains were shown as through workings in the BR(WR) timetable of the time although, significantly, they were in the BR(SR) one.

The last through coaches from Waterloo ran on Saturday 5 September 1964, although BR(WR) did provide a through service from Paddington to Bude on summer Saturdays in 1965 (Appendix 3.2). The BR(WR) timetable for the period 14 June 1965 to 17 April 1966 shows eight arrivals at Bude on summer Saturdays, including the through train from Paddington at 4.11pm. In contrast only one train, from Halwill, ran through to Padstow, while two others, both from Exeter St David's, terminated at Wadebridge. Two evening trains from Halwill ran only as far as Launceston. The number of trains to Padstow from Exeter St David's increased to two on summer Saturdays. There was no Sunday service. The timetable from 18 April 1966 to 5 March 1967, however, does not include one for the lines at all! Instead it shows bus routes from Okehampton to Wadebridge via Launceston, and to Bude via Halwill, although the line did not close until 3 October 1966. The Taunton to Barnstaple line (Chapter 3.11) is treated in a similar fashion, which would appear to demonstrate BR(WR)'s eagerness to close these lines. The Beeching Report had revealed that the branch carried fewer than 5,000 passengers a week, and the only stations with annual passenger receipts above £5,000 were Okehampton, Holsworthy, Launceston, Wadebridge and Padstow.

The lines of the 'Withered Arm' had seen a transformation in their motive power during the 1960s. At the start of the decade ex-LSWR Class 'T9' 4-4-0s and Class 'O2' 0-4-4 tanks, which dated from the late 19th century, were still well in evidence, supplemented by ex-SR Class 'N' 2-6-0s together with unrebuilt 'Light Pacifics'. The long reign of the ex-LSWR engines ended in 1961 when more modern standard classes, particularly Ivatt Class 2 2-6-2 and BR Standard Class 4 2-6-4 tanks

Ex-SR 'N' Class 2-6-0 No 31406 waits at Padstow on a very wet Saturday 31 August 1963 with the 6.00pm train to Okehampton. It was built at Ashford Works in 1933 and worked in the South East until displaced by the Kent Coast electrification, when it was transferred to the West Country. The engine was withdrawn in September 1964 with the end of steam on the former SR lines. *Author*

During the summer months Padstow received through coaches from Waterloo off the 'Atlantic Coast Express' each weekday until September 1964. In the early 1960s a number of additional through trains also ran on Saturdays. Here unrebuilt 'West Country' 'Pacific' No 34033 *Chard* has arrived at Padstow with the 7.30am train from Waterloo on 1 July 1961. Due to weight restrictions the rebuilt members of the class could not be used on the North Cornwall line. *Terry Gough*

joined the 2-6-0s and 'Pacifics'. Trains on these lines continued to be steam-worked by Exmouth Junction's remaining Standard Class 4 tanks until the end of 1964, after which DMUs came to dominate services. Although the line from Meldon Junction to Wadebridge closed from 3 October 1966, trains from Bodmin Road continued to run between Wadebridge and Padstow until this line too closed from 30 January 1967.

The last steam working occurred on 5 September 1965 when Ivatt Class 2 2-6-2 tank No 41283 worked a Great Western Society special to commemorate 100 years of the Plymouth to Launceston branch. By 1965 the ex-GWR line from Lydford to Plymouth had closed completely, but that from Lydford to Launceston was still open for goods traffic. The special started at Exeter St David's and ran via Okehampton to Lydford (SR) to reach the Launceston branch; it returned to Exeter via Halwill, including a trip to Bude and back. It therefore became the last steam-hauled train to leave both Launceston and Bude.

Months after the end of regular steam working, Ivatt 2-6-2 Class 2 tank No 41283 of Templecombe shed stands at Halwill with the Great Western Society special celebrating the centenary of the ex-GWR Plymouth to Launceston branch on 5 September 1965. The train had travelled from Exeter St David's via Okehampton, Lydford and Launceston. After running round its train at Halwill, it then ran to Bude and back. This was the last ever BR steam departure from both Launceston and Bude *Author*

Steam was to return to Launceston some 18 years later when on 26 December 1983 the 1ft 11½in-gauge Launceston Steam Railway opened. Trains now run from a new Launceston station to the west of the original SR station, westwards for some 2½ miles to a newly constructed station at New Mills.

A section of the trackbed west of Launceston opened as the 1ft 11½in-gauge Launceston Steam Railway on Boxing Day 1983. The railway currently terminates at New Mills where there is a large children's play area and other facilities. Several of the narrow-gauge engines on the line originally worked in North Wales slate quarries. One of these, *Covercoat*, built in 1898 by the Hunslet Engine Company of Leeds for the Dinorwic slate quarry, is seen after arrival at Launceston from New Mills in September 2003. *Author*

Another Woolwich Arsenal-built 'N' Class 2-6-0, No 31836, heads the 4.24pm train from Okehampton to Bude near Halwill in 5 July 1961. The engine is unusually displaying the incorrect white discs on its smokebox, which indicate that the train is for Padstow – as a Bude train it should be carrying a single white disc on the left side of its smokebox, as in the next picture. *Terry Gough*

One of Exmouth Junction's fleet of BR Standard Class 3 2-6-2 tanks, No 82017, leaves Dunsland Cross on 5 July 1961 with the 1.55pm train from Bude to Okehampton, which comprises two ex-SR coaches. No 82017 was built at Swindon in 1952 and ended its days at Nine Elms in April 1965. *Terry Gough*

Another of Exmouth Junction's recently acquired BR Standard Class 3 2-6-2 tanks arrives at Whitstone & Bridgerule in April 1961 with a Bude to Halwill train. Unlike their classmates on BR(WR), which ran in green livery, those supplied to BR(SR) retained their black liveries throughout their careers. *M. E. J. Deane collection, courtesy of Ian Bennett*

In this view of Bude station in April 1961 'N' Class 'Mogul' No 31843, also carrying the wrong white discs, runs back from Bude's small engine shed prior to taking out a train of vans for Halwill. No 31843 was built at Ashford in 1924 and withdrawn in September 1964. *M. E. J. Deane collection, courtesy of Ian Bennett*

The Standard Class 3 2-6-2 tanks were displaced from Exmouth Junction by the arrival of more powerful Standard Class 4 2-6-4s in the summer of 1962. Here No. 80067 stands in Bude staion with the 9.30am to Halwill and Okehampton on 7 September 1963. In the background Class N 'Mogul' No. 31840 backs into the small engine shed. It had just arrived on the 8.53am from Halwill. No. 80067 was later transferred to Templecombe shed and worked trains on the ex-Somerset & Dorset line until withdrawn in June 1965. No 31840 was built in 1924 and withdrawn in September 1964.*Author*

The Great Western Society special celebrating the centenary of the ex-GWR Launceston branch is seen again at Bude on 5 September 1965. Ivatt 2-6-2 Class 2 tank No 41283 has run round its train and now waits to depart for Exeter St David's, the last steam-hauled train ever to do so. A BR(WR) DMU forming a service train can be seen above the heads of the crowd of people standing on the platform waiting to give the special a good send-off. No 41283 was withdrawn after the closure of the ex-Somerset & Dorset line in March 1966. *Author*

(7496)
2nd - SPECIAL ARRANGEMENT
Great Western Society
(South West Group)
5th SEPTEMBER, 1965
Launceston Branch Centenary Tour
Exeter St. Davids   Okehampton
Lydford,   Lifton,   LauncestonG.W.,
Bude, Okehampton, ExeterSt.Davids
(W)   For conditions see over

0144   0144

3.11 Taunton – Barnstaple Junction (October 1966)

The first section of the 44¾-mile broad-gauge line from Taunton to Barnstaple was opened by the Devon & Somerset Railway (D&SR) from Norton Fitzwarren to Wiveliscombe in 1871, the second, between Wiveliscombe and Barnstaple (Victoria Road) two years later. A station at Norton Fitzwarren opened in the same year. Although nominally independent, the D&SR was actually worked by the Bristol & Exeter Railway from the start; the GWR took over the B&E in 1876 but did not absorb the D&SR until 1901.

The line was initially single throughout with passing loops at most stations. In the 1930s the line was doubled as far as Milverton as part of an initiative by the GWR to increase line capacity for the heavy summer holiday traffic. At the same time the main line eastwards through Taunton was quadrupled as far as Cogload Junction. In 1960 the ex-GWR station at Barnstaple (Victoria Road) was closed to passengers and all trains were diverted to the ex-SR station at Barnstaple Junction, which had previously only been used by through trains to Ilfracombe via Taunton. The main-line station at Norton Fitzwarren closed a year later in October 1961. The main station on the line was Dulverton, which for many years was also the interchange station for the Exe Valley line trains to Tiverton and Exeter (Chapter 1, line 1.8).

The survey of passenger traffic carried out for the Beeching Report in April 1961 showed that the line carried fewer than 5,000 passengers a week, and apart from Dulverton the stations each produced receipts of less than £5,000 per annum. It was therefore one of the first lines that BR(WR) wished to be rid of, and closure proposals were first published soon after the Beeching Report itself in March 1963. Complete closure of the line was announced for 30 September. Strong objections to the TUCC followed, while Somerset County Council initially refused to fund the road improvements to allow the

The Taunton to Barnstaple line was the last in the West Country to use ex-GWR 'Moguls', the first of the class having been designed by G. J. Churchward and built at Swindon in 1911. No 7333 arrives at Venn Cross with a train from Barnstaple Junction to Taunton in the early 1960s. This engine was one of C. B. Collett's updated versions of Churchward's original design with cab-side windows; it was built at Swindon in 1932 and withdrawn in October 1963. *M. E. J. Deane collection, courtesy of Ian Bennett*

introduction of alternative bus services. As a result the line was to survive for another three years.

For many years the line had seen heavy holiday traffic from South Wales and the Midlands to Ilfracombe. On summer Saturdays in 1962 the only through arrival was the 10.55am from Wolverhampton Low Level (Appendix 3.1), although additional trains left Ilfracombe for both Manchester Exchange and Cardiff. Trains both to and from Wolverhampton and Cardiff also ran in the summer of 1964 – however,

Two of Churchward's original 'Moguls' pass at Venn Cross on 31 August 1964, a few weeks before the end of steam on the line. No 6363, built in 1925, heads the 11.25am train from Taunton to Barnstaple, while 1917-built No 5336 approaches with the 10.40am service from Barnstaple Junction. Both engines were withdrawn a month later. *Author*

Table 64 of the BR(WR) summer timetable fails to mention them. The Cardiff train (which actually started in Swansea) is only shown in Table 1, covering all West of England main line trains, although the through train from Wolverhampton Low Level does appear in Table 14 of the contemporary BR(WR) timetable. These omissions were corrected in the timetable for 1965, where Table 44 shows there were six passenger trains over the route each weekday, most of which had connections to or from

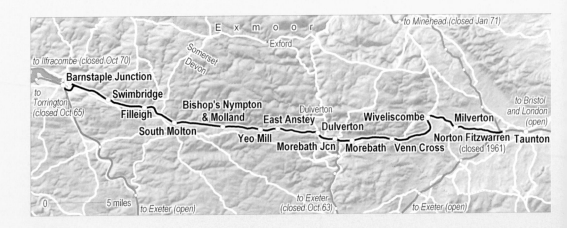

Another original Churchward 'Mogul' prepares to leave Dulverton with a train from Taunton to Barnstaple Junction during the summer of 1962. *M. E. J. Deane collection, courtesy of Ian Bennett*

In the early 1960s several BR Standard Class 3 2-6-2 tanks were allocated to Taunton shed and worked on the line alongside the much older ex-GWR 'Moguls'. Here No 82008 enters Dulverton with the 12.25pm train from Ilfracombe to Taunton on 7 September 1963. No 82008 was built at Swindon in 1952 and withdrawn in February 1964. On the right ex-GWR 0-4-2 tank No 1450 can be seen waiting to propel its train down the Exe Valley to Exeter St David's at 3.15pm. *Author*

Ilfracombe. On summer Saturdays this was increased to ten up and nine down trains, including the through trains from South Wales and Wolverhampton (Appendix 3.2). There was no Sunday service.

Things regressed again in 1966 as, although the line remained open until October, the Western Region timetable from 18 April 1966 to 5 March 1967 does not include a train service for it at all. Instead a bus service is shown from Taunton to Dulverton and from Barnstaple to South Molton. Rail passengers for Ilfracombe are directed to travel via Exeter St David's.

The line was the last ex-GWR line west of Taunton to be steam-worked by tender engines. For many years services were dominated

Ex-GWR 'Mogul' No 7333
is seen again as it waits at
Milverton with a train from
Taunton to Barnstaple
Junction in the early 1960s.
*M. E. J. Deane collection,
courtesy of Ian Bennett*

G. W. R.

BARNSTAPLE

by ex-GWR 2-6-0 'Moguls', some dating from the First World War. In the early 1960s several BR Standard Class 3 2-6-2 tanks were allocated to Taunton depot and were also used on the line. Steam disappeared in October 1964 to be replaced by the ubiquitous DMUs, with North British or 'Hymek' diesel-hydraulics working the remaining summer through trains in 1965. The last run by a steam engine occurred on 27 March 1965 when the now preserved ex-GWR 0-6-0 No 3205 worked 'The Exmoor Ranger', a special organised by the Plymouth Railway Circle and RCTS, from Barnstaple Junction to Taunton. The train had earlier visited the ex-GWR station at Barnstaple (Victoria Road) as part of its complex itinerary.

Since closure much of the former trackbed has been obscured by new road building. The section just west of Norton Fitzwarren has, however, recently been used by the heritage West Somerset Railway as part of the new triangle to turn steam locomotives at the eastern end of its line.

North British-built
Type 2 diesel-hydraulic
No D6347 heads the
11.10am Ilfracombe to
Wolverhampton Low Level
train on the double-track
section east of Milverton
on 24 July 1965. That was
the last year the line saw
through summer trains. No
D6347 was withdrawn in
November 1968.
Owen Mogg

Western Region Timetable 14 June 1965 - 17 April 1966

Note that two trains (shown as 'B' and 'C' on the timetable) from Wolverhampton and Carmarthen to Ilfracombe used this route on summer Saturdays in 1965. (see Appendix 3) The train from Wolverhampton also ran in 1966 but via Exeter St. David's. This was the last nationally published timetable for the lines. They were omitted from the Western RegionTimetable for the period 18 April 1966 to 5 March 1967. This indicates that buses have replaced the rail services although the lines did not actually close until October 1966 (see page 152)

Table 44 — **Weekdays** — **Saturdays**

NOT on Saturdays 19 June to 4 September

19 June to 4 September

Taunton to Barnstaple and Ilfracombe

Miles	Station		Weekdays FSX FSO	Saturdays B C
—	**TAUNTON**	d	07 52 .. 11 10 13 28 16 40 17 50 .. 19 45 21 10 ..	06 10 07 00 08 50 11 20 .. 13 08 13 28 16 00 17 57 21 25
6	MILVERTON	d	08 07 .. 11 23 13 41 16 53 18 03 .. 19 58 21 23	07 13 09 03 11 33 .. 13 23 13 43 16 13 18 10 21 37
9	WIVELISCOMBE	d	08 14 .. 11 30 12 49 17 00 18 10 .. 20 05 21 30 ..	06 30 07 20 09 10 11 40 .. 13 30 13 55 16 20 18 18 21 45
14	VENN CROSS	d	08 24 .. 11 40 13 59 17 10 18 20 .. 20 15 21 40	07 31 09 21 11 52 .. 14 07 16 31 18 31 21 56
17	MOREBATH HALT	d	08 29 .. 11 45 14 04 17 15 18 25 .. 20 20 21 45	07 37 09 27 11 58 .. 16 37 18 37 22 02
19	MOREBATH JUNCTION HALT	d	08 33 .. 11 49 14 08 17 19 18 29 .. 20 24 21 49	09 31 12 02 .. 16 41 18 41 22 06
21	DULVERTON	d	08 39 .. 11 54 14 12 17 23 18 33 .. 20 29 21 54	06 55 07 50 09 40 12 12 .. 13 56 14 25 16 46 18 46 22 11
24	EAST ANSTEY	d	08 46 .. 12 01 14 19 17 30 18 41 .. 20 36 22 01	07 59 09 50 12 21 .. 14 05 14 34 16 56 18 56 22 20
26	YEO MILL HALT	d	08 50 .. 12 05 14 23 17 34 18 45 .. 20 40 22 05	09 54 12 25 .. 17 00 19 00 22 24
30	BISHOP'S NYMPTON & MOLLAND	d	08 57 .. 12 13 14 31 17 41 18 52 .. 20 47 22 12	07 12 08 09 10 01 12 35 .. 14 17 14 45 17 07 19 07 22 31
34	SOUTH MOLTON	d	09 04 .. 12 21 14 40 17 49 19 00 .. 20 55 22 20	07 23 08 18 10 11 12 44 .. 14 25 14 54 17 15 19 17 22 39
37	FILLEIGH HALT	d	09 12 .. 12 29 14 50 17 59 19 08 .. 21 03 22 28	07 33 08 27 10 20 12 53 .. 15 03 17 24 19 25 22 48
40	SWIMBRIDGE	d	09 19 .. 12 36 14 57 18 04 19 15 .. 21 10 22 35	07 41 08 34 10 28 13 00 .. 15 12 17 31 19 32 22 55
45	**BARNSTAPLE JUNCTION**	a	09 26 .. 12 43 15 06 18 11 19 22 .. 21 17 22 42	07 50 08 43 10 37 13 11 .. 14 50 15 24 17 42 19 43 23 06
60½ 40	**ILFRACOMBE**	a	10 16 .. 13 32 16 52 19 14 21 25 ..	08 35 09 27 11 23 13 56 .. 15 38 16 20 19 21 21 25

Weekdays

NOT on Saturdays 19 June 4 to September

Saturdays — 19 June to 4 September

Ilfracombe to Barnstaple and Taunton

Miles	Station		Weekdays A A	Saturdays D E
—	40 **ILFRACOMBE**	d	.. 11c00 .. 13 50 16e56 18 15 ..	07 55 09 25 10 20 11 10 11 45 .. 15 10 16 30 18 00 18 15
15	**BARNSTAPLE JUNCTION**	d	06 40 08 37 11 55 .. 14 45 17 55 19 04 ..	06 48 08 42 10 10 11 07 12 00 12 30 .. 15 58 17 16 18 46 19 48
20	SWIMBRIDGE	d	06 50 08 47 12 05 .. 14 58 18 05 19 16 ..	07 01 .. 11 20 .. 16 11 17 32 18 59 20 00
23	FILLEIGH HALT	d	06 58 08 54 12 12 .. 15 05 18 12 19 23 ..	07 09 .. 11 28 .. 16 19 17 40 19 07 20 08
26	SOUTH MOLTON	d	07 07 09 05 12 23 .. 15 13 18 20 19 31 ..	07 21 09 13 10 35 11 40 12 27 12 57 .. 16 27 17 48 19 18 20 15
30	BISHOP'S NYMPTON & MOLLAND	d	07 15 09 13 12 31 .. 15 21 18 28 19 39 ..	07 29 .. 11 48 .. 13 05 .. 16 35 17 56 19 26 20 23
34	YEO MILL HALT	d	07 21 09 19 12 37 .. 15 27 18 34 19 45 ..	07 35 .. 11 55 .. 16 41 18 02 19 32 20 29
36	EAST ANSTEY	d	07 27 09 29 12 43 .. 15 33 18 42 19 51 ..	07 41 .. 12 01 .. 16 47 18 19 38 20 34
39	DULVERTON	d	07 35 09 36 12 50 .. 15 40 18 50 19 58 ..	07 48 09 37 10 58 12 13 12 52 13 23 .. 16 57 18 15 19 46 20 42
41	MOREBATH JUNCTION HALT	d	07 39 09 40 12 54 .. 15 44 18 53 20 02 ..	07 52 .. 12 17 .. 17 01 18 19 19 50 20 46
43	MOREBATH HALT	d	07 43 09 44 12 58 .. 15 48 18 57 20 06 ..	07 56 .. 12 21 .. 17 05 18 23 19 54 20 50
46½	VENN CROSS	d	07 51 09 52 13 06 .. 15 56 19 05 20 16 ..	08 04 .. 12 29 13 42 .. 17 13 18 31 20 02 20 58
51	WIVELISCOMBE	d	08 00 10 01 13 15 .. 16 05 19 14 20 25 ..	08 13 10 03 11 23 12 40 13 17 13 53 .. 17 23 18 41 20 12 21 08
54	MILVERTON	d	08 06 10 07 13 21 .. 16 11 19 20 20 31 ..	08 19 .. 12 46 .. 14 00 .. 17 29 18 47 20 18 21 14
60	**TAUNTON**	a	08 17 10 18 13 32 .. 16 22 19 31 20 42 ..	08 30 10 21 11 38 12 58 13 33 14 11 .. 17 40 18 58 20 31 21 25

Heavy figures denote through carriages; light figures denote connecting services. For general notes see page 3

A From Torrington
B From Wolverhampton
C From Carmarthen
D To Cardiff
E To Wolverhampton from 26 June

b Until 25 September arr 16 00
c Until 25 September
e Mondays to Fridays until 25 September

The last 2.45pm service from Barnstaple Junction to Taunton crosses Waterrow Viaduct, between Venn Cross and Wiveliscombe, on 1 October 1966. The viaduct was designed by Brunel for the opening of the broad-gauge line in 1873, and has since been demolished. *Author*

A BR Derby-built Class 116 two-car DMU departs from Milverton forming the 4.40pm service from Taunton to Barnstaple on 1 October 1966. This was the last day of passenger services, which were withdrawn from Monday 3 October. The land occupied by the railway is now part of the Milverton bypass. *Author*

135a
GREAT WESTERN RAILWAY
MILVERTON
TO
SHEFFIELD, L.M.S.
CARRIAGE PAID
No. of Packages
Route via BRISTOL

3.12 Bere Alston – Callington (November 1966)

The station at the Devon village of Bere Alston first opened in June 1890, together with the line from Plymouth to Lydford of the grandly titled Plymouth, Devonport & South Western Junction Railway (PDSWJR). For the first time the LSWR was able to run through trains from London Waterloo to Plymouth via Tavistock on track of which it had complete control, rather than over GWR metals via Yelverton.

The PDSWJR/LSWR then sought to build a branch line linking Callington, on the Cornish side of the River Tamar, to Bere Alston on its new main line. As a first step, in June 1891 the PDSWJR acquired the 3ft 6in-gauge East Cornwall Mineral Railway (ECMR). This had opened in 1872 to link quarries at Gunnislake with Calstock Quay on the river via a rope-worked incline. The Callington branch was developed in two parts. In the east the Bere Alston & Calstock Light Railway would cross the Tamar on a viaduct some 120 feet above the river. This would then join the ECMR near the top of the incline. Meanwhile the ECMR would be converted to standard gauge. Work started in 1900 but it was not until Colonel Stephens, well known for the development of light railways under the 1896 Light Railways Act, was appointed as consulting engineer in 1905 that the line was completed. The 9½ miles from Bere Alston to Callington eventually opened in March 1908. The ECMR's rope-worked incline to the quay at Calstock was replaced by a wagon lift adjacent to the western end of the viaduct, which was dismantled in 1934.

Although the PDSWJR's main line was worked by the LSWR, the Callington branch operated as a separate entity. The PDSWJR acquired

A typical LSWR train of the late 19th century is seen at Bere Alston on 14 July 1956. Class 'O2' 0-4-4 tank No 30225, built in 1892, heads a train for Callington. At the time No 30225 was allocated to the former LSWR shed at Plymouth Friary; this depot was transferred to BR(WR), as 83H, in 1958, but closed in September 1963. The 'O2s' would soon be replaced on the branch by more modern Ivatt Class 2 2-6-2 tanks. *Frank Hornby*

Ex-LSWR Class 'O2' 0-4-4 tank No 30225 is pictured after arrival at Callington with its train from Bere Alston on 14 July 1956. Although No 30225 was the last of the class to be withdrawn on mainland Britain, in December 1962, several survived on the Isle of Wight until 1966, and one is now preserved at Havenstreet on the Island. *Frank Hornby*

two big 0-6-2 tanks, *Lord St Leven* and *Earl of Mount Edgcumbe*. On nationalisation they became BR(SR) Nos 30758 and 30757 respectively and mainly worked freight on the branch until the mid-1950s. The PDSWJR became part of the Southern Railway in 1923, and soon ex-LSWR Class 'O2' 0-4-4 tanks took over passenger services, remaining associated with the branch until replaced by Ivatt Class 2 2-6-2 tanks in the 1960s. The 'O2s' had first appeared in 1889 and were some 14 tons lighter than the 'M7' tanks of 1897, which in 1962 were still working BR(SR) branch lines in East and North Devon.

Unlike other ex-SR lines in Devon and Cornwall, the Callington branch saw little holiday traffic and most trains were lightly loaded. The Beeching Report had revealed that the branch carried fewer than 5,000 passengers a week and that no station had annual passenger receipts

No 41310, one of the Ivatt Class 2 2-6-2 tanks that replaced the Class 'O2' tanks, is pictured approaching Bere Alston with a train from Callington in May 1960. *M. E. J. Deane collection, courtesy of Ian Bennett*

above £5,000. Its complete closure was therefore proposed. In the event it was the viaduct that saved at least part of the branch as a case was made that closure of the line would deprive local communities around the Cornish town of Gunnislake of easy access to Plymouth. Notice of closure as far as Gunnislake was therefore withdrawn. The 5-mile section from Gunnislake to Callington was closed from 7 November 1966, when Gunnislake became its western terminus.

In 1966 there were seven return workings up the branch from Bere Alston, with an eighth through working from Callington to Plymouth on Saturday evenings. In addition, an afternoon train ran to Gunnislake and back from Bere Alston. There was no Sunday service. By then services were worked by DMUs, which had replaced the Ivatt tanks from the winter timetable of 1963.

In the event, the line to Gunnislake was one of only two ex-SR

A small engine shed was provided at Callington by the Plymouth, Devonport & South Western Junction Railway in 1908. It later became a sub-shed of the SR depot at Plymouth Friary and outlasted the SR depot, not being closed by BR(WR) until services were dieselised in September 1964. At the time it still had an allocation of three Ivatt tanks, and one of these, No 41310, is seen being serviced at the depot in May 1960. The engine was withdrawn in October 1964. *M. E. J. Deane collection, courtesy of Ian Bennett*

Another Ivatt Class 2 2-6-2 tank No 41317 arrives at Calstock with the 4.23pm train from Callington to Bere Alston on 4 July 1961. This engine was also allocated to Plymouth Friary. *Terry Gough*

Although DMUs replaced steam on the branch in the autumn of 1964, the distinctive overall roof at Callington survived. Here a two-car Class 119 unit stands at the station as the 12.53pm service to Bere Alston on 6 September 1965. Services between Gunnislake and Callington were withdrawn from 7 November 1966. *Author*

A First Great Western Class 153 single-unit 'Super Sprinter' crosses the River Tamar at Calstock as the 1.45pm service from Gunnislake to Plymouth on 14 May 2009. *Author*

Western Region Timetable 18 April 1966 - 5 March 1967

Table 41 **(Second class only)**

Weekdays only

Plymouth and Bere Alston to Callington

Miles					E	D SO	E	D SO	E	D SO			
—	35 PLYMOUTH	d	06 00	07 50	09 50	09 55	11 30	11 55	13 10	13 10	16 10	16 50	18 10
—	BERE ALSTON	d	06 35	08 20	10 20	10 25	12 05	12 20	13 40	13 46	16 40	17 25	18 50
1¾	CALSTOCK	d	06 41	08 26	10 26	10 31	12 11	12 26	13 46	13 52	16 46	17 31	18 56
4½	GUNNISLAKE	d	06 53	08 38	10 38	10 43	12 23	12 38	13 58	14 04	16a58	17 43	19 08
5½	CHILSWORTHY	d	06 58	08 43	10 43	10 48	12 28	12 43	14 03	14 09	..	17 48	19 13
6½	LATCHLEY	d	07 02	08 47	10 47	10 52	12 32	12 47	14 07	14 13	..	17 52	19 17
7¾	LUCKETT	d	07 07	08 52	10 52	10 57	12 37	12 52	14 12	14 18	..	17 57	19 22
9¼	CALLINGTON	a	07 13	08 58	10 58	11 03	12 43	12 58	14 18	14 24	..	18 03	19 28

Weekdays only

Callington to Bere Alston and Plymouth

Miles					E	D SO		E	D SO				SO
—	CALLINGTON	d	05 48	07 27	09 35	09 40	11 15	12 53	13 01	15 55	..	18 08	19 40
1¾	LUCKETT	d	05 54	07 33	09 41	09 46	11 21	12 59	13 07	16 01	..	18 14	19 46
3	LATCHLEY	d	05 58	07 37	09 45	09 50	11 25	13 03	13 11	16 05	..	18 18	19 50
4	CHILSWORTHY	d	06 03	07 42	09 50	09 55	11 30	13 08	13 16	16 10	..	18 23	19 55
5	GUNNISLAKE	d	06 07	07 46	09 54	09 59	11 34	13 12	13 20	16 14	17 01	18 27	19 59
7¾	CALSTOCK	d	06 19	07 58	10 06	10 11	11 46	13 24	13 32	16 26	17 13	18 39	20 11
9½	BERE ALSTON	a	06 26	08 05	10 13	10 18	11 53	13 31	13 39	16 33	17 20	18 46	20 18
—	35 PLYMOUTH	a	06 56	08 38	11 06	11 13	12 25	14e33	14 10	17 03	17 47	19 35	20 50

Heavy figures denote through carriages;
light figures denote connecting services
For general notes see page 3

A [bus symbol] (Western National)
B Until 11 June and from 5 September
C 13 June to 2 September
D 18 June to 3 September
E **Not** Saturdays 18 June to 3 September

b 13 June to 2 September
e On Saturdays arr 14 10

First Great Western Class 150/2 'Sprinter' No 150263 arrives at Bere Ferrers forming the 11.35am service from Gunnislake to Plymouth on the same day. Bere Ferrers is situated on the former LSWR main line to Plymouth, the track of which was singled following closure of the line between here and Okehampton in May 1968. The signal box visible in the background is not functional but forms part of the Railway Heritage Centre that has been established here. *Author*

The branch line from Plymouth to Gunnislake was one of those that frustrated Dr Beeching by remaining open despite his attempts to close it. A healthy crowd of passengers waits at Gunnislake to board Great Western Railway's 09.29 service to Plymouth on Friday 28 December 2018. Class 150 'Sprinter' No 150247 has just arrived as the 08.40 service from Plymouth. Sadly Dr Beeching succeeded in depriving the people of Callington of their train service in November 1966. *Author*

branch lines in the West Country listed in the Beeching Report to avoid complete closure, the other being the Exmouth branch (see Chapter 3.20). The retention of this service also resulted in at least part of the ex-SR main line into Plymouth being kept open. In 1964 all trains on this route had been diverted via the ex-GWR line through

Western Passenger Timetable 4 May 1970 - 2 May 1971

Table 31

Mondays to Fridays also Saturdays from 3 October

Plymouth to Bere Alston, Gunnislake and Liskeard

Miles	Miles			2	2	2 SX	2 SO		2		2	2		2			2		2				2	
0	0	**PLYMOUTH**	d	05 15	05 40	06 28	06 28	06 55	07 00	07 22	07 25	08 30	08 50	09 10	..	11 08	11 25	..	12 10	..	12 50	..	13 15	..
1¼	—	DEVONPORT	d		05 44	06 32	06 32		07 04		07 30	08 34		09 14			11 29		12 14				13 19	
1¾	—	DOCKYARD	d		05 46	06 34	06 34		07 06		07 32	08 36		09 16			11 31		12 16				13 21	
2¼	—	KEYHAM	d		05 48	06 36	06 36		07 08		07 34	08 38		09 18			11 33		12 18				13 23	
—	3	ST BUDEAUX VICTORIA RD	d						07 11					09 21			11 36						13 26	
—	7¾	BERE FERRERS	d						07 18					09 28			11 43						13 33	
—	10	BERE ALSTON	d	05 40					07 29					09 39			11 54						13 44	
—	11¾	CALSTOCK	d						07 35					09 45			12 00						13 50	
—	14½	**GUNNISLAKE**	a	05 58					07 47					09 57			12 12						14 02	
3	—	ST. BUDEAUX FERRY RD	d		05 50	06 38	06 38	07 02			07 36	08 40							12 20					
4¼	—	SALTASH	d		05a55	06 44	06a43	07 07		07 33	07 41	08 45	09 00						12 25					
9¼	—	ST GERMANS	d			06 51					07 48	08 52							12 32					
14¾	—	MENHENIOT	d			07 00					07 57	09 01							12 41					
17¾	—	**LISKEARD**	a			07 07		07 24		07 50	08 03	09 07	09 18			11 34			12 47		13 16			

			2				2			2		2		2	2			A SX	2					2
PLYMOUTH	d	14 07	14 25	..	14 55	..	16 05	16 38	..	16 42	17 10	17 15	..	18 00	18 08	..	18 50	19 40	20 00	..	20 45	..	21 25	21 40
DEVONPORT	d		14 29				16 09	16 42		16 46		17 19		18 04	18 12									
DOCKYARD	d		14 31				16 11	16 44		16 48		17 21		18 06	18 14									
KEYHAM	d		14 33				16 13	16 47		16 51		17 23		18 08	18 16				20 05					21 45
ST BUDEAUX VICTORIA RD	d									16 54					18 19				20 09					21 49
BERE FERRERS	d									17 01					18 26				20 16					21 56
BERE ALSTON	d									17 12					18 37				20 27					22a03
CALSTOCK	d									17 18					18 43				20 33					
GUNNISLAKE	a									17 30					18 55				20 45					
ST. BUDEAUX FERRY RD	d		14 35				16 15	16 49				17 25		18 10										
SALTASH	d		14a40				16a20	16 55				17a30		18 15									21 36	
ST GERMANS	d							17 02			17 27			18 22										
MENHENIOT	d							17 11						18 31										
LISKEARD	a	14 33			15 22			17 17			17 38			18 37			19 16	20 09			21 11		21 53	

Liskeard, Gunnislake and Bere Alston to Plymouth

Miles	Miles			2	SO	2	SX	2	2		2 SX		2			SX	2			2	A SX			
0	—	**LISKEARD**	d	..	06 00	..	06 23	..	..	..	07 30	08 04	..	08 10	..	08 56	09 35	..	09 51	..	10 43	11 33	12 23	..
3	—	MENHENIOT	d		06 05		06 28				07 36			08 15			09 40							
8½	—	ST GERMANS	d		06 13		06 36				07 44			08 23			09 48							
13	—	SALTASH	d	06 00	06 22		06 45	06 52	07 20		07 53			08 31			09 56							
14¾	—	ST BUDEAUX FERRY RD	d	06 04	06 26		06 49	06 56	07 24		07 57			08 35			10 00							
—	0	**GUNNISLAKE**	d			06 05							07 50							10 02				
—	2¾	CALSTOCK	d			06 17							08 02							10 14				
—	4½	BERE ALSTON	d			06 28							08 13							10 25				
—	7¼	BERE FERRERS	d			06 34							08 19							10 31				
—	11½	ST BUDEAUX VICTORIA RD	d			06 41							08 26							10 38				
15½	12½	KEYHAM	d	06 06	06 28	06 45	06 51	06 58	07 26		07 59		08 29	08 37			10 02			10 41				
16	—	DOCKYARD	d	06 09	06 31	06 48	06 54	07 01	07 29		08 02			08 40			10 05			10 44				
16½	—	DEVONPORT	d	06 11	06 33	06 50	06 56	07 03	07 31		08 05		08 32	08 42			10 07			10 46				
17¾	14½	**PLYMOUTH**	a	06 15	06 37	06 54	07 00	07 07	07 35		08 09	08 32	08 37	08 46		09 25	10 11		10 19	10 50	11 12	12 01	12 51	

		2		2			2	2			2		2		2		2	FO B	2		2	2		
LISKEARD	d	..	..	13 10	..	14 02	..	..	15 27	..	..	16 47	..	17 28	..	18 11	19 00	19 17	..	19 38	..	..	23 06	..
MENHENIOT	d			13 15								16 53				18 17	19 05							
ST GERMANS	d			13 23								17 00				18 25	19 13							
SALTASH	d			13 31				15 10			16 28	17 08	17 35			18 34	19 21			19 56				
ST BUDEAUX FERRY RD	d			13 35				15 14			16 32	17 12	17 39			18 39	19 25							
GUNNISLAKE	d	12 20					14 12								17 35				19 05		20 48			
CALSTOCK	d	12 32					14 24								17 47				19 17		21 00			
BERE ALSTON	d	12 43					14 35								17 58				19 28		21 10	22 10		
BERE FERRERS	d	12 49					14 41								18 04				19 34		21 16	22 16		
ST BUDEAUX VICTORIA RD	d	12 56					14 48								18 11				19 41		21 23	22 23		
KEYHAM	d	12 59		13 37			14 51	15 16			16 34	17 15	17 41		18 14	18 42	19 27		19 44		21 26	22 26		
DOCKYARD	d	13 02		13 40			14 54	15 19			16 37	17 17	17 44		18 17		19 30		19 47					
DEVONPORT	d	13 04		13 42			14 56	15 21			16 39	17 19	17 46		18 19	18 46	19 32		19 49					
PLYMOUTH	a	13 08		13 46		14 30	15 00	15 25	15 55		16 43	17 24	17 50	17 56	18 23	18 50	19 36	19 45	19 53	20 08	21 34	22 34	23 35	

Heavy figures denote through carriages
For general notes see pages 5 and 6

A Until 30 October
B 12 June to 4 September

Western Passenger Timetable 4 May 1970 - 2 May 1971

Table 31—continued
Plymouth to Bere Alston, Gunnislake and Liskeard
Until 26 September — **Saturdays**

		A	G	C	②		C		②			②		②			②		J		C
PLYMOUTH	d	02(45	03(40	04(45	05 15	05 35	06(10	06 28	06 55	07 00	07 15	07 35	08 30	08 50	09	10 11 08	11 25	12 01	12 20	12 52	13 15	13(33	14 05	14 35	14 55	15 14	15(46
DEVONPORT	d					05 39		06 32		07 04	07 19		08 34		09 14		11 29	12 05			13 19		14 39			
DOCKYARD	d					05 41		06 34		07 06	07 21		08 36		09 16		11 31	12 07			13 21		14 41			
KEYHAM	d					05 43		06 36		07 08	07 23		08 38		09 18		11 33	12 09			13 23		14 43			
ST BUDEAUX VIC. RD	d									07 11					09 21		11 36				13 26					
BERE FERRERS	d									07 18					09 28		11 43				13 33					
BERE ALSTON	d					05 40				07 29					09 39		11 54				13 44					
CALSTOCK	d									07 35					09 45		12 00				13 50					
GUNNISLAKE	a					05 58				07 47					09 57		12 12				14 02					
ST BUDEAUX FERRY RD	d					05 45		06 38	07 02		07 25		08 40					12 11					14 45			
SALTASH	d					05a50		06a43	07 07		07 30		08 45	09 00				12 16					14a50			
ST GERMANS	d										07 37		08 52					12 23								
MENHENIOT	d										07 46		09 01					12 32								
LISKEARD	a	03(15	04(10	05(15			06(38			07 24		07 52	08 03	09 07	09 17		11 34		12 38	12 47	13 19		14(01	14 34		15 22	15 43	16(15

Saturdays —continued | **Sundays**

			C	②		②	C	②	②			N	L		L		K		L		
PLYMOUTH	d	16(02	16 05	16 40	16 42	17 05	17 20	18 00	18 26	18 55	19(25	20 20	20 45	22 00	07 00	09(30	11(30	15(05	15(35	17(15	18 20	19 25	22 15
DEVONPORT	d		16 09		16 46	17 09		18 04	18 30														
DOCKYARD	d		16 11		16 48	17 11		18 06	18 32			20 25		22 05									
KEYHAM	d		16 13		16 51	17 13		18 08	18 34														
ST BUDEAUX VIC. RD	d			16 54				18 37			20 28		22 08										
BERE FERRERS	d			17 01				18 44			20 36		22 16										
BERE ALSTON	d			17 07				18 55			20 46		22a23										
CALSTOCK	d			17 18				19 01			20 52												
GUNNISLAKE	a			17 30				19 13			21 04												
ST BUDEAUX FERRY RD	d		16 15			17 15		18 10															
SALTASH	d		16a20			17a20		18 15															
ST GERMANS	d							17 38	18 22														
MENHENIOT	d							18 31															
LISKEARD	a	16(31		17 08			17 51	18 37		19 22	19(54		21 12		07 28	09(54	11(58	15(33	16(03	17(43	18 48	19 53	22 43

Liskeard, Gunnislake and Bere Alston to Plymouth
Until 26 September — **Saturdays**

			②			B		②		C	D	E		G	②		C	H		②
LISKEARD	d	06 00			08 04		08 10	09 04	09(28	09 35	10 02		10(36	10(51	11(11	11 38	12(02		13 01	13(12	13(34	13 42	14 02	
MENHENIOT	d	06 05					08 15			09 40									13 47		
ST GERMANS	d	06 13					08 23			09 48									13 55		
SALTASH	d	06 00 06 22		06 52 07 32			08 31			09 56									14 03		15 10
ST BUDEAUX FERRY RD	d	06 04 06 26		06 56 07 36			08 35			10 00									14 07		15 14
GUNNISLAKE	d		06 05			07 50					10 02							12 23			14 12
CALSTOCK	d		06 17			08 02					10 14							12 35			14 24
BERE ALSTON	d		06 28			08 13					10 25							12 46			14 35
BERE FERRERS	d		06 34			08 19					10 31							12 52			14 41
ST BUDEAUX VIC. RD	d		06 41			08 26					10 38							12 59			14 48
KEYHAM	d	06 06 06 28	06 45 06 58	07 38		08 29 08 37				10 02	10 41							13 02		14 09	14 51 15 16
DOCKYARD	d	06 09 06 31	06 48 07 01	07 41		08 40				10 05	10 44							13 05		14 12	14 54 15 19
DEVONPORT	d	06 11 06 33	06 50 07 03	07 43		08 32 08 42				10 07	10 46							13 07		14 14	14 56 15 21
PLYMOUTH	a	06 15 06 37	06 54 07 07	07 47 08 32	08 07 08 46	09 32	09(56	10 11	10 30	10 50	11(05	11(20	11(40	12 06	12(30	13 11	13 27	13(41	14(06	14 18	14 30	15 00	15 25

Saturdays —continued | **Sundays**

		C			②			②	B			C	②	②			L		N		L	
LISKEARD	d	15(08	15 27			17 28		18 15	19 05	19 38		20(56			23 06	11 47	13 03		13(47		15(55		16 51	19 36	21(19		23 06
MENHENIOT	d							18 20	19 10													
ST GERMANS	d							18 28	19 18													
SALTASH	d		16 28	17 35				18 36	19 26	19 56												
ST BUDEAUX FERRY RD	d		16 32	17 39				18 40	19 30													
GUNNISLAKE	d					17 35			19 25			21 08										
CALSTOCK	d					17 47			19 37			21 20										
BERE ALSTON	d					17 58			19 48			21 31 22 30										
BERE FERRERS	d					18 04			19 54			21 37 22 36										
ST BUDEAUX VIC. RD	d					18 11			20 01			21 44 22 43										
KEYHAM	d		16 34 17 41		18 14 18 42	19 32		20 04			21 47 22 46											
DOCKYARD	d		16 37 17 44		18 17		19 35		20 07													
DEVONPORT	d		16 39 17 46		18 19 18 46	19 37		20 09														
PLYMOUTH	a	15(37	15 50	16 43 17 50	17 56	18 23	18 50	19 41	20 08	20 13	21(25	21 54	22 53	23 35	12 20	13 35	14(20	16(20	17 20	20 05	21(48	23 35

Heavy figures denote through carriages
For general notes see pages 5 and 6

A	4 July to 29 August
B	13 June to 12 September
C	13 June to 5 September
D	30 May to 19 September
E	From 13 June
G	23 May to 5 September
H	4 July to 5 September
J	23 May to 12 September
K	From 4 October
L	Until 27 September
N	14 June to 6 September

Devonport Albert Road, and the ex-SR line through Devonport King's Road was closed. Trains regained their old route at St Budeaux. The line between Bere Alston and Okehampton, however, was closed in May 1968 (Chapter 3.16). Since then the line has been operated as a branch line from Plymouth to Gunnislake. In 1994 the original station at Gunnislake was replaced by a new station to the east, allowing the demolition of a low bridge over the main A390 road just east of the old station. The autumn of 2019 saw nine trains run between Plymouth and Gunnislake each weekday, one originating at Liskeard. They were operated by Great Western Railway with 'Sprinter' DMUs. Eight trains ran on Saturdays and five on Sundays.

The line is now the last survivor of the Col Stephens light railway empire on the national network. A small railway museum has been established at Bere Ferrers station where information on Col Stephens and his railways is displayed.

3.13 Bodmin Road – Bodmin General, Bodmin North – Wadebridge and Padstow (January 1967)

For a small Cornish town Bodmin had quite a complex rail network. The Bodmin & Wadebridge Railway (BWR), which opened in July 1834, was among the first steam-worked lines to carry passengers in Britain. Although the line was promoted as a purely local venture, the LSWR saw it as part of a route into Cornwall to rival the broad-gauge lines that were under the influence of the GWR. It therefore purchased the BWR in 1847. This was certainly a long-term investment, as the LSWR line from Okehampton did not arrive in Wadebridge until May 1895. Padstow was finally reached in March 1899. Meanwhile the 3½-mile line, from the GWR main line at Bodmin Road to Bodmin General, had opened in May 1887. The next step in the development of railways around Bodmin occurred a year later when a line was built around the town from Bodmin General to meet the former BWR line at Boscarne Junction. This allowed GWR trains to reach Wadebridge, although they were not permitted to stop at either of the intermediate halts en route. This situation continued into the early years of nationalisation.

BR(WR) took over responsibility for both lines from 1 January 1963. Despite this the pattern of services in the summer of 1964 remained much as it had been for decades. Six trains a day ran from Bodmin Road to Bodmin General only, while five further trains ran through to either Wadebridge or Padstow. In addition, three trains ran from the ex-GWR

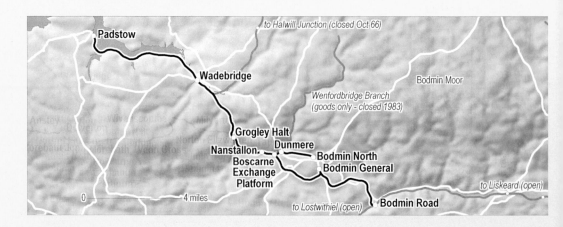

Until 1960 the line between Wadebridge and Bodmin North was the home of two 19th-century ex-LSWR classes of tank engine: passenger trains were in the hands of Class 'O2' 0-4-4s, while Class '0298' 2-4-0 Beattie well tanks of 1874/75 could be seen on both passenger and china clay traffic. These were soon replaced by ex-GWR pannier tanks, and here Class '5700' pannier tank No 4694, built in 1945 at Swindon and recently allocated to Wadebridge depot, is pictured at Boscarne Junction with the 2.52pm train from Padstow to Bodmin North on 3 July 1961. *Terry Gough*

station at Bodmin General to Padstow, while five more ran from the ex-LSWR Bodmin North station to either Wadebridge or Padstow. From June 1964 the service was completely revised. A new halt, Boscarne Exchange Platform, was built at Boscarne Junction, and here passengers on four of the five weekday departures from Bodmin North had to change onto trains from Bodmin Road to Padstow; the fifth departure, at 5.50pm, ran through to Wadebridge. There was no Sunday service.

The motive power over the former LSWR and GWR lines was typical for the West Country as a whole. For many years GWR-line trains had been hauled by that company's 'Small Prairie' tanks, while those on the ex-LSWR lines were in the hands of a variety of tank engines dating from the latter part of the 19th century, typically 'O2' Class 0-4-4s. In addition, Wadebridge was home to the last three Beattie Class '0298' 2-4-0 well tanks, which, although subsequently rebuilt, dated from 1874. These ancient machines were mainly used on china

Ex-GWR motive power had traditionally worked over the ex-LSWR line with trains from Wadebridge to Bodmin General and Bodmin Road. Here 'Small Prairie' No 4569 is seen near Grogley Halt on 10 September 1960 with the 3.24pm service from Wadebridge to Bodmin General and Bodmin Road. No 4569 was built at Swindon in 1924 and withdrawn in July 1964. *Peter Gray*

clay traffic on the old BWR line to Wenfordbridge. However, they were also frequently seen on passenger trains, particularly the one-coach locals from Wadebridge to Padstow, trains that at times could also be hauled by unrebuilt 'Light Pacifics'.

Although single-unit railcars and North British Type 2 diesel-hydraulics replaced steam on trains from Bodmin Road in September 1961, the well tanks remained in use until July 1962, when they were replaced by ex-GWR Class '1366' pannier tanks. The Class 'O2' tanks had already

Wadebridge depot's recently acquired ex-GWR pannier tank No 4694 is seen again at Bodmin North during 1960. After arrival from Padstow it has run round its train of ex-SR Maunsell coaches before returning to the Cornish coast.
M. E. J. Deane collection, courtesy of Ian Bennett

been replaced on services from Bodmin North by ex-GWR Class '5700' pannier and Ivatt Class 2 2-6-2 tanks. Steam was finally eliminated at the end of the of 1964. The shuttle service from Bodmin North was worked by two AC railcars, which had been displaced from the Cirencester and Tetbury branches in April 1964.

The Beeching Report had revealed that the branch carried fewer than 5,000 passengers a week and that only Padstow, Wadebridge and Bodmin stations had annual passenger receipts above £5,000. The investment in the new exchange platform at Boscarne Junction in September 1964 is therefore rather surprising. Passenger services from both Bodmin Road and Bodmin North to Padstow were withdrawn from 30 January 1967, the last train being worked by NB Type 2 diesel-hydraulic No D6309.

The ex-GWR pannier tanks did not last long on passenger trains from Wadebridge as they were soon replaced by Ivatt Class 2 2-6-2 tanks. Here No 41275 stands at Bodmin North with the 4.05pm train to Padstow on a very wet Saturday 31 August 1963. *Author*

Today Bodmin Road, now renamed Bodmin Parkway, remains open on the main line from Plymouth to Penzance (Chapter 2.4), with services operated by Great Western Railway and CrossCountry trains. The line from Wenfordbridge to the BR(WR) main line via Bodmin remained in use for china clay traffic until 1983. Since then the line from Bodmin Parkway to Bodmin General and Boscarne Junction has been reopened by the heritage Bodmin & Wenford Railway, and ex-GWR 'Small Prairie' tanks can once again be seen at work. The railway is also host to one of the two preserved Class '0298' well tanks, No 30587, while the second, No 30585, has made several appearances. The trackbed between Padstow and Boscarne Junction is now a footpath/cycleway.

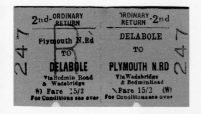

Services to Bodmin North were revised from 15 June 1964 when a new halt named Boscarne Exchange Platform opened at Boscarne Junction, where passengers could change onto trains between Bodmin Road, Bodmin General and Padstow. Two of the four-wheeled railbuses built by AC Cars Ltd in 1958 were allocated to Wadebridge for use on the line; they had been built for the Tetbury and Cirencester branches, which had both closed in April 1964. One of the railbuses is pictured at Bodmin North on 21 June 1965. *Frank Hornby*

BR(WR) had introduced DMUs on its services to Bodmin and Padstow in September 1961. Here a single-unit railcar stands at Bodmin Road station on the Plymouth to Penzance main line, forming the 3.37pm service to Bodmin General and Padstow on 7 September 1965. Bodmin Road station survives today as Bodmin Parkway and again sees steam trains operated by the heritage Bodmin & Wenford Railway. *Author*

Ex-GWR 'Small Prairie' tank No 5552 recreates a scene from the 1960s as it leaves Bodmin Parkway with a train for Bodmin General during the Autumn Gala on the Bodmin & Wenford Railway on 7 September 2003. No 5552 was built at Swindon in 1928 and withdrawn in 1960. It then spent the next 26 years at Barry scrapyard before being purchased and restored. *Author*

Ex-GWR Class '1366' pannier tanks replaced the three Class '0298' 2-4-0 well tanks at Wadebridge in the summer of 1962, and all three were withdrawn in December of that year. However, two, Nos 30585 and 30587, both built by Beyer Peacock in 1874, were subsequently preserved. No 30587 is now part of the National Collection and is based at the Bodmin & Wenford Railway, while No 30585, although based at the Buckingham Railway Centre, has made several visits to Bodmin. The two well tanks are seen together at Bodmin on 9 October 2010 during the railway's Autumn Gala. *Author*

Western Region Timetable 18 April 1966 - 5 March 1967

Table 43 (Second class only unless otherwise shown)

Weekdays

NOT on Saturdays 18 June to 3 September

Bodmin Road to Padstow

Miles	Miles								D SX			D SX			A	
	—	**BODMIN ROAD**	d	07 45	..	09 48	..	11 40	13 53	..	15 45	..	16 27	..	18 00	19 45
3½	—	BODMIN GENERAL ¶	a	07 53	..	09 56	..	11 48	14 01	..	15 55	..	16 35	..	18 08	19 53
			d	07 55	..	09c58	..	11 50	14 03	..	16 05	..	16 37	..	18c10	19 55
	1½	BODMIN NORTH HALT	d	..	..	10 14	..	..	..	..	..	..	..	..	18 26	..
		DUNMERE HALT	d	..	..	10 17	..	..	..	..	..	..	..	..	18 29	..
6½	2⅝	NANSTALLON HALT	d	08 03	..	10 21	..	11 58	14 11	..	16 13	..	16 44	..	18 33	20 02
8	3⅝	GROGLEY HALT	d	08 07	..	10 25	..	12 02	14 15	..	16 17	..	16 48	..	18 37	20 06
11	6½	WADEBRIDGE	a	08 14	..	10 32	..	12 09	14 22	..	16 24	..	16 55	..	18 44	20 13
			d	08 31	..	10 34	..	12 11	14 23	..	16 26	17 15	17 15	..	18 45	20 15
16½	12½	**PADSTOW**	a	08 40	..	10 43	..	12 20	14 32	..	16 35	..	17b05	17 24	18 54	20 24

Saturdays
18 June to 3 September

					C								
BODMIN ROAD	d	07 45	08 35	..	..	09 20	..	10 00	..	11 25	12 15	..	13 15	14 15
BODMIN GENERAL ¶	a	07 53	08 43	..	..	09 28	..	10 08	..	11 33	12 23	..	13 23	14 23
	d	07 55	08 49	..	..	09 30	..	10 10	..	11 37	12 30	..	13 28	14 26
BODMIN NORTH HALT	d	..	..	..	09 33	..	..	..	..	..	..	..	..
DUNMERE HALT	d	..	..	..	09 36	..	..	..	..	..	..	..	..
NANSTALLON HALT	d	08 01	08 56	..	..	09 39	..	10 17	..	11 47	12 40	..	13 38	14 33
GROGLEY HALT	d	08 05	09 00	..	..	09 43	..	10 21	..	11 51	12 44	..	13 42	14 37
WADEBRIDGE	a	08 12	09 07	..	..	09 50	..	10 28	..	11 58	12 51	..	13 49	14 44
	d	08 18	..	..	..	09 51	..	10 31	..	11 59	12 52	..	13 50	..
PADSTOW	a	08 27	..	..	..	10 00	..	10 40	..	12 08	13 01	..	13 59	..

Saturdays
18 June to 3 September—continued

Sundays
(Southern National)

BODMIN ROAD	d	15 10	..	16 10	..	17 05	..	18 00 20 05	..	11 30	..	19 30	..	23 00
BODMIN GENERAL ¶	a	15 18	..	16 18	..	17 13	..	18 08 20 13	..					
	d	15 20	..	16 24	..	17c15	..	18 14 20 16	..					
BODMIN NORTH HALT	d	..	..	..	17 32	..	..						
DUNMERE HALT	d	..	..	..	17 35	..	..						
NANSTALLON HALT	d	15 28	..	..	17 39	..	18 22 20 23						
GROGLEY HALT	d	15 32	..	..	17 43	..	18 26 20 27						
WADEBRIDGE	d	15 39	..	16 39	..	17 50	..	18 33 20 34	..	12 03	..	20 03	..	23 33
	d	15 41	..	16 40	..	17 51	..	18 36 20 36						
PADSTOW	a	15 50	..	16 49	..	18 00	..	18 45 20 45	..	12 34	..	20 34	..	00 04

Heavy figures denote through carriages; light figures denote connecting services
For general notes see page 3

On Sundays passengers with through rail tickets may travel by Southern National Omnibus between Bodmin Road, Wadebridge and Padstow

A   13 June to 2 September
C   To Bodmin Road (arr 09 56)
D   First and second class

b   Saturdays only
c   Via Bodmin North
¶   1 mile to Bodmin North Station

Western Region Timetable: 18 April 1966 – 5 March 1967

3.14 and 3.15 Sidmouth Junction - Sidmouth and Tipton St. John's and Exmouth (March 1967)

A station at Feniton opened with the line from Yeovil to Exeter in 1860 (Chapter 2.6). Then situated in the middle of nowhere, it was renamed Ottery & Sidmouth Road, Ottery St Mary, then Ottery Road. The LSWR, as elsewhere on the East Devon coast, saw the potential of Sidmouth as a popular seaside town and therefore encouraged the construction of a branch line. The 8¼-mile single line opened in July 1874 when Ottery Road became Sidmouth Junction, a name it was to retain for over 90 years. Although nominally built by the Sidmouth Railway, it was worked from the start by the LSWR. The Sidmouth Railway nevertheless retained its independence until the railway amalgamations of 1923. Two intermediate stations were opened at Ottery St Mary and Tipton St John's, 5 miles from Sidmouth Junction, both with passing loops.

South of Tipton St John's the line climbed steeply for 2 miles at 1 in 45 to reach the terminus at Sidmouth. As a result the station at Sidmouth was inconveniently situated above and about 1 mile from the seafront. It has been suggested that the rather select resort of Sidmouth actually wished to deter day trippers from what it considered to be the lower classes!

The neighbouring resort of Budleigh Salterton a few miles west along the coast was quite happy to encourage such trippers and in May 1897 the Budleigh Salterton Railway (BSR) opened its 6½-mile line from Tipton St John's. There were two intermediate stations on the line, neither with passing loops; that at East Budleigh opened with the line, with a further station at Newton Poppleford opening two years later. The line was again worked by the LSWR, with the BSR losing its independence in 1912. By then the LSWR had already extended the line a further 5 miles to Exmouth in June 1903, with a crossing point at the intermediate station at Littleham. The line skirted the northern edge of the

For many years the lines from Sidmouth Junction to Sidmouth and Exmouth were home to ex-LSWR Class 'M7' 0-4-4 tanks. Despite the introduction of Ivatt Class 2 and BR Standard Class 3 2-6-2 tanks, they were not all replaced until BR(WR) took over the line at the beginning of 1963. One of the 'M7s', No 30253, approaches Tipton St John's, the junction of the Sidmouth and Exmouth lines, in May 1961, with a train for Sidmouth. No 30253 was built at Nine Elms in 1897 and withdrawn in October 1961. *M. E. J. Deane collection, courtesy of Ian Bennett*

One of the Ivatt Class 2 2-6-2 tanks that replaced the 'M7s' on services from Sidmouth Junction, No 41306, heads the 11.12am train from Sidmouth to Tipton St John's on 9 August 1960. The passenger accommodation comprises an SR two-coach set built in the mid-1920s. *Terry Gough*

town and approached Exmouth station on a long curving viaduct. A station at Exmouth had opened in 1861 with the arrival of the Exeter & Exmouth Railway (Chapter 3.20) and until 1924 the two lines from Exeter and Tipton St John's had to share the two faces of a single island platform. The station was then completely rebuilt and the number of platform faces doubled.

Once the line from Tipton St John's had opened, through coaches from Waterloo to Exmouth were detached at Sidmouth Junction together with those for Sidmouth, a tradition that was to continue for many years. The weekday train service to Sidmouth and Exmouth during the winter of 1962/63, including the arrival of the 'Atlantic Coast Express' at 2.06 and 2.27pm respectively, is given in BR(SR) Table 35 (see pp. 63 & 64). Until 1963 coaches for Exmouth and Sidmouth were detached from the 11.00am departure from Waterloo, the 'Atlantic Coast Express', on weekdays throughout the year. On summer Saturdays there were three through trains from Waterloo (Appendix 3.1). An interesting through working that ran on summer Saturdays until September 1962 was from Cleethorpes, with coaches for both Sidmouth and Exmouth (Appendix 3.1). From Birmingham the train ran via the former Midland line to

Tipton St John's station is pictured on 13 September 1966, almost three years after dieselisation. A number of trains from Exmouth terminated here or reversed to reach Sidmouth. On the right a Class 118 DMU has arrived from Sidmouth Junction for Sidmouth, while on the left a Derby-built Class 116 unit provides a connecting service for Exmouth. *J. M. Tolson, Frank Hornby collection*

Bath Green Park, then traversed the old Somerset & Dorset main line to Templecombe where it joined the ex-LSWR main line to Sidmouth Junction. The train left Cleethorpes at 7.00am and arrived in Sidmouth and Exmouth at 5.17pm and 5.40pm respectively. The through trains reversed at Sidmouth Junction; most then ran double-headed by two tank engines to Tipton St John's, where the train divided, the first section departing for Exmouth via Budleigh Salterton, the second for Sidmouth.

A Class 116 DMU approaches Tipton St John's over the level crossing at the south end of the station forming the 4.30pm service from Sidmouth to Sidmouth Junction on 12 February 1964. *Author*

Ivatt Class 2 2-6-2 tank No 41292 arrives at Sidmouth with a train from Sidmouth Junction in May 1961. *M. E. J. Deane collection, courtesy of Ian Bennett*

BRIT. TRANSP'T COMMISSION (S)
PARKING TICKET FOR MOTOR CAR
OR THREE WHEELED VEHICLE AT
3487 **SIDMOUTH JUNCTION** 3487
Registration No.......................
Fee 6d.
Available on day of issue only
For conditions see over

Alternatively, some trains were booked to work to their destinations separately from Sidmouth Junction. The same procedure was following when diesel-hydraulics took over the through workings in 1965.

By the summer timetable for 1963, the first since the transfer of the line to BR(WR), the old 'M7' 0-4-4 tanks had already been replaced by Ivatt Class 2 2-6-2 tanks. These were assisted from 1963 by the larger BR Standard Class 4 2-6-4 tanks, but steam was replaced by DMUs from the end of

BR Standard Class 3 2-6-2 tank No 82018 stands at Tipton St John's in 1956 with a train for Exmouth comprising two ex-LSWR coaches. At the time most trains were still hauled by Class 'M7' 0-4-4 tanks, several of which survived until the early 1960s. No 82018 was one of the fleet of 2-6-2 tanks allocated new to Exmouth Junction depot in 1952/54, and was withdrawn from Nine Elms depot in June 1966. A. J. Pike, Frank Hornby collection

October 1963. The through workings to and from Waterloo during the winter months did not reappear, but those to Sidmouth and Exmouth did resume on summer Saturdays in both 1964 and 1965. In the former year these saw the reappearance of the 2-6-4 and 2-6-2 tanks, but by the summer of 1965 BR(WR) diesel-hydraulics were in charge of the branch-line workings. Three through trains then ran from Waterloo on Saturdays (Appendix 3.2). This was perhaps surprising as they were the only through trains from Waterloo to any West Country resort, compared with 17 in 1962. One of the through trains saw steam power return to the ex-SR main line, which had been officially dieselised since 7 September 1964; this was the 3.05pm departure from Sidmouth Junction to Waterloo with coaches that had left Exmouth and Sidmouth at 2.13pm and 2.27pm respectively. This train ran for the last time on 28 August. The last through public service of all was the 10.00am from Waterloo, which last ran on Saturday 25 September 1965.

The Beeching Report had revealed that the two branches carried fewer than 5,000 passengers a week, although Sidmouth Junction, Sidmouth, Budleigh Salterton and Exmouth stations all had annual passenger receipts above £5,000. Closure proposals were therefore

In September 1962 Exmouth Junction lost its allocation of Standard Class 3 tanks, and thereafter branch services were dominated by Ivatt Class 2 engines. One of these, No 41308, stands in Exmouth station with the 1.28pm train to Tipton St John's on 12 August 1960. *Terry Gough*

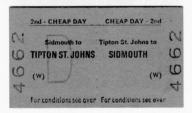

published, with closure subsequently announced for 6 March 1967. Prior to closure seven trains ran from Sidmouth Junction to Sidmouth, with an eighth on Fridays at 11.00pm. A connection to Exmouth was provided for this and most other trains at Tipton St John's. In addition, three trains ran from Exmouth to Sidmouth, which involved reversing at Tipton St John's. The withdrawal of these trains from 6 March 1967 left the Exeter to Exmouth line as the only ex-SR branch line to survive east of Exeter.

The last steam locomotives over the branch lines were scheduled to work an LCGB special on 28 February 1965. 'Merchant Navy' 'Pacific' No 35022 *Holland-America Line* hauled the train from Waterloo to Axminster. Here participants had the option of travelling on the Lyme Regis and Seaton branches hauled by Ivatt 2-6-2 tank No 41206. The main train was taken forward to Sidmouth Junction where ex-GWR pannier tank No 4666 hauled the rear three coaches to Sidmouth. On the return the two trains combined at Tipton St John's and continued double-headed to Exmouth. From Exmouth the train ran direct to Exeter

No 41308 is seen again at East Budleigh station between Exmouth and Tipton St John's with the 1.28pm train from Exmouth on 9 August 1960. By that year the ex-LSWR coaches had been replaced by former SR two-coach Maunsell sets built in the mid-1920s. DMUs took over branch-line services from Sidmouth Junction from October 1963. *Terry Gough*

A three-car Class 118 DMU, one of the units that replaced steam in October 1963, stands in Exmouth station forming a service to Sidmouth Junction on 14 September 1966. On the left is the recently closed single-road engine shed, a sub-shed of Exmouth Junction; the concrete structure had replaced an earlier shed in the late 1920s. *J. M. Tolson, Frank Hornby collection*

Central, where *Holland-America Line* took over again for the return to Waterloo. The tour was so successful that a second train was run on 7 March using locos Nos 41291 and 4666.

Sidmouth Junction station on the main line reopened as Feniton in 1971, but little of the two branch lines remains today. One section, between Exmouth and Littleham, is now a footpath/cycleway.

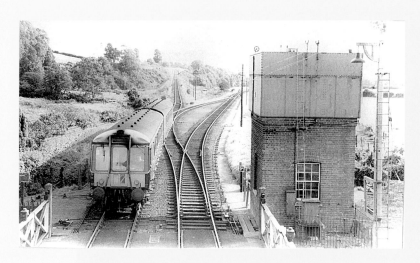

The junction for the Sidmouth and Exmouth lines immediately south of Tipton St John's station is well shown in this picture. A DMU, which appears to comprise a single-unit railcar and trailer, arrives as a service from Exmouth on 13 September 1966. As it is destined for Sidmouth, it will reverse in the station and take the steeply inclined line visible on the left. *J. M. Tolson, Frank Hornby collection*

Through trains from Sidmouth and Exmouth to Waterloo

Although by the summer of 1963 the former BR(SR) lines west of Salisbury were part of BR(WR), the schedule of holiday trains on Saturdays remained as before, including the through trains from Waterloo to Sidmouth and Exmouth. Here, on 10 August 1963, Ivatt Class 2 2-6-2 tank No 41307 and BR Standard Class 4 2-6-4 tank No 80042 double-head the 11.45am train from Waterloo to Sidmouth and Exmouth away from Exmouth Junction. The train will divide at Tipton St John's with Nos 80042 and 41307 taking forward the Sidmouth and Exmouth portions of the train respectively. *Peter Gray*

By the summer of 1965 most of the through trains to West Country branch lines had been withdrawn. Exceptions were three through trains that ran from and to Waterloo with coaches for and from both Sidmouth and Exmouth. Here 'Hymek' Type 3 No D7095 and North British Type 2 No D6324, both diesel-hydraulics, arrive at Sidmouth Junction with the through coaches from Sidmouth (departing at 2.27pm) and Exmouth (2.13pm) to Waterloo on 24 July 1965. The two portions will have combined at Tipton St John's. In the background steam can be seen escaping from BR Standard Class 5 4-6-0 No 73022, which was waiting in the yard to take the train to Waterloo. *Author*

The return workings for the two diesel-hydraulics on 24 July 1965 were trains to Sidmouth and Exmouth, which arrived at Sidmouth Junction as the 12.00pm train from Waterloo behind a 'Warship' diesel-hydraulic. 'Hymek' No D7095 is seen again as it backs onto the Sidmouth portion, due to depart at 3.27pm. In the background No D6324 waits to take out the coaches for Exmouth. This train last ran on Saturday 28 August 1965. *Author*

North British Type 2 diesel-hydraulic No D6324 has now backed onto the through Exmouth coaches at Sidmouth Junction, due out at 3.35pm. Like other BR(WR) diesel-hydraulics, Nos D7095 and D6324 had short lives, being withdrawn in October 1972 and September 1968 respectively. *Author*

BR Standard Class 5 4-6-0 No 73022 waits to leave Sidmouth Junction with the 3.05pm departure for Waterloo on that same Saturday 24 July 1965, which included the through coaches from both Sidmouth and Exmouth. This was the only Waterloo train scheduled for steam haulage west of Salisbury during 1965. A three-car Derby-built Class 116 DMU can be seen waiting in the bay platform to form the 3.00pm service for Sidmouth. *Author*

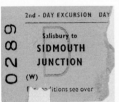

Another North British Type 2 diesel-hydraulic, No D6342, has arrived at Exmouth with the through coaches off the 10.00am train from Waterloo on Saturday 4 September 1965. The train was retimed from Saturday 11 September and last ran two weeks later, thus ending the long tradition of through holiday trains from Waterloo forever. No D6342 was withdrawn in December 1968. *Author*

Western Region Timetable 18 April 1966 - 5 March 1967

Note By the summer of 1966 only local trains ran between Sidmouth Junction, Sidmouth and Exmouth. This compares with three trains from Waterloo on Saurdays in 1965. In addition a through train ran from Cleethorpes via Birmingham on Saturdays in 1962. (see Appendix 3)

Table 38 **(Second class only)**

Weekdays

NOT on Saturdays 18 June to 3 Septembe

Sidmouth Junction to Sidmouth and Exmouth

Miles							A			A		B			B	A		B	B				B	
—	SIDMOUTH JUNCTION..	d	07 30	..	..	08 33	..	10 40	..	..	13 00	..	..	14 55	..	..	16 45	..	..	..	18 29	18 57	..	..
3	OTTERY ST MARY	d	07 36	....	....	08 39	....	10 46	....	....	13 06	....	....	15 01	....	....	16 51	....	....	....	18 35	19 03	....	....
5	TIPTON ST JOHN'S	a	07 40	..	..	08 43	..	10 50	..	..	13 10	..	..	15 05	..	..	16 55	..	..	..	18 39	19 07	..	..
—	TIPTON ST JOHN'S	d	07 41	....	....	08 44	10 17	....	10 55	12 17	13 11	....	14 15	15 06	....	16 34	16 56	....	....	....	18 42	19 08	....	....
8¼	SIDMOUTH	a	07 49	..	..	08 52	10 25	..	11 03	12 25	13 19	..	14 23	15 14	..	16 42	17 04	..	..	..	18 50	19 16	..	..
—	TIPTON ST JOHN'S	d	....	07 44	....	....	....	10 51	....	....	....	13 15	....	....	15 10	....	....	17 00	17 38	....	....	....	19 10	....
6¼	NEWTON POPPLEFORD HALT	d	..	07 47	..	..	..	10 54	..	..	..	13 18	..	..	15 13	..	..	17 03	17 41	..	..	..	19 13	..
9½	EAST BUDLEIGH	d	....	07 52	....	....	....	10 59	....	....	....	13 23	....	....	15 18	....	....	17 08	17 46	....	....	....	19 18	....
11½	BUDLEIGH SALTERTON	d	..	07 57	08 58	..	..	11 04	..	..	..	13 28	..	..	15 23	..	..	17 13	17 53	..	..	..	19 23	..
14¾	LITTLEHAM	d	....	08 05	09 06	....	....	11 12	....	....	....	13 36	....	....	15 31	....	....	17 21	18 01	....	....	....	19 31	....
16½	EXMOUTH	a	..	08 09	09 10	..	..	11 16	..	..	..	13 40	..	..	15 35	..	..	17 25	18 05	..	..	..	19 35	..

Weekdays

NOT on Saturdays 18 June to 3 Sept.—*cont.*

		C	C		FO		FO		
SIDMOUTH JUNCTION..	d	21 10	..	..	23 00	..	..	..	..
OTTERY ST MARY	d	21 16	....	....	23 06	....	....	....	....
TIPTON ST JOHN'S	a	21 20	..	..	23 10	..	..	..	..
TIPTON ST JOHN'S	d	21 21	....	....	23 11	....	....	....	....
SIDMOUTH	a	21 29	..	..	23 19	..	..	..	..
TIPTON ST JOHN'S	d	....	21 25	....	....	....	23 15	....	....
NEWTON POPPLEFORD HALT	d	..	21 28	..	..	..	23 18	..	..
EAST BUDLEIGH	d	....	21 33	....	....	....	23 23	....	....
BUDLEIGH SALTERTON	d	..	21 38	..	..	..	23 28	..	..
LITTLEHAM	d	....	21 46	....	....	....	23 36	....	....
EXMOUTH	a	..	21 50	..	..	..	23 40	..	..

Saturdays

18 June to 3 September

							A									
SIDMOUTH JUNCTION..	d	07 30	..	..	08 39	09 03	..	..	10 40	..	..	11 49	..	..	13 00	..
OTTERY ST MARY	d	07 36	....	....	08 47	09 09	....	....	10 46	....	....	11 55	....	....	13 06	....
TIPTON ST JOHN'S	a	07 40	..	..	08 51	09 13	..	..	10 50	..	..	11 59	..	..	13 10	..
TIPTON ST JOHN'S	d	07 41	....	....	08 52	....	10 18	....	....	10 55	....	12 00	....	....	13 11	....
SIDMOUTH	a	07 49	..	..	09 00	..	10 26	..	..	11 03	..	12 08	..	..	13 19	..
TIPTON ST JOHN'S	d	....	07 44	....	....	09 14	....	....	10 51	....	....	....	12 10	....	....	13 15
NEWTON POPPLEFORD HALT	d	..	07 47	..	..	09 17	..	..	10 54	..	..	..	12 13	..	..	13 18
EAST BUDLEIGH	d	....	07 52	....	....	09 22	....	....	10 59	....	....	....	12 18	....	....	13 23
BUDLEIGH SALTERTON	d	..	07 57	..	..	09 27	..	..	11 04	..	..	..	12 23	..	..	13 28
LITTLEHAM	d	....	08 05	....	....	09 35	....	....	11 12	....	....	....	12 31	....	....	13 36
EXMOUTH	a	..	08 09	..	..	09 39	..	..	11 16	..	..	..	12 35	..	..	13 40

Saturdays

18 June to 3 September—continued

					B				B						B									
SIDMOUTH JUNCTION..	d	13 53	14 55	..	..	..	..	16 45	..	..	..	18 29	18 57	..	..	21 10	..	..	..	23 00	..	..	..	..
OTTERY ST MARY	d	13 59	15 01	....	....	....	....	16 51	....	....	....	18 35	19 03	....	....	21 16	....	....	....	23 06	....	....	....	....
TIPTON ST JOHN'S	a	14 03	15 05	..	..	..	..	16 55	..	..	..	18 39	19 07	..	..	21 20	..	..	..	23 10	..	..	..	..
TIPTON ST JOHN'S	d	14 04	15 06	....	....	16 10	....	16 56	....	18 10	....	18 42	19 08	....	....	21 21	....	....	....	23 11	....	....	....	....
SIDMOUTH	a	14 12	15 14	..	..	16 18	..	17 04	..	18 18	..	18 50	19 16	..	..	21 29	..	..	..	23 19	..	..	..	..
TIPTON ST JOHN'S	d	....	....	....	15 10	....	....	....	17 00	....	....	....	....	....	19 10	....	....	21 25	....	....	23 15	....	....	....
NEWTON POPPLEFORD HALT	d	..	..	..	15 13	..	..	..	17 03	..	..	..	..	..	19 13	..	..	21 28	..	..	23 18	..	..	..
EAST BUDLEIGH	d	....	....	....	15 18	....	....	....	17 08	....	....	....	....	....	19 18	....	....	21 33	....	....	23 23	....	....	....
BUDLEIGH SALTERTON	d	..	..	..	15 23	..	..	..	17 13	..	..	..	..	..	19 23	..	..	21 38	..	..	23 28	..	..	..
LITTLEHAM	d	....	....	....	15 31	....	....	....	17 21	....	....	....	....	....	19 31	....	....	21 46	....	....	23 36	....	....	....
EXMOUTH	a	..	..	..	15 35	..	..	..	17 25	..	..	..	..	..	19 35	..	..	21 50	..	..	23 40	..	..	..

Sundays

22 May to 25 September only

					A		B		A		B	A				A								
SIDMOUTH JUNCTION..	d	10 15	..	11 43	..	13 00	..	..	..	14 50	..	..	17 05	..	17 40	..	..	18 55	..	..	20 05	..	..	..
OTTERY ST MARY	d	10 21	....	11 49	....	13 06	....	....	....	14 56	....	....	17 11	....	17 46	....	....	19 01	....	....	20 11	....	....	....
TIPTON ST JOHN'S	a	10 25	..	11 53	..	13 10	..	..	..	15 00	..	..	17 15	..	17 50	..	..	19 05	..	..	20 15	..	..	..
TIPTON ST JOHN'S	d	10 26	....	11 54	12 14	13 11	....	....	14 32	15 01	....	16 34	....	....	17 51	18 34	....	....	19 10	....	20 16	....	....	....
SIDMOUTH	a	10 34	..	12 02	12 22	13 19	..	..	14 40	15 09	..	16 42	..	..	17 59	18 42	..	..	19 18	..	20 24	..	..	..
TIPTON ST JOHN'S	d	....	10 29	....	....	....	13 15	....	....	....	15 05	....	17 18	....	....	....	....	19 06	....	....	....	20 20	....	....
NEWTON POPPLEFORD HALT	d	..	10 32	..	..	..	13 18	..	..	..	15 08	..	17 21	..	..	..	..	19 09	..	..	..	20 23	..	..
EAST BUDLEIGH	d	....	10 37	....	....	....	13 23	....	....	....	15 13	....	17 26	....	....	....	....	19 14	....	....	....	20 28	....	....
BUDLEIGH SALTERTON	d	..	10 42	..	..	..	13 28	..	..	..	15 18	..	17 31	..	..	..	..	19 19	..	..	..	20 33	..	..
LITTLEHAM	d	....	10 50	....	....	....	13 36	....	....	....	15 26	....	17 39	....	....	....	....	19 27	....	....	....	20 41	....	....
EXMOUTH	a	..	10 54	..	..	..	13 40	..	..	..	15 30	..	17 43	..	..	..	..	19 31	..	..	..	20 45	..	..

Heavy figures denote through carriages;
light figures denote connecting services
For general notes see page 3

A From Exmouth
B From Sidmouth
C 13 June to 2 September

3.16
Okehampton –
Plymouth
(May 1968)

The LSWR had since 1862 sought to build a standard-gauge line from Exeter around the northern fringes of Dartmoor to Plymouth. Okehampton was reached in 1871 and by 1876 LSWR trains were able to run through to Plymouth on mixed-gauge track down the GWR's branch from Lydford and Tavistock via Yelverton. This was a highly unsatisfactory situation that the LSWR sought to overcome through its association with the grandly titled Plymouth, Devonport & South Western Junction Railways (PDSWJR). The final section, built by the PDSWJR, finally opened between Lydford and Plymouth in June 1890, although the LSWR's own station at Plymouth Friary did not open until June 1891.

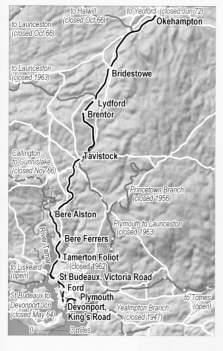

The 23¾-mile route ran south-westwards through Tavistock to Bere Alston, adjacent to the River Tamar. It then followed the east bank of the river beneath Brunel's famous bridge before heading east through Devonport into Plymouth. Both the LSWR and PDSWJR became part of the Southern Railway in 1923.

Once this route had opened the LSWR was able to compete with the GWR for the transatlantic passenger and mail traffic that embarked/disembarked at Plymouth. This was popular with passengers as it allowed them to arrive in London a day or more earlier than by remaining on board their liner until it docked in Southampton. At the time GWR trains had to run via Bristol, which compensated for the LSWR's longer route around Dartmoor, but once the GWR's 'Somerton cut-off' opened in 1906 its shorter route gave it an unassailable advantage. As a result in the 1930s the GWR's 'Cornish Riviera' ran non-stop from Paddington to Plymouth in 4 hours, while the fastest train via what was now the SR route took 5hr 25min. At this time both services were steam-hauled, but by 1962 the 'Cornish Riviera' express was in the hands of BR(WR) 'Warship' Class diesel-hydraulics. The train nevertheless still took 4hr 15min to run from Paddington to Plymouth with a stop at Exeter

The line from Okehampton to Plymouth formed part of the LSWR main line between London and Plymouth. A number of trains therefore worked through to and from London, including the 'Atlantic Coast Express', while there was also a daily through train from Plymouth to Brighton. Despite its main-line status ex-LSWR Class 'T9' 4-4-0s were used regularly until 1960. Here No 30710 is seen near Tavistock on 8 July 1958; this engine was built in 1899 and withdrawn in August 1959. *Terry Gough*

More modern motive power is seen as a rebuilt 'West Country' 'Pacific' passes Meldon Quarry with the 2.25pm Plymouth to Waterloo train on 11 August 1960. It was not unusual for through trains on this route to comprise only three coaches, especially during the winter months. In summer further coaches from Padstow and Bude would be added at Okehampton, and finally a restaurant car would appear at Exeter Central. *Terry Gough*

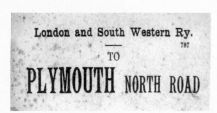

London and South Western Ry.
—
787
TO
PLYMOUTH NORTH ROAD

St David's. On the ex-SR route the steam-hauled 'Atlantic Coast Express' reached Plymouth from Waterloo in 5hr 22min. Allowing for the additional stop made by the 'Cornish Riviera', neither time had changed significantly since the 1930s.

In the winter of 1962 six trains left Waterloo for Plymouth, including at 11.00am the 'Atlantic Coast Express'. In addition, a through train from Brighton to Plymouth used the route daily. The weekday train service during the winter of 1962/63, including the arrival of the 'ACE' at 3.02 and 4.22 pm respectively, is given in BR(SR) Table 35 (see pp. 63 & 64). On summer Saturdays the number of through trains had traditionally been increased (Appendix 3.1), but in 1964, when the line was operated by BR(WR), the number decreased to just three. Worse was to follow when, from 7 September 1964, all daytime trains from Waterloo terminated at Exeter. Only the 1.10am newspaper train still ran through to Plymouth via Okehampton, together with the Brighton to Plymouth train. The 'Light Pacifics' and ex-SR 'N' Class 2-6-0s that had dominated services over the route for many years were replaced by DMUs and diesel-hydraulics. Most trains then ran from Exeter Central to Plymouth stopping at all stations, with

Unrebuilt Bulleid 'Battle of Britain' 'Pacific' No 34064 *Fighter Command* drifts into Bere Alston station with a mixed goods train from Plymouth in May 1960. The line to the right is to Callington. Although Callington station closed in November 1966, the line remains open as far as Gunnislake, together with that from Plymouth. In 1962 No 34064 was experimentally fitted with a Giesl oblong ejector, but the engine was withdrawn four years later. *M. E. J. Deane collection, courtesy of Ian Bennett*

Steam largely disappeared from passenger trains on this route in September 1964. The last steam-hauled passenger train to traverse it as far as Lydford was the Great Western Society special of 5 September 1965 celebrating the centenary of the ex-GWR Plymouth to Launceston branch. The train has already been pictured towards the end of its itinerary at Lydford, Halwill and Bude. Here Ivatt Class 2 2-6-2 tank No 41283 is pictured earlier in the day taking water at Okehampton. *Author*

a number running between Tavistock and Plymouth only. By this time the old PDSWJR route into Plymouth through Devonport King's Road and Ford had already closed, in May 1964, and trains to Plymouth from Okehampton and beyond were diverted to use the ex-GWR route through Keyham and Devonport Albert Road to rejoin their old route at a new junction at St Budeaux.

Despite its previous importance as part of the ex-LSWR main line from Waterloo to Plymouth, the Beeching Report had revealed that the route carried fewer than 5,000 passengers a week and that only Okehampton, Lydford and Tavistock stations had annual passenger receipts above £5,000. BR(WR) would have closed the whole route from Okehampton to Plymouth but, as described earlier, the branch from Bere Alston to Gunnislake remained open (Chapter 3.12). To avoid the branch being isolated from the rest of the national rail network, the Plymouth line between St Budeaux Victoria Road and Bere Alston also had to be retained. The section east to Okehampton was, however, closed from 6 May 1968. The 'newspaper' and Brighton to Plymouth trains had already been diverted to run via Newton Abbot, and the latter continued to do so for many years.

Mineral trains continued to run west of Okehampton as far as Meldon Quarry until 2011. In addition, the heritage Dartmoor Railway runs passenger trains to Meldon Quarry during the summer months (Chapter 2.8). Some 10 miles of the route between Okehampton and Lydford, including the section over the spectacular Meldon Viaduct, is now a cycle/footpath known as the 'Granite Way'. A feasibility study for reopening the line between Bere Alston and Tavistock has been carried out for Devon County Council, but as yet no action has been taken. In addition, the possibility of reopening the whole line has also been considered following the breaching of the sea wall at Dawlish on the ex-GWR main line in April 2014. For the present this option had been ruled out due to the high cost, particularly that of replacing Meldon Viaduct.

As the ex-LSWR main line to Plymouth approached the city it followed the east bank of the River Tamar. Here a BR two-car DMU crosses a tributary of the river between St Budeaux and Tamerton Foliot forming a service for Gunnislake on 12 August 1991. The main line was closed north of Bere Alston from 6 May 1968, and by this time the remaining section from St Budeaux to Bere Alston had been singled. *Terry Gough*

Western Region Timetable 18 April 1966 - 5 March 1967

Note By the summer of 1967 only two through trains used this route, from Waterloo and Brighton respectively. They are shown as 'A' and 'G' in this timetable This compares with eight through trains on Saturdays in 1962. (see Appendix 3)

Table 35

Weekdays

NOT on Saturdays 18 June to 3 September

Exeter to Plymouth (via Okehampton) and Ilfracombe

Miles					A		R SX			R			R			R	A	SO				E		D SX
—	**EXETER CENTRAL**	d		05 09	05 13	05 23	06 55			08 08		08 55	09 44		11 30	11 44	13 16							
¾	**EXETER ST DAVID'S**	a			05 16	05 26	06 58			08 11		08 58	09 47		11 33	11 47	13 20							
—		d			05 22	05 34	—				08 39	09 05		10 13	11 41					13 25		13 31		13 35
5	NEWTON ST CYRES	d					Stop				08 50			10 25										
7½	CREDITON	d				05 48					08 57	09 18		10 31	11 54							13 44		13 49
11¼	YEOFORD	d				05 56					09 04	09 25		10 38	12 01							13 51		13 56
16	BOW	d										09 34		10 47										
19¼	NORTH TAWTON	d										09 41		10 54						13 53				
22	SAMPFORD COURTENAY HALT	d										09 46		10 59										
25¾	OKEHAMPTON (FOR BUDE) Z	a			05 56							09 53		11 06						14 03				
—		d			06 06			07 25				09 56		11 12						14 05				
32½	BRIDESTOWE HALT	d			06 20			07 40				10 09		11 25						14 18				
35½	LYDFORD	d			06 27			07 45				10 15		11 31						14 24				
37	BRENTOR	d			06 31			07 49				10 18		11 35						14 27				
42	TAVISTOCK NORTH	d	06 18		06b49		07 12	07 59	09 00			10 28		11 47				13 32	13 55	14 38				
48½	BERE ALSTON	d	06 30		07 01		07 24	08 11	09 12			10 42		12 00				13 44	14 07	14c50				
51¼	BERE FERRERS	d	06 35		07 07		07 30	08 17	09 18			10 48		12 06				13 50	14 13	14c56				
55¼	ST BUDEAUX, VICTORIA ROAD HALT	d	06 43		07 15		07 38	08 25	09 26			10 56		12 14				13 58	14 21	15c04				
56½	KEYHAM	d	06 46		07 18		07 41	08 28	09 29			10 59		12 17				14 01	14 24	15c07				
57¼	DOCKYARD HALT	d	06 48		07 21		07 43											14 03	14 26					
57½	DEVONPORT, ALBERT ROAD	d	06 51		07 24		07 46	08 31	09 32			11 02		12 20				14 06	14 29	15c11				
58¾	**PLYMOUTH**	a	06 55		07 28		07 50	08 38	09 36			11 06		12 24				14 10	14 33	15c15				
14¼	COPPLESTONE	d				06 02					09 11				12 07							13 57		14 02
15¾	MORCHARD ROAD HALT	d				06 06					09 15				12 11									
18¼	LAPFORD	d				06 11					09 22				12 15							14 04		14 10
22	EGGESFORD	d				06 18					09 29				12 22							14 11		14 19
26	KING'S NYMPTON	d				06 25					09 36				12v29							14 17		14 22
29	PORTSMOUTH ARMS	d				06 31					09 41				12v34									
33	UMBERLEIGH	d				06 38					09 48				12v41							14 28		14 33
35¼	CHAPELTON HALT	d									09 53				12v46									
39¾	BARNSTAPLE JUNCTION (FOR BIDEFORD) Z	a		06 07		06 48					09 59				12v53							14 37		14 42
—		d		06 17		06 58					10 03				12v55							14 39		14 44
40½	BARNSTAPLE TOWN	d		06 21		07 02					10 07				12v59							14 43		14 48
44¾	WRAFTON	d		06 29		07 10					10 14				13v06							14 50		14 55
45¾	BRAUNTON	d		06 33		07 15					10 17				13v09							14 53		14 58
51½	MORTEHOE & WOOLACOMBE	d		06 47		07 30					10 30				13v22							15 06		15 13
54¾	**ILFRACOMBE**	a		06 55		07 40					10 39				13v31							15 15		15 20

		K SO	R		SX	G ⊗			A						A			Q SO				R SX	A	A
EXETER CENTRAL	d		14 51			15 11	15 39	15 50	17 01		17 22		17 45		19 06					19 35	19 45	20 12	21 26	23 11
EXETER ST DAVID'S	a		14 54			15 15	15 42	15 53	17 05		17 25		17 48		19 10					19 38	19 48	20 15	21 30	23 15
	d	14 22				15 19	15 45	16 04			17 27		17 58							19 40	19 52			
NEWTON ST CYRES	d						15 55				17 37		18 08							19 50				
CREDITON	d	14 36					16 01	16 17			17 43		18 14							19 56				
YEOFORD	d	14 43					16 08	16 24			17 50		18 21							20 03	20 11			
BOW	d						16 17				17 59										20 20			
NORTH TAWTON	d						16 23				18 05										20 26			
SAMPFORD COURTENAY HALT	d						16 29				18 11										20 32			
OKEHAMPTON (FOR BUDE) Z	a					15 54	16 36				18 18										20 39			
	d					15 58	16 38				18 22										20 49			
BRIDESTOWE HALT	d						16 51				18 35										21 02			
LYDFORD	d						16 56				18 41										21 07			
BRENTOR	d						17 00				18 44										21 11			
TAVISTOCK NORTH	d				16 05	16 25	17 10			18 04	18 56						19 50				21 21			
BERE ALSTON	d				16 17	16 38	17 22			18 16	19 10						20 02	20 25			21 33			
BERE FERRERS	d				16 23		17 27			18 22	19 16						20 08	20 31			21 39			
ST BUDEAUX, VICTORIA ROAD HALT	d				16 31		17 35			18 30	19 24						20 16	20 40			21 47			
KEYHAM	d				16 34	16 53	17 38			18 33	19 27						20 19	20 43			21 50			
DOCKYARD HALT	d				16 36																			
DEVONPORT, ALBERT ROAD	d				16 39		17 41			18 36	19 31						20 22	20 46			21 53			
PLYMOUTH	a				16 43	17 03	17 45			18 40	19 35						20 26	20 50			21 57			
COPPLESTONE	d	14 49						16 30					18 27							20 09				
MORCHARD ROAD HALT	d							16 34					18 31							20 13				
LAPFORD	d	14 57						16 41					18 36							20 17				
EGGESFORD	d	15 06						16 47					18 45							20 24				
KING'S NYMPTON	d	15 12						16 54					18 51							20 30				
PORTSMOUTH ARMS	d							16 59					18 57							20 36				
UMBERLEIGH	d	15 23						17 06					19 03							20 43				
CHAPELTON HALT	d							17 10					19 08							20 47				
BARNSTAPLE JUNCTION (FOR BIDEFORD) Z	a	15 32						17 17					19 14							20 54				
	d	15 35		16 15				17 20					19 17							20 56				
BARNSTAPLE TOWN	d	15 39		16 19				17 24					19 21							21 00				
WRAFTON	d	15 47		16 26				17 31					19 28							21 07				
BRAUNTON	d	15 50		16 29				17 34					19 31							21 10				
MORTEHOE & WOOLACOMBE	d	16 08		16 42				17 48					19 45							21 23				
ILFRACOMBE	a	16 15		16 51				17 56					19 53							21 32				

Heavy figures denote through carriages; light figures denote connecting services
For general notes see page 3

For the complete service between St Budeaux and Plymouth see Table 34

A From London Waterloo

D 23 May to 23 September. From London Paddington
E Until 21 May and from 26 September
G From Brighton
K 28 May, 4 and 11 June and 10, 17 and 24 Sept. From London Paddington
Z Western/Southern National Omnibus between: Okehampton, Bude and Barnstaple Gas Board Offices and Bideford. See also pages 9 to 20

Q From Callington
R From Exmouth
b Arr 06 39
c Saturdays only
v Four minutes later on Saturdays 28 May, 4 and 11 June and 10, 17 and 24 September.

Western Region Timetable 18 April 1966 - 5 March 1967
Note By the summer of 1967 only two through trains used this route, from Waterloo and Brighton respectively. They are shown as 'A' and 'G' in this timetable This compares with eight through trains on Saturdays in 1962. (see Appendix 3))

Table 35—continued

Exeter to Plymouth (via Okehampton) and Ilfracombe

Saturdays   18 June to 3 September

Station			A						H	N		J ⊗		J			
EXETER CENTRAL	d	05 09	05 13	05 23	07 17		08 57	09 40	09 51	10 25			13 20			
EXETER ST DAVID'S	a		05 16	05 26	07 20		09 00	09 43	09 54	10 28			13 23			
	d		05 22	05 34	07 23		09 08	09 48		10 26	11 23	13 21	13 31			
NEWTON ST CYRES	d						09 18	09 59								
CREDITON	d		05 48				09 24	10 05								
YEOFORD	d		05 56				09 31	10 12	10 44							
BOW	d						09 40	10 53								
NORTH TAWTON	d						09 46	10 59								
SAMPFORD COURTENAY HALT	d						09 52	11 05								
OKEHAMPTON (FOR BUDE) Z	a		05 56				09 59	11 12				14 09				
	d		06 06		07 25		10 03	11 16				14 12				
BRIDESTOWE HALT	d		06 20		07 40		10 16	11 29				14 25				
LYDFORD	d		06 27		07 45		10 21	11 34				14 30				
BRENTOR	d		06 31		07 49		10 25	11 38				14 34				
TAVISTOCK NORTH	d	06 18	06b49	07 12	07 59	09 05	10 36	11 48	13 32	14 10	14 45				
BERE ALSTON	d	06 30	07 01	07 24	08 11	09 17	10 49	12 01	13 45	14 23	14 58				
BERE FERRERS	d	06 35	07 07	07 30	08 17	09 23	10 55	12 07	13 50	14 29	15 04				
ST BUDEAUX VICTORIA ROAD HALT	d	06 43	07 15	07 38	08 25	09 31	11 03	12 15	13 58	14 37	15 12				
KEYHAM	d	06 46	07 18	07 41	08 28	09 34	11 06	12 18	14 01	14 40	15 15				
DOCKYARD HALT	d	06 48	07 21	07 43					14 03	14 43					
DEVONPORT ALBERT ROAD	d	06 51	07 24	07 46	08 31	09 37	11 09	12 21	14 06	14 45	15 20				
PLYMOUTH	a	06 55	07 28	07 50	08 38	09 41	11 13	12 25	14 10	14 49	15 24				
COPPLESTONE	d		06 02					10 18								
MORCHARD ROAD HALT	d		06 06					10 22								
LAPFORD	d		06 11					10 27								
EGGESFORD	d		06 18					10 34								
KING'S NYMPTON	d		06 25					10 41								
PORTSMOUTH ARMS	d		06 31					10 46								
UMBERLEIGH	d		06 38					10 53								
CHAPELTON HALT	d							10 58								
BARNSTAPLE JUNCTION (FOR BIDEFORD) Z	a	06 07	06 48		08 21			11 05	12 37	14 29					
	d	06 17	06 58	07 55	08 24	09 20		11 08	12 41	14 33					
BARNSTAPLE TOWN	d	06 21	07 02	07 59	08 29	09 24		11 12	12 46	14 38					
WRAFTON	d	06 29	07 10	08 06	08 35	09 31		11 20	12 54	14 46					
BRAUNTON	d	06 33	07 15	08 09	08 38	09 34		11 23	12 59	14 51					
MORTEHOE & WOOLACOMBE	d	06 47	07 30	08 23	08 52	09 48		11 37	13 18	15 10					
ILFRACOMBE	a	06 55	07 40	08 31	09 00	09 56		11 45	13 26	15 18					

Station		K	J	P ⊗		A		A		A	E		A	A
EXETER CENTRAL	d			15 11	15 39	15 59	17 01	17 21	17 45	19 09	19 33	19 43	21 26	23 11
EXETER ST DAVID'S	a	13 55	14 12	15 15	15 42	16 02	17 05	17 24	17 48	19 13	19 36	19 46	21 30	23 15
	d	13 55	14 12	15 18	15 50	16 06		17 34	17 53	19 40		19 52		
NEWTON ST CYRES	d					16 16		18 03		19 50				
CREDITON	d		14 28		16 03	16 22	17 47	18 09		19 56		20 11		
YEOFORD	d		14 36		16 10	16 29		18 16		20 03		20 11		
BOW	d					16 19		18 01		20 20				
NORTH TAWTON	d					16 26		18 07		20 26				
SAMPFORD COURTENAY HALT	d					16 31		18 13		20 32				
OKEHAMPTON (FOR BUDE) Z	a			15 55		16 38		18 20		20 39				
	d			15 58		16 41		18 22		20 49				
BRIDESTOWE HALT	d					16 54		18 35		21 02				
LYDFORD	d					16 59		18 41		21 07				
BRENTOR	d							18 44		21 11				
TAVISTOCK NORTH	d			16 25	17 11	18 04		18 56	19 45	21 17				
BERE ALSTON	d			16 38	17 23	18 19	19 10	19 57	20 25	21 33				
BERE FERRERS	d				17 29	18 22	19 16	20 03	20 31	21 39				
ST BUDEAUX VICTORIA ROAD HALT	d				17 37	18 30	19 24	20 11	20 40	21 47				
KEYHAM	d			16 53	17 40	18 33	19 27	20 14	20 43	21 50				
DOCKYARD HALT	d													
DEVONPORT ALBERT ROAD	d				17 43	18 36	19 31	20 17	20 46	21 53				
PLYMOUTH	a			17 03	17 47	18 40	19 35	20 21	20 50	21 57				
COPPLESTONE	d		14 42		16 35		18 22		20 09					
MORCHARD ROAD HALT	d				16 39		18 26		20 13					
LAPFORD	d		14 51		16 44		18 31		20 17					
EGGESFORD	d		14 58		16 51		18 38		20 24					
KING'S NYMPTON	d		15 04		16 58		18 45		20 30					
PORTSMOUTH ARMS	d				17 03		18 50		20 37					
UMBERLEIGH	d		15 16		17 10		18 57		20 43					
CHAPELTON HALT	d				17 14		19 01		20 47					
BARNSTAPLE JUNCTION (FOR BIDEFORD) Z	a		15 25		17 24		19 08		20 54					
	d	14 57	15 34	16 40	17 24		19 11		20 56					
BARNSTAPLE TOWN	d	15 00	15 39	16 44	17 29		19 15		21 00					
WRAFTON	d	15 13	15 47	16 51	17 35		19 22		21 07					
BRAUNTON	d	15 18	15 52	16 54	17 38		19 25		21 11					
MORTEHOE & WOOLACOMBE	d	15 37	16 11	17 08	17 52		19 39		21 23					
ILFRACOMBE	a	15 45	16 19	17 16	18 00				21 32					

Heavy figures denote through carriages; light figures denote connecting services
For general notes see page 3

For the complete service between St Budeaux and Plymouth see Table 34

A From London Waterloo
E From Callington
H From Exmouth to Manchester
J From London Paddington
K From Wolverhampton
N From Salisbury
P From Brighton
Z Western/Southern National Omnibuses between —Okehampton and Bude and Barnstaple Gas Board Offices and Bideford. See also pages 9 to 20
b Arr 06 39

Western Region Timetable 18 April 1966 - 5 March 1967
Note By the summer of 1967 only two through trains used this route, from Waterloo and Brighton respectively. They are shown as 'A' and 'G' in this timetable This compares with eight through trains on Saturdays in 1962. (see Appendix 3)

Table 35—continued

Exeter, Plymouth (via Okehampton) and Ilfracombe

Sundays
Until 15 May and from 2 October

		E	C	G		C		C	B		C		C	C		B		C
EXETER CENTRAL	d	09 30	10 15	10 59	13(10	...	13 45	...	14 57	15 04	...	16 34	...	17 54	19 30	...	20 11	...	20 46
EXETER ST DAVID'S	a	09 33	10 18	11 02	13(14	...	13 48	...	15 00	15 08	...	16 37	...	17 57	19 33	...	20 15	...	20 49
	d	09 35					14 05			15 25					19 50		20 25		
NEWTON ST CYRES	d																		
CREDITON	d	09 50					14 20			15 40					20 05		20 40		
YEOFORD	d																		
BOW	d																		
NORTH TAWTON	d																		
SAMPFORD COURTENAY HALT	d																		
OKEHAMPTON (FOR BUDE) Z	a									16 04							21 04		
	d									16 06							21 06		
BRIDESTOWE HALT	d																		
LYDFORD	d																		
BRENTOR	d																		
TAVISTOCK NORTH	d									16 33							21 33		
BERE ALSTON	d									16 46							21 46		
BERE FERRERS	d																		
ST BUDEAUX VICTORIA ROAD HALT	d																		
KEYHAM	d																		
DOCKYARD HALT	d																		
DEVONPORT ALBERT ROAD	d																		
PLYMOUTH	a									17 05							22 05		
COPPLESTONE	d																		
MORCHARD ROAD HALT	d																		
LAPFORD	d		10 06				14 36								20 21				
EGGESFORD	d		10 12				14 42								20 27				
KING'S NYMPTON	d		10 19				14 49								20 34				
PORTSMOUTH ARMS	d																		
UMBERLEIGH	d		10 29				14 59								20 44				
CHAPELTON HALT	d																		
BARNSTAPLE JUNCTION (FOR BIDEFORD) Z	a		10 39				15 09								20 54				
	d		10b48				15b28								21c33				
BARNSTAPLE TOWN	d																		
WRAFTON	d																		
BRAUNTON	d																		
MORTEHOE & WOOLACOMBE	d																		
ILFRACOMBE	a		11b36				16b16								23c20				

Table 35—continued

Exeter, Plymouth (via Okehampton) and Ilfracombe

Sundays
22 May to 25 September

		E	C	D			C		B	C	D		C		C	C		C	D
EXETER CENTRAL	d	08 30	09 25	10 05	...	10 28	10 56	13 10	...	13 42	...	14 57	15 04	...	15 47	17 00	17 15	17 43	...	20 05	20 14	...
EXETER ST DAVID'S	a	08 33	09 28	10 08	...	10 32	10 59	13 14	...	13 45	...	15 00	15 08	...	15 50	17 03	17 18	17 46	...	20 08	20 18	...
	d	08 35	09 30	10 10				13 20	13 35		14 45			15 25			17 05		19 50			20 25
NEWTON ST CYRES	d																			
CREDITON	d	08 49	09 45	10 25				13 35			14 59			15 40		17 20			20 05			20 40
YEOFORD	d	08 56	09 52	10 32				13 42	13 53					15 47		17 27			20 12			20 47
BOW	d			10 01				13 51						15 56								20 56
NORTH TAWTON	d			10 07				13 57						16 02								21 02
SAMPFORD COURTENAY HALT	d																			
OKEHAMPTON	d			10 17				14 07						16 12								21 12
(FOR BUDE) Z	d			10 19				14 09						16 14								21 17
BRIDESTOWE HALT	d			10 32				14 22						16 27								21 24
LYDFORD	d			10 37				14 27						16 32								21 32
BRENTOR	d			10 41				14 31						16 36								21 36
TAVISTOCK NORTH	d			10 51				14 41						16 47								21 47
BERE ALSTON	d			11 03				14 53						16 59								21 59
BERE FERRERS	d			11 09				14 59						17 05								22 05
ST BUDEAUX VICTORIA ROAD HALT	d			11 17				15 07						17 13								22 13
KEYHAM	d																			
DOCKYARD HALT	d																			
DEVONPORT ALBERT ROAD	d																			
PLYMOUTH	a			11 24				15 14						17 20								22 20
COPPLESTONE	d	09 01		10 38							15 09					17 33			20 18			
MORCHARD ROAD HALT	d	09 05		10 42												17 37			20 22			
LAPFORD	d	09 10		10 47					14 04		15 17					17 41			20 26			
EGGESFORD	d	09 16		10 53					14 11		15 23					17 48			20 33			
KING'S NYMPTON	d	09 23		11 00					14 17		15 29					17 54			20 39			
PORTSMOUTH ARMS	d	09 28		11 05					14 23							18 00			20 45			
UMBERLEIGH	d	09 34		11 12					14 29		15 39					18 07			20 51			
CHAPELTON HALT	d	09 38		11 16												18 11			20 56			
BARNSTAPLE JUNCTION	d	09 44		11 23					14 39		15 48					18 18			21 02			
(FOR BIDEFORD) Z	d	09 48		11 26					14 46		15 50					18 21			21 04			
BARNSTAPLE TOWN	d	09 53		11 30					14 50		15 54					18 25			21 08			
WRAFTON	d	10 00		11 37					14 57		16 01					18 32			21 15			
BRAUNTON	d			11 47					15 00		16 04					18 35			21 18			
MORTEHOE & WOOLACOMBE	d	10 18		11 54					15 14		16 19					18 49			21 32			
ILFRACOMBE	a	10 26		12 02					15 22		16 27					18 57			21 40			

3.17 Barnstaple Junction - Ilfracombe (October 1970)

An unrebuilt 'Bulleid' 'Pacific' approaches Barnstaple Town station on the curving bridge over the River Taw with a local train to Ilfracombe in the early 1960s. The two-coach train comprises one Maunsell and one Bulleid coach. The bridge was demolished in 1978. *M. E. J. Deane collection, courtesy of Ian Bennett*

By the late 19th century the popular seaside town of Ilfracombe was already attracting up to 40,000 visitors a year, most of whom arrived by sea down the Bristol Channel. It was therefore an obvious destination for the LSWR, which by then controlled the line from Exeter to Barnstaple, to extend its empire. As elsewhere a local company, the Barnstaple & Ilfracombe Railway, was encouraged to promote and build the line, which opened as a light railway in July 1874 but was purchased by the LSWR a year later.

Soon after leaving Barnstaple Junction, situated to the south of the town across the River Taw, the 15-mile single line crossed the river on a curving 213-yard-long viaduct to reach the more centrally situated station at Barnstaple Town, until 1935 also the terminus of the 2-foot-gauge Lynton & Barnstaple

Bristol Channel

Ilfracombe

Woolacombe

Mortehoe & Woolacombe

Braunton
Wrafton

Braunton
Burrows

Barnstaple Town

Barnstaple Junction

Barnstaple (Victoria Road) (closed Jun 60)

to Taunton (closed Oct 66)

0 —— 2 miles

to Torrington (closed Oct 65)

to Exeter (open)

In this panoramic view of Ilfracombe station, another unrebuilt 'Bulleid' 'Pacific' can be seen about to leave the station with a train for Waterloo in the early 1960s. The goods yard seems to be little used while at least one rake of coaches can be seen in the extensive sidings behind the 'Pacific'. The small engine shed and turntable were just behind the photographer. *M. E. J. Deane collection, courtesy of Ian Bennett*

Railway. Beyond Barnstaple there were three intermediate stations at Wrafton, Braunton and Mortehoe, the latter renamed Mortehoe & Woolacombe in 1950. The 5¾ miles between Braunton and Mortehoe were steeply graded at up to 1 in 74, followed by a 3¼-mile 1 in 36 descent to the terminus at Ilfracombe, situated 225 feet above the town. Banking engines were therefore needed from both Braunton and Ilfracombe for the heavier trains to reach Mortehoe, 600 feet above sea level. By 1891 the line had been doubled between Barnstaple Town and Ilfracombe and brought up to main-line standards. This allowed the first through working of coaches from both London Waterloo and Paddington. Further improvements by the SR in 1925 accommodated the arrival at Ilfracombe of a large number of through trains, especially on summer Saturdays.

In the summer of 1962 there were ten Saturday departures from Waterloo to Ilfracombe, including the daily 11.00am 'Atlantic Coast Express'. A further through train ran from Portsmouth & Southsea via Salisbury. In addition there were six arrivals via the ex-GWR line from Taunton, one of which was a through train from Wolverhampton Low Level. (Appendix 3.2). The weekday train service to Barnstaple & Ilfracombe during the winter of 1962/63, including the arrival of the 'Atlantic Coast Express' at 3.09 & 3.55pm respectively, is given in BR(SR) Table 35 (see pp. 63 & 64). The summer trains from Waterloo ran until 6 September 1964, although Table 64 of the BR(WR) summer timetable, like that for Bude and Padstow, gives no clue to their existence. Following the complete revision of services from 7 September, there were just eight arrivals at Ilfracombe from Exeter, stopping at all stations after Crediton. In addition there was a morning and afternoon train from Barnstaple Junction. On summer Sundays three trains ran from Exeter with a morning train from Barnstaple.

Unusually running tender-first, unrebuilt 'Battle of Britain' 'Pacific' No 34086 *219 Squadron* drifts down the 1 in 36 descent towards Ilfracombe with a late-morning train from Waterloo in September 1963. Tender-first working on the line was unusual as a 65-foot turntable was available at Ilfracombe engine shed. *Neil Carter*

On a dull 30 August 1963, unrebuilt 'Battle of Britain' 'Pacific' No 34075 *264 Squadron* runs round the 8.10am train from Salisbury via Exeter Central at Ilfracombe. On the right 'West Country' No 34107 *Blandford Forum* waits with the 2.20pm train for Waterloo. *Author*

Summer Saturdays in 1965 saw three through trains from London Paddington to Ilfracombe via Exeter St David's (Appendix 3.2), replacing those from Waterloo. The long-standing summer Saturday through train to Wolverhampton continued to run via Dulverton in 1965 (also Appendix 3.2), but in 1966 this too was diverted via Exeter St David's. In 1967 the line west of Barnstaple Town was singled with a passing loop at Braunton. From 4 May 1970 there were just five departures for Exeter each weekday, although the service was strengthened to seven trains on summer Saturdays, including the one through train to and from Paddington. There was no Sunday service. The public timetable for the period carried the warning that the Minister of Transport had given his consent to withdrawal of rail services between Barnstaple Junction and

G.W.R.

Ilfracombe

Ilfracombe's single-road shed and 65-foot turntable were situated just south of the station; the original shed had been replaced by this concrete structure in 1928/29. An 'N' Class 'Mogul' stands outside the shed while unrebuilt 'Battle of Britain' 'Pacific' No 34075 *264 Squadron* waits to come 'on shed' after arrival with its train from Salisbury in September 1963. The shed was a sub-shed of Barnstaple Junction and closed in September 1964. *Neil Carter*

Ilfracombe and that passengers should confirm train times before travelling. The Beeching Report had revealed that the branch carried fewer than 5,000 passengers a week, although Ilfracombe, Braunton and Barnstaple stations all had annual passenger receipts above £5,000. The double track between Barnstaple Town and Ilfracombe was singled in 1967, with closure announced in December 1969, and implemented from 5 October 1970.

The unrebuilt 'Light Pacifics' and ex-SR Class 'N' 2-6-0s, which had long been in charge of services over the route, were replaced by DMUs and diesel-hydraulics in September 1964. Steam reappeared on 27 March 1965 when, as mentioned in Chapters 3.5 and 3.11, the 'Exmoor Ranger' railtour visited the line. The last steam-hauled train over the route was the Southern Counties Touring Society's 'Exeter Flyer' from Waterloo on 3 October 1965. This was hauled from Exeter Central to Barnstaple Junction by BR Standard Class 4 2-6-4 tanks Nos 80043 and 80039. At Barnstaple Junction No 80043 took half of the train to Ilfracombe and back, while No 80039 hauled the remaining coaches to Torrington. That day also coincided with the last day of passenger traffic on the Torrington branch.

Despite an abortive attempt by a preservation group to purchase the Ilfracombe line, it was dismantled soon after closure. Part is now used as a footpath/cycleway and forms a section of the 'Tarka Trail'.

During the line's brief period of diesel operation a three-car Class 116 DMU arrives at Barnstaple Town's single platform forming the 1.35pm service from Exeter St David's to Ilfracombe during August 1970. The line from Barnstaple Junction closed from 5 October of that year despite a long campaign to retain it. *Geoff Radley*

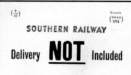

The same DMU is seen again on the same day at Braunton. The signal box, level crossing and lattice-post ex-LSWR home signal are visible beyond the unit. In the days of steam, banking engines were attached to the rear of Ilfracombe trains for the steep incline up to Mortehoe. This crossing was the cause of major traffic disruption, especially on summer Saturdays. *Geoff Radley*

A few years later, in the mid-1970s, after attempts to purchase the line had failed, the tracks through Barnstaple Town station have been lifted and dereliction has set in. The station canopy remains, together with several of the attractive ex-LSWR lamp-posts. The platform edge on the left was once used by trains on the 1ft 11in-gauge Lynton & Barnstaple Railway. *M. E. J. Deane collection, courtesy of Ian Bennett*

Western Region Timetable 4 May 1970 to 2 May 1971

Note that one train (shown as 'A' on the timetable) ran from Paddington to Ilfracombe on certain summer Saturdays in 1970. This compares with ten through trains from Waterloo during the summer of 1962 and three from Paddington in 1965. (see Appendix 3)

Table 29

Mondays to Fridays, also Saturdays from 3 October

Exeter to Okehampton, Barnstaple and Ilfracombe

Miles							B																	
0	EXETER CENTRAL	d			08f03			10c21						13 16	13 16	14 50		14e50	16 56		17 42		19g11	
¾	EXETER ST. DAVID'S	a			08f06			10c25						13 20	13 20	14 54		14e54	17 00		17 45		19g14	
		d	04 05	04 17	08 24		08 45	10 40		11 23				13 35	13 45	15 28		16 00	17 36		17 46		19 45	20 36
5	NEWTON ST CYRES	d					08 52	10 47								15 35			17 43		17 54		19 52	
7¾	CREDITON	d	04 16	04 28	08 34		08 58	10 53		11 34				13 46	13 55	15 41		16 12	17 49		18 00		19 58	20 47
11¼	YEOFORD	d			08 41		09 05	11 00		11 41					14 02	15 48		16 19	17 56		18 07		20 05	20 54
16	BOW	d			08 50			11 09							14 11	15 57			18 05				20 14	
19½	NORTH TAWTON	d			08 57			11 15							14 18	16 03			18 11				20 20	
22	SAMPFORD COURTENAY	d			09 02			11 21							14 23	16 09			18 17				20 26	
25¾	OKEHAMPTON (FOR BUDE Z)	a		04 54	09 10			11 29							14 31	16 17			18 25				20 34	
14½	COPPLESTONE	d					09 11											16 24			18 12			
15¾	MORCHARD ROAD	d					09 15											16 28			18 16			
18¼	LAPFORD	d	04 33				09 20			11 54				14 04				16 33			18 21			21 07
22	EGGESFORD	d					09 28			12 02				14 11				16b43			18 29			21 15
26	KING'S NYMPTON	d					09 34			12 08				14 18				16 49			18 35			21 21
29	PORTSMOUTH ARMS	d					09 40											16 55			18 41			
33	UMBERLEIGH	d	04 57				09 46			12 19				14 29				17 02			18 47			21 32
35½	CHAPELTON	d					09 51											17 06			18 52			
39¾	BARNSTAPLE JUNCTION (FOR BIDEFORD Z)	a	05 08				09 59			12 30				14 40				17 15			19 00			21 43
		d	05 21				10 02							14 42				17 20			19 03			
40½	BARNSTAPLE TOWN	d	05 25				10 06							14 46				17 24			19 07			
44¾	WRAFTON	d	05 33				10 13							14 53				17 31			19 14			
45¾	BRAUNTON	d	05 37				10 17							14 57				17 35			19 18			
51½	MORTEHOE & WOOLACOMBE	d	05 52				10 31							15 11				17 50			19 32			
54¾	ILFRACOMBE	a	06 00				10 39							15 19				17 58			19 40			

Saturdays

Until 26 September

E								A			J						
EXETER CENTRAL	d				08 03		10 26	11 06	13 16	13 16		15 10		16 56	17 42	19 11	
EXETER ST DAVID'S	a				08 06		10 30	11 09	13 20	13 20		15 13		17 00	17 45	19 14	
	d	04 05	04 17	07 35	08 30	09 22	10 40	11 13	13 45	13 27	14(30	15 30	16 00	17 42	17 53	19 45	20 36
NEWTON ST CYRES	d					09 30	10 47					15 37		17 49	18 00	19 52	
CREDITON	d	04 16	04 28	07 46	08 40	09 35	10 53	11 25	13 55	13 38	14(41	15 43	16 11	17 55	18 06	19 58	20 47
YEOFORD	d			07 53	08 47	09 41	11 00	11 32	14 02			15 50	16 18	18 02	18 13	20 05	20 54
BOW	d				08 56		11 09		14 11			15 59		18 11		20 14	
NORTH TAWTON	d				09 03		11 15		14 18			16 05		18 17		20 20	
SAMPFORD COURTENAY	d				09 08		11 21		14 23			16 11		18 23		20 26	
OKEHAMPTON (FOR BUDE Z)	a		04 54		09 16		11 29		14 31			16 19		18 31		20 34	
COPPLESTONE	d					09 47							16 24		18 18		
MORCHARD ROAD	d					09 51							16 27		18 22		
LAPFORD	d	04 33		08 06		09 56		11 46		13 56	14(58		16 32		18 27		21 07
EGGESFORD	d			08 14		10 03		11 53		14 04	15(09		16b42		18 34		21 15
KING'S NYMPTON	d			08 20		10 09		12 00		14 11	15(15		16 49		18 41		21 21
PORTSMOUTH ARMS	d					10 14							16 54		18 46		
UMBERLEIGH	d	04 57		08 31		10 21		12 12		14 22	15(26		17 01		18 53		21 32
CHAPELTON	d					10 25							17 05		18 58		
B'STAPLE JNC (FOR B'FORD Z)	a	05 08		08 42		10 30		12 21		14 33	15(37		17 10		19 06		21 43
	d	05 21		08 47		10 35		12 26		14 37			17 15		19 08		
BARNSTAPLE TOWN	d	05 25		08 51		10 39		12 31		14 42			17 20		19 12		
WRAFTON	d	05 33		08 58		10 48		12 39		14 49			17 28		19 19		
BRAUNTON	d	05 37		09 02		10 52		12 44		14 53			17 32		19 23		
MORTEHOE & WOOLACOMBE	d	05 52		09 17		11 08		13 03		15 08			17 48		19 38		
ILFRACOMBE	a	06 00		09 25		11 15		13 10		15 16			17 56		19 46		

Sundays

		C (G)	C (H)	(bus) G		H	(bus)	G		H
EXETER CENTRAL	d									
EXETER ST DAVID'S	a									
	d	11(05		14n00	14 10		17n15		17 52	
NEWTON ST CYRES	d									
CREDITON	d	11(15			14 21				18 03	
YEOFORD	d									
BOW	d									
NORTH TAWTON	d									
SAMPFORD COURTENAY	d									
OKEHAMPTON (FOR BUDE Z)	a			15n26			18n41			
COPPLESTONE	d			Stop			Stop			
MORCHARD ROAD	d									
LAPFORD	d	11(32			14 38				18 20	
EGGESFORD	d	11(39			14 45				18 27	
KING'S NYMPTON	d	11(46			14 52				18 34	
PORTSMOUTH ARMS	d									
UMBERLEIGH	d	11(56			15 02				18 44	
CHAPELTON	d									
B'STAPLE JNC (FOR B'FORD Z)	a	12(07			15 13				18 55	
	d	12j48	13j00	15j28		15j40		19j28		19j10
BARNSTAPLE TOWN	d									
WRAFTON	d									
BRAUNTON	d									
MORTEHOE & WOOLACOMBE	d									
ILFRACOMBE	a	13j36	13j48	16j16		16j30		20j16		20j00

Heavy figures denote through carriages; light figures denote connecting services
For general notes see pages 5 and 6

A On certain dates is a through train from London Paddington (Table 1)
B From Paignton (Table 1)
C 14 June to 6 September
G 7 June to 30 August
H Until 31 May and from 6 September
J 13 June to 5 September
Z By Bus. See pages 11 to 27

b Arr 3 minutes earlier
c 5 minutes later on Saturdays
e On Saturdays Exeter Central dep 15 40 and arr Exeter St David's 15 43
f On Mondays to Fridays Exeter Central dep 08 08 and arr Exeter St. David's 08 11
g On Saturdays Exeter Central dep 18 58 and arr Exeter St David's 19 02
j (bus) (Southern National) between Barnstaple Junction Station Approach (approximately 4 minutes walk from the station) and Ilfracombe (Bus Station). Also calls intermediately at Wrafton Cross and Braunton (George Hotel)
n (bus) (Devon General) bus between Exeter St David's and Okehampton square

The Minister of Transport has given his consent to withdrawal of the rail service between Barnstaple Jcn and Ilfracombe. At the time of going to press a date for closure has not been determined. Passengers are advised to confirm train times before travelling.

3.18 Taunton – Minehead (January 1971)

The 24¾-mile line from Taunton to Minehead left the GWR's West of England main line at Norton Fitzwarren, 2 miles west of Taunton, together with the branch from Taunton to Barnstaple. The broad-gauge railway was built as two separate entities. The first section from Norton Fitzwarren to Watchet was opened by the West Somerset Railway (WSR) in March 1862, although from the start it was leased to the Bristol & Exeter Railway (B&E). At the time the prosperity of the railway rested on the export and import of materials from Watchet Harbour, including coal from South Wales. At this time the standard gauge West Somerset Mineral Railway (WSMR) was also carrying iron ore from the Brendon Hills to the harbour at Watchet.

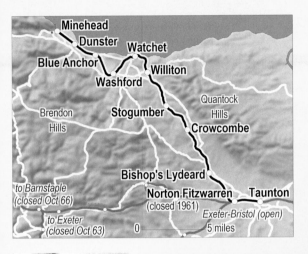

Minehead was already emerging as a holiday resort and pressure began to mount for the line to be extended there. The B&E, however, refused to sponsor the line, which was eventually opened by the Minehead Railway (MR) in July 1874. It was the penultimate line to be built to the broad gauge (the last was to be the St Ives branch, Chapter 3.25). Between Watchet and Washford the line ran parallel with the WSMR, which had refused to share its tracks with the MR. The MR was amalgamated with the GWR (successor to the B&E) in July 1897, but the WSR remained a legally independent company until amalgamated with the GWR in 1923.

The line was single throughout with passing loops at Bishop's Lydeard, Crowcombe Heathfield, Williton and Blue Anchor. In the 1930s work was carried out to increase capacity for the heavy summer holiday traffic to the West Country. East of Norton Fitzwarren the main line through Taunton was quadrupled as far as Cogload Junction, and on the Minehead

G. W. R.

W.&B. L/6.

MINEHEAD

Ex-GWR 'Large Prairie' 2-6-2T No 6155 arrives at Minehead with a train from Taunton in March 1961. The photo makes an interesting contrast to the situation today. The fields that the line crosses between Minehead and Dunster are completely undeveloped, as Butlins holiday camp did not open until May 1962. The location of the water tower, water crane and signals are also all different. No 6155 was built at Swindon in 1933 and, in 1961, was a Taunton engine; it was withdrawn in October 1965. *M. E. J. Deane collection, courtesy of Ian Bennett*

Another of Taunton shed's ex-GWR 'Large Prairie' 2-6-2Ts, No 4157, pulls away from Williton with a train for Taunton in March 1961. The station's footbridge was removed after closure and has only recently been replaced by an ex-GWR covered footbridge from Trowbridge station in Wiltshire. The engine was built at Swindon in 1947 and withdrawn in June 1965. *M. E. J. Deane collection, courtesy of Ian Bennett*

branch the track was doubled from Norton Fitzwarren to Bishop's Lydeard and from west of Dunster to Minehead. In addition, passing loops were provided in the countryside at Leigh Bridge, west of Crowcombe, and at Kentsford Crossing, west of Watchet. The Barnstaple line, which also left the main line at Norton Fitzwarren, was doubled as far as Milverton at the same time (Chapter 3.11).

The Beeching Report had revealed that the branch carried up to 10,000 passengers a week, significantly more than most West Country branch lines, while both Minehead and Watchet stations had annual passenger receipts above £5,000. Nonetheless, proposals to close the line were made in 1968. However, at the subsequent public hearing the local TUCC concluded that hardship would result from the line's closure. The Transport Minister of the day, Fred Mulley, begged to differ and services finally ended on the 3 January 1971. The station at Norton Fitzwarren had closed ten years earlier.

An ex-GWR Class '5700' 0-6-0 pannier tank arrives at Stogumber with a train for Taunton in January 1961. The scene at Stogumber is also now transformed: although the small station buildings remain, the area once covered by the large goods shed is now the restored station's well-tended gardens. *M. E. J. Deane collection, courtesy of Ian Bennett*

A three-car Class 116 DMU, which includes cars Nos W51135, W59445 and W51148, waits in Minehead station to form the 11.40am service to Taunton on 28 August 1963. DMUs had taken over local services on the branch in September 1962. Trains were withdrawn from 4 January 1971 after a long campaign to retain the service. *Author*

G. W. R.

Crowcombe

Local passenger trains on the line had for many years been hauled by ex-GWR pannier and 'Prairie' tanks, while the heavier trains were in the hands of 'Moguls'. DMUs replaced steam in September 1962 although steam returned on the summer Saturday through workings in 1963. In the summer of 1962 four through trains arrived at Minehead on Saturdays: two from Paddington and one each from Swansea and Wolverhampton Low Level (Appendix 3.1). Summer traffic on the branch was boosted significantly when Butlins opened its Minehead Holiday Camp in 1962. Through trains continued to use the branch until 1970, the final year before closure. There were then 13 arrivals at Minehead on summer Saturdays, including one from Paddington and one from Oxford (Appendix 3.3). The summer Sunday service comprised four trains, including a through train from Bristol Temple Meads. The winter service prior to closure comprised nine trains a day from Taunton with the

'Hymek' Type 3 diesel-hydraulic No D7087 arrives at Bishop's Lydeard with the 3.15pm train from Minehead on 7 August 1965. From the length of the train this would appear to be the stock of the 2.40pm arrival at Minehead, the Saturdays-only through train from Wolverhampton Low Level. *Owen Mogg/PT*

The West Somerset Railway succeeded in reopening the line between Minehead and Williton in 1976. Here ex-GWR Class '6400' pannier tank No 6412 has just arrived at Williton with the empty stock for the 'Quantock Flyer' special train to Minehead on 19 March 1977. No 6412 was purchased direct from BR by the embryo Dart Valley Railway in 1964 and was later acquired by the WSR. It has since returned to the Dart Valley Railwa. *Author*

additional train on Fridays and Saturdays. There was no Sunday service during the winter.

In 1964 the holiday camp became the temporary home of ex-LMS 'Coronation' Class Pacific No 6229 *Duchess of Hamilton* (BR No 46229); it is now part of the National Collection and displayed at the National Railway Museum at York in its pre-war streamlined state.

Unlike so many other lines, the story here has a happy ending as just four months after closure the West Somerset Railway Co Ltd was inaugurated on 5 May 1971. The first (new) WSR train, a Directors' Special, ran from Bishop's Lydeard to Minehead on 21 December 1975 hauled by ex-British Leyland Bagnall 0-6-0 saddle tank *Victor*. A public service between Minehead and Blue Anchor began on 28 March 1976. After overcoming many difficulties, the WSR has developed into the magnificent preserved railway it is today. Ex-GWR 'Prairie' tanks can again be seen hauling rakes of chocolate and cream coaches along the southern flanks of the Quantock Hills.

The restoration of the Minehead branch as the heritage West Somerset Railway has presented endless opportunities to recreate scenes from the 1950s and 1960s. This is exemplified here by visiting ex-GWR 'Small Prairie' 2-6-2T No 5553, seen arriving at Blue Anchor with a train for Bishop's Lydeard during the WSR's Spring Gala on 27 March 2012. The train is made up of BR Mark 1 coaches painted in the ex-GWR chocolate and cream livery introduced by BR(WR) in 1956 for its crack expresses. No 5553 was built in 1928 and withdrawn in November 1961; it was restored after more than 20 years in Barry scrapyard. *Author*

In addition to regular trains between Minehead and Bishop's Lydeard, the WSR is able to accept through trains from the national network. Here a post-privatisation Great Western Trains HST arrives at Crowcombe Heathfield during the railway's Spring Gala on 22 March 1997. This was the first HST to traverse the line and was the subject of much interest from photographers. Waiting to leave the up platform with a WSR train for Bishop's Lydeard is ex-GWR 'Large Prairie' No 4160, rescued from Barry scrapyard in 1974. *Author*

Western Region Timetable 4 May 1970 to 2 May 1971

Note that one train (shown as 'C' on the timetable) ran from Paddington to Minehead on certain summer Saturdays in 1965. This compares with two through trains from Paddington during the summer of 1962. (see Appendix 3)

Table 27

Mondays to Fridays
also Saturdays from 3 October

Taunton to Minehead

Miles														FSO	B FSX	
0	TAUNTON	d	06 35	07 29	..	09 15	..	11 15	..	13 15	..	14 45	..	16 42	..	17 48	..	20 16	..	21 10	..	21 10	..	..
5	BISHOP'S LYDEARD	d	06 43	07 38	..	09 23	..	11 24	..	13 23	..	14 53	..	16 50	..	17 56	..	20 24	..	21 18	..	21 25	..	..
9	CROWCOMBE	d	06 51	07 46	..	09 31	..	11 32	..	13 31	..	15 01	..	16 58	..	18 04	..	20 32	..	21 26	..	21 45	..	..
11½	STOGUMBER	d	06 59	07 52	..	09 37	..	11 38	..	13 37	..	15 07	..	17 04	..	18 10	..	20 38	..	21 32	..	..	..	..
15	WILLITON	d	07 05	08 01	..	09 46	..	11 45	..	13 44	..	15 16	..	17 13	..	18 17	..	20 45	..	21 41	..	22 01	..	..
16¾	WATCHET	d	07 09	08 05	..	09 50	..	11 49	..	13 48	..	15 20	..	17 17	..	18 21	..	20 49	..	21 45	..	22 10	..	..
19	WASHFORD	d	07 15	08 11	..	09 56	..	11 55	..	13 54	..	15 26	..	17 23	..	18 27	..	20 55	..	21 51	..	22 19	..	..
21½	BLUE ANCHOR	d	07 20	08 16	..	10 01	..	12 00	..	13 59	..	15 31	..	17 28	..	18 32	..	21 00	..	21 56	..	..	..	..
23	DUNSTER	d	07 24	08 20	..	10 05	..	12 04	..	14 03	..	15 35	..	17 32	..	18 36	..	21 04	..	22 00	..	..	..	..
24¾	MINEHEAD	a	07 29	08 25	..	10 10	..	12 09	..	14 08	..	15 40	..	17 37	..	18 41	..	21 09	..	22 05	..	22b42	..	..

Saturdays
Until 26 September

						K			C									
TAUNTON	d	06 15	07 20	..	08 30	..	09 20	..	10 24	11 13	12 52	..	14 05	..	15 15	..	17 00	..	17 54	..	19 10	..	21 10
BISHOP'S LYDEARD	d	06 23	07 28	..	..	..	09 28	..	..	11 21	13 00	..	14 13	..	15 23	..	17 08	..	18 02	..	19 18	..	21 18
CROWCOMBE	d	06 31	07 36	..	..	..	09 36	..	..	11 29	13 08	..	14 21	..	15 31	..	17 16	..	18 10	..	19 26	..	21 26
STOGUMBER	d	06 39	07 42	..	..	..	09 42	..	..	11 35	13 16	..	14 27	..	15 37	..	17 22	..	18 16	..	19 32	..	21 32
WILLITON	d	06 46	07 51	..	08 56	..	09 51	..	10 51	11 46	13 27	..	14 36	..	15 46	..	17 31	..	18 26	..	19 41	..	21 41
WATCHET	d	06 50	07 55	..	09 00	..	09 55	..	10 55	11 51	13 31	..	14 40	..	15 50	..	17 35	..	18 30	..	19 45	..	21 45
WASHFORD	d	06 56	08 01	..	09 06	..	10 01	..	11 01	11 57	13 37	..	14 46	..	15 56	..	17 41	..	18 36	..	19 51	..	21 51
BLUE ANCHOR	d	07 01	08 06	..	09 11	..	10 06	..	11 06	12 03	13 42	..	14 51	..	16 01	..	17 46	..	18 41	..	19 56	..	21 56
DUNSTER	d	07 05	08 10	..	09 15	..	10 10	..	11 10	12 07	13 46	..	14 55	..	16 05	..	17 50	..	18 45	..	20 00	..	22 00
MINEHEAD	a	07 10	08 15	..	09 20	..	10 15	..	11 15	12 12	13 51	..	15 00	..	16 10	..	17 55	..	18 50	..	20 05	..	22 05

Sundays
14 June to 6 September

Sundays
Until 7 June and from 13 September

				D						B		B		B		B		B	
TAUNTON	d	09 00	..	11 43	..	14 10	..	16 35	..	19 15	..	21 10	..	14 55	..	16 50	..	18 50	..	21 10	..
BISHOP'S LYDEARD	d	09 08	..	11 51	..	14 18	..	16 43	..	19 23	..	21 25	..	15 10	..	17 05	..	19 05	..	21 25	..
CROWCOMBE	d	09 16	..	11 59	..	14 26	..	16 51	..	19 31	..	21 45	..	15 30	..	17 25	..	19 25	..	21 45	..
STOGUMBER	d	09 22	..	12 05	..	14 32	..	16 57	..	19 37	..		..		..		..		..		..
WILLITON	d	09 29	..	12 12	..	14 39	..	17 04	..	19 44	..	22 01	..	15 46	..	17 41	..	19 41	..	22 01	..
WATCHET	d	09 33	..	12 16	..	14 43	..	17 08	..	19 48	..	22 10	..	15 55	..	17 45	..	19 50	..	22 10	..
WASHFORD	d	09 39	..	12 22	..	14 49	..	17 14	..	19 54	..	22 19	..	16 04	..	17 59	..	19 59	..	22 19	..
BLUE ANCHOR	d	09 44	..	12 27	..	14 54	..	17 19	..	19 59	..		..		..		..		..		..
DUNSTER	d	09 48	..	12 31	..	14 58	..	17 23	..	20 03	..		..		..		..		..		..
MINEHEAD	a	09 53	..	12 36	..	15 03	..	17 28	..	20 08	..	22b42	..	16b27	..	18b22	..	20b22	..	22b42	..

Heavy figures denote through carriages
For general notes see pages 5 and 6

B (Western National) from Taunton Rail Station Bridge to Minehead Bus Station. Calls at Bishop's Lydeard (Police Station), Crowcombe (Carew Arms), Williton (Egremont Hotel), Watchet (Rail Station) and Washford (Sheppards Corner)

C On certain dates is a through service from London Paddington (See Table 1)

D From Bristol T.M.

K On certain dates is a through service from Oxford (See Table 1)

b Minehead Bus Station

3.19 Maiden Newton - Bridport (May 1975)

The 9¼-mile broad-gauge branch line from Maiden Newton to the Dorset town of Bridport was opened by the Bridport Railway in November 1857. As the name suggested, the town included a small port for seagoing vessels on the River Brit.

An intermediate station was built at Powerstock, although the hamlet of Toller had to wait another five years for its station. Both had just one platform with no passing loop. A station had been opened at Maiden

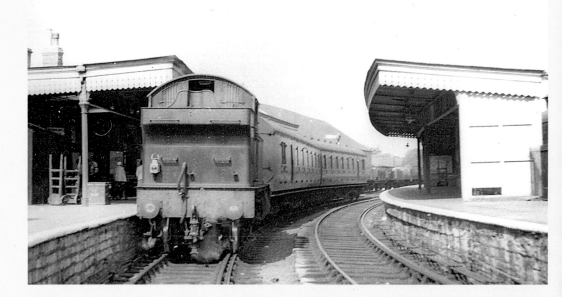

Ex-GWR 'Small Prairie' No 4562 stands at Bridport station on 20 August 1952 with a train from Maiden Newton composed of a typical ex-GWR two-coach suburban 'B' set. No 4562 was one of the early members of Class '4500', built in 1924 with a flat top to its side tanks. It was allocated to Weymouth depot for use on the Bridport branch for many years until withdrawal in October 1960. *A. J. Pike, Frank Hornby collection*

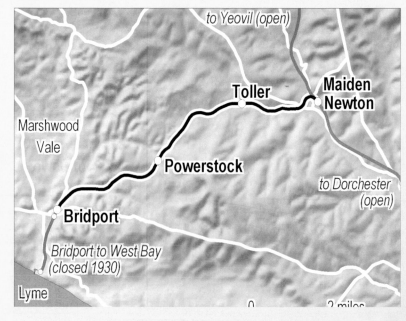

CHEAP DAY - 2nd

Bridport to
MAIDEN
NEWTON

(W)

For conditions see over

5645

Ex-GWR Class '5700' pannier tank No 3763 is serviced at the small engine shed at Bridport before working a train to Maiden Newton on 20 August 1952. The ex-GWR depot was a sub-shed of Weymouth, which at nationalisation was part of BR(WR)'s Bristol Locomotive Division. It was transferred to BR(SR), together with the sub-shed at Bridport, in February 1958, and closed in June 1959. A. J. Pike, Frank Hornby collection

Newton by the Wilts, Somerset & Weymouth Railway Company with the opening of its line between Yeovil and Weymouth in the previous January. Passengers from Bridport therefore had immediate access to broad-gauge trains to London, Bristol and Weymouth. In 1858 an agreement was reached with the GWR to work the line, followed by a lease in 1881, by which time the branch had been converted to standard-gauge track. The GWR finally acquired the line in 1902.

In 1884 the line was extended 2 miles to West Bay on the coast in the hope of attracting tourists with a halt at East Street (Bridport). The tourists never materialised, however, and the line closed to passengers in 1930, although it remained open for freight until 1962. Following nationalisation the branch changed regions twice: being an ex-GWR branch it was initially allocated to BR(WR), but in April 1950 was transferred to the Southern Region. Motive power, which was provided by Weymouth shed, remained under BR(WR) control until 1958. The branch was transferred back to BR(WR) from January 1963, although Weymouth remained within BR(SR).

A decade after nationalisation motive power on the branch was still dominated by ex-GWR 'Small Prairies' and pannier tanks hauling one of the ubiquitous ex-GWR two-coach 'B' sets. Maiden Newton station comprised two through platforms with a bay for Bridport branch trains. As there were no run-round facilities in the bay, the coaches were propelled into a siding on a rising gradient; the engine then ran clear and the coaches were allowed to run back into the bay by gravity with the guard controlling the brake. DMUs took over the services from June 1959, although one return working remained steam-operated, latterly by Ivatt Class 2 2-6-2 tanks from Weymouth depot. The last steam-hauled

Maiden Newton station was photographed on the same day, showing the main line from Castle Cary to Weymouth on the right while the single-track line to Bridport disappears to the left. The Bridport branch coaches are in the siding beside it; these would be run into the station by gravity before the next departure for Bridport. The main line through the station was singled in 1966, although a passing loop was retained. *A. J. Pike, Frank Hornby collection*

train was the 'Bridport Belle', a Locomotive Club of Great Britain special on 22 January 1967. The nine-coach train was topped and tailed over the branch by Ivatt tanks Nos 41295 and 41320. On the return journey the train stalled on the notorious Witherstone Bank, and was eventually rescued by diesel-electric No D6541 (later BR No 33023).

Even before publication of the Beeching Report the former GWR Weymouth main line through Yeovil Pen Mill was being downgraded. By 1962 the through trains from Paddington to Weymouth had disappeared and only a semi-fast service between Bristol, Westbury or Yeovil and Weymouth survived. Good connections were nevertheless maintained at

Bridport station and signal box are pictured on 22 August 1963, with passengers gathering on the up platform to await the next train for Maiden Newton. By the end of 1969 the facilities had been reduced to a minimum, the run-round loop had been removed and the station had become an unstaffed halt. *Author*

A two-car Class 119 DMU, Nos W51105 and W51077, waits in the Bridport bay at Maiden Newton while a Weymouth-bound train arrives at the down main line platform on 22 August 1963. DMUs took over all but one service on the Bridport branch in June 1959. All services were withdrawn from 5 May 1975 after a long campaign to save the line. *Author*

Maiden Newton. At the time of closure the service still comprised nine trains each weekday. There were no Sunday trains.

The Beeching Report had revealed that the branch carried fewer than 5,000 passengers a week and only Bridport and Maiden Newton stations had annual passenger receipts above £5,000. The branch was inevitably listed for closure in the Report while, as discussed in Chapter 2.1, services on the main line from Castle Cary to Weymouth were to be 'modified'. The latter proposal involved the closure of all intermediate stations including Maiden Newton, so the future of rail services in this part of the West Country looked bleak.

The last steam-powered train from Bridport, the 'Bridport Belle' railtour from Waterloo, is pictured near Powerstock on 22 January 1967. The train is headed by Ivatt Class 2 2-6-2 tank No 41320 with No 41284 at the rear. It stalled on Witherstone Bank in poor weather and had to be rescued by Type 3 diesel-electric No D6541 (later BR No 33023). Running very late, the train eventually reached Maiden Newton where rebuilt Bulleid 'Pacific' No 34030 *Watersmeet* was waiting to return it to Waterloo. *Trevor Owen, Colour-Rail*

The first direct threat to services was the proposal by BR(WR) to close all intermediate stations on the main line including Maiden Newton in September 1964. This was in advance of any closure notice being posted for the branch itself! After a Public Inquiry permission to close Maiden Newton and certain other stations between Yeovil Pen Mill and Weymouth was refused by the Minister, Barbara Castle (see Chapter 2.1). The closure notice for the branch itself was announced in May 1965, but this and later proposals were successfully fought off, but facilities were reduced to a minimum, with Bridport becoming an unstaffed halt. The fact that the branch survived so long had much to do with effective local lobbying, which was strongly supported by the local paper, the Bridport News. In June 1967 Barbara Castle announced that the line would not close due to doubts over whether the local road network could cope with the extra buses needed to replace the trains. In June 1971 BR again formally proposed the closure of the line, and again there was strong local opposition, but after some further prevarication the will of BR at last prevailed and the branch closed from 5 May 1975.

With the closure of the Bridport branch the implementation of the Beeching Report was finally complete in the West Country. Just four branch-line services had survived the Beeching Axe, at least in part.

Western Region Timetable 1 May 1972 to 6 May 1973

Table 7—continued   **Mondays to Fridays, also Saturdays**
                                                    from 30 September

South Wales, Bristol and Bath to Westbury, Bridport, Weymouth, Southampton and Portsmouth

Heavy figures denote through carriages;
light figures denote connecting services
For general notes see pages 5 and 6

A Until 7 October

b Mondays to Fridays 29 May to 1 Sept. arrive 15 mins. earlier
c Arrive 07 30

¶ For complete service between Weymouth and Dorchester see Southern timetable

‡ For details of sailings between Weymouth and Channel Islands see Table 33

Western Passenger Timetable: 1 May 1972 to 6 May 1973

Western Region Timetable 1 May 1972 to 6 May 1973

Table 7—continued

Mondays to Fridays, also Saturdays
from 30 September

South Wales, Bristol and Bath to Westbury, Bridport, Weymouth, Southampton and Portsmouth

SWANSEA	1 d	..	12 55	..	..	..	14 55	..	17 20	..	..
CARDIFF GENERAL	24 d	..	14 15	..	..	16 22	..	18 50	..	..
NEWPORT	24 d	..	14 29	..	..	16 36	..	19 04	..	..
9 BIRMINGHAM NEW STREET	d	..	13 15	..	15 15	..	18 15	..	..
9 GLOUCESTER EASTGATE	d	..	13 10	..	16 11	..	19 10	..	..
BRISTOL TEMPLE MEADS	23, 24 d	15 42	..	17 12	..	17 45	..	20 22	21 05	..
BATH SPA	23 d	16 02	..	17 32	..	18 05	..	20 37	21 24	..
FRESHFORD	d	16 17	..	17 47	..	18 21	..	..	
AVONCLIFF	d	16 20	..	17 50	..	18 24	..	..	
BRADFORD-ON-AVON	d	16 23	..	17 53	..	18 27	..	20 55	21 43	..
CHIPPENHAM	d	..	..	..	..	..	..	
TROWBRIDGE	d	16 31	..	18 01	..	18 35	..	21 02	21 51	..
WESTBURY	d	16 39	..	18 10	..	18 43	..	21 11	22 02	..
	d	16 42	17 00	18 10	..	18 43	..	21 12	21 15	22 10
FROME	d		17 10	18 10	18 27	..	..	21 23	..
BRUTON	d		17 23	18 44	..	..		
CASTLE CARY	d		17 27	18 52	..	..		
YEOVIL PEN MILL	d		17 45	19 09	..	..	21 43	..
THORNFORD BRIDGE	d		17 53	19 16	..	..	22 04	..
YETMINSTER	d		17 56	19 19	..	..		
CHETNOLE	d		18 00	19 23	..	..	22 13	..
MAIDEN NEWTON	d		18 12	19 36	..	..	22 28	..
MAIDEN NEWTON	d	16 35	..	18 20	..	20 05	..	
TOLLER	d	16 41	..	18 26	..	20 11	..	
POWERSTOCK	d	16 47	..	18 32	..	20 17	..	
BRIDPORT	a	16 57	..	18 42	..	20 27	..	
DORCHESTER WEST	¶ d		18 24	19 54	..	..	22 40	..
UPWEY AND BROADWAY	¶ d		18 33	20 03	..	..	22 48	..
RADIPOLE	¶ d		18 37	20 06	..	..	22 51	..
WEYMOUTH ‡	¶ a		18 40	20 09	..	..	22 54	..
DILTON MARSH	a	16 47	..	18 51	..	21 20	22 17	..
WARMINSTER	a	16 54	..	18 58	..	21 27	22 26	..
SALISBURY	a	17 23	..	19 20	..	21 50	22 53	..
SOUTHAMPTON	a	18 23	..	20 23	..	22 38	..	
BOURNEMOUTH	a	19c18	..	..	..	23 37	..	
PORTSMOUTH & SOUTHSEA	a	19 15	..	21 15	..	23 31	..	
PORTSMOUTH HARBOUR	a	19 30	..	21 31	..	..	
RYDE PIER HEAD	a	20 35	..	..	..	..	
BRIGHTON	a	21 07	..	23 07	..	..	

Heavy figures denote through carriages;
light figures denote connecting services
For general notes see pages 5 and 6

c Arrive 19 37 on Saturdays
g Arrive 18 21

¶ For complete service between Weymouth and Dorchester see Southern timetable

‡ For details of sailings between Weymouth and Channel Islands see Table 33

Table 7—continued

Saturdays
Until 23 September

South Wales, Bristol and Bath to Westbury, Bridport, Weymouth, Southampton and Portsmouth

SWANSEA	1 d	..	..	06 00	..	06 50 06 50	..	07 50 07 50	09 05 09 05	..
CARDIFF GENERAL	24 d	..	..	..	08 10 08 20	..	09 07 09 53	10k53	..
NEWPORT	24 d	..	06 14	..	08 24 08 35	..	09 20 10 07	11 06 11k06	..
9 BIRMINGHAM NEW STREET	d	02 05	..	07 20 07h55	..	..	09 15	..
9 GLOUCESTER EASTGATE	d	03 48	..	07 39 08 19 08 19	..	..	10 33	..
BRISTOL TEMPLE MEADS	23, 24 d	05 43	06 55 07 40	08 25	..	09 18 08 45 09 18 09 40	10 30	11 35 12 00	..
BATH SPA	23 d	06 00	07 13 08 00	08 40	..	09 22 09 33 09 55	10 45	11 00 11 54 12 15	..
FRESHFORD	d		08 05	..	..		12 30	..
AVONCLIFF	d		08 08	..	..		12 33	..
BRADFORD-ON-AVON	d	06 18	07 31 08 21	..	..	10 13 11 03	12 36	..
CHIPPENHAM	d	..	..	..	..	..	..	
TROWBRIDGE	d	06 25	07 38 08 28	09 03	..	09 44 10 20	11 23	12 44	..
WESTBURY	d	06 34	07 47 08 37	09 12	..	09 51 10 02 10 29	11 19 12 45	12 56	..
	d	06 42	07 47 08 37	09 12 09 44	..	09 53 10 03 10 31	11 39 12 07 12 24	13 08	..
FROME	d		09 05	..	..	11 30	13 16	..
BRUTON	d	07 09	09 05	..	..	11 46	13 25	..
CASTLE CARY	d	07 13	09 10	09 36	..	10 26 10 53	11 51	13 29	..
YEOVIL PEN MILL	d	07 28	09 26	09 52	..	10 41 11 11	12c13	13 45	..
THORNFORD BRIDGE	d	07 46	09 29	..	..		13 52	..
YETMINSTER	d	07 50	09 35	..	..		13 55	..
CHETNOLE	d	07 55	09 40	..	..		13 59	..
MAIDEN NEWTON	d	08 08	09 52	10 15	..	11 03 11 30	12 35	14 12	..
MAIDEN NEWTON	d	07 15 08 15	..	10 18	..	11 34 12 39	..
TOLLER	d	07 21 08 21	..	10 24	..	11 40 12 45	..
POWERSTOCK	d	07 27 08 27	..	10 30	..	11 46 12 51	..
BRIDPORT	a	07 37 08 37	..	10 40	..	11 56 13 01	..
DORCHESTER WEST	¶ d	08 20	10 04	10 28	..	11 17 11 41	12 48	14 24	..
UPWEY AND BROADWAY	¶ d	08 29	10 12	..	..		14 32	..
RADIPOLE	¶ d	08 33	10 15	..	..		14 35	..
WEYMOUTH ‡	¶ a	08 36		10 40	..	11 29 11 54	13 00	14 38	..
DILTON MARSH	a	07 53	09 49	..	10 00	..	11 52 12 12	..
WARMINSTER	a	08 00	09 56	..	10 07	..	12 02 12 19 12 36	..
SALISBURY	a	08 22	10 19	..	11 00	..	12 15 12 41 13 02	..
SOUTHAMPTON	a	09 23	..	11 14	..	13 23 13 31	..
BOURNEMOUTH	a	10 10	..	12 10	..	14 04 14 10	..
PORTSMOUTH & SOUTHSEA	a	10 15	..	11 58	..	14 10	..
PORTSMOUTH HARBOUR	a	10 31	..	12 02	..	14 23	..
RYDE PIER HEAD	a	11l30	..	12p45	..	14h55	..
BRIGHTON	a	12 07	..	13 50	..	16 07	..

Heavy figures denote through carriages;
light figures denote connecting services
For general notes see pages 5 and 6

b From 10 June to 2 September ⊞ from Derby dep 06 40 (Table 9)
c Arr 12 07
e Arr 07 30
f From 27 May to 2 September arr 15 mins. earlier
g Until 20 May and from 9 September arr 45 minutes later

h Until 20 May and from 9 September arr 35 minutes later
k Via Bath Spa

¶ For complete service between Weymouth and Dorchester see Southern timetable

‡ For details of sailings between Weymouth and Channel Islands see Table 33

Western Region Timetable 1 May 1972 to 6 May 1973

Table 7—continued

Saturdays
Until 23 September

South Wales, Bristol and Bath to Westbury, Bridport, Weymouth, Southampton and Portsmouth

SWANSEA 1 d							
CARDIFF GENERAL 24 d	10 55	12 55		14 55	17 20		
NEWPORT 24 d	12 45	14 15		16 35	18 50		
	12 58	14 29		16 49	19 04		
9 BIRMINGHAM NEW STREET d	12 00	12b37		15 15 16 08	18 15		
9 GLOUCESTER EASTGATE d	12 12	13 36		16 11	19 10		
BRISTOL TEMPLE MEADS 23, 24 d	13 43	15 42		17 12 17 45	20 22	21 05	
BATH SPA 23 d	14 00	16 02		17 32 18 03	20 37	21 24	
FRESHFORD d		16 17		17 47 18 19			
AVONCLIFF d		16 20		17 50 18 22	20 55	21 43	
BRADFORD-ON-AVON d		16 24		17 53 18 27			
CHIPPENHAM d							
TROWBRIDGE d	14 23	16 22		18 01 18 35	21 02	21 51	
WESTBURY a	14 31	16 39 16 39		18 10 18 43	21 11	22 02	
WESTBURY d	14 32	16 42 17 00		18 10 18 43	21 12	21 15 22 10	
FROME d		17 10		18e27	21 23		
BRUTON d		17 23		18 44			
CASTLE CARY d		17 27		18 52	21 43		
YEOVIL PEN MILL d		17 45		19 09	22 04		
THORNFORD BRIDGE d		17 53		19 16			
YETMINSTER d		17 56		19 19	22 13		
CHETNOLE d		18 00		19 23			
MAIDEN NEWTON d		18 12		19 36	22 28		
MAIDEN NEWTON d	14 43 16 35	18 20		20 05			
TOLLER d	14 49 16 41	18 26		20 11			
POWERSTOCK d	14 55 16 47	18 32		20 17			
BRIDPORT a	15 05 16 57	18 42		20 27			
DORCHESTER WEST ¶ d		18 24		19 54	22 40		
UPWEY AND BROADWAY ¶ d		18 33		20 03	22 48		
RADIPOLE ¶ d		18 37		20 06	22 51		
WEYMOUTH ‡ ¶ a		18 40		20 09	22 54		
DILTON MARSH a		16 47		18 51	21 20 22 17		
WARMINSTER a	14 45	16 54		18 58	21 27 22 26		
SALISBURY a	15 08	17 23		19 20	21 50 22 52		
SOUTHAMPTON a	15 45	18 23		20 23	22 38		
BOURNEMOUTH a	16 54	19 37		21 37	23 37		
PORTSMOUTH & SOUTHSEA a	16 34	19 15		21 15	23 31		
PORTSMOUTH HARBOUR a	16 38	19 31		21 31			
RYDE PIER HEAD a	17 30	20 35		22c05			
BRIGHTON a	18 07	21 07		23 07			

Heavy figures denote through carriages:
light figures denote connecting service
For general notes see pages 5 and 6

b From 10 June to 2 September dep 13 57
c 27 May to 2 September
e Arr 18 22

¶ For complete service between Weymouth and Dorchester see Southern timetable

‡For details of sailings between Weymouth and Channel Islands see Table 33

3.20 Exeter – Exmouth (Open)

The line between Exeter and Exmouth was the first branch line to a
seaside resort on the East Devon coast when it was opened by the Exeter
& Exmouth Railway (E&ER) in May 1861. Originally the 10½-mile line was to
be broad gauge to link up with the South Devon Railway (SDR) in Exeter, but
as with the line to Crediton the SDR was once again thwarted by the actions
of the LSWR. Agreement was reached with the E&ER for the LSWR to build
the first 4¼ miles of the branch to Topsham from a junction with its standard-
gauge main line 1¼ miles from Exeter. The next 5 miles were built by the
E&ER, although in 1866 the company was absorbed by the LSWR. Intermediate
stations were provided at Topsham, Exton (originally Woodbury Road) and
Lympstone. The line was double track as far as Topsham with a passing loop
at Lympstone. Only a single island platform was available at Exmouth until the
station was rebuilt and doubled in size in 1925. Prior to this additional halts
had opened at Polsloe Bridge, and at Clyst St Mary & Digby in 1907 and 1908
respectively, although the latter was closed by BR in September 1948.

The passenger traffic on the branch was always significantly heavier than
that on other branch lines in East Devon. Although this ruled out push-pull
operation, at nationalisation the line was still worked by Class 'M7' 0-4-4
tanks with rakes of ex-LSWR coaches. In 1952 Exmouth Junction engine shed

A typical Exmouth branch train is pictured prior to the introduction of the new BR Standard Class 3 2-6-2 tank engines and suburban coaches that took over the service to Exmouth in 1956. Both the engine and coaches seen here are of LSWR origin, as Class 'M7' 0-4-4 tank No 30670 leaves Exeter Central with a train for Exmouth in the mid-1950s. No 30670 was built in 1897 and withdrawn in March 1963. *Denis Horton*

received an allocation of brand-new BR Standard Class 3 2-6-2 tanks. At first, however, these could not run south of Topsham because of weight restrictions, but in 1956 bridges on the line were strengthened and an improved service was introduced using new BR non-corridor coaching stock. These locos dominated services on the branch until the more powerful Standard Class 4 2-6-4 tanks appeared in June 1962. The reign of the Class 4 tanks was, however, short as from 15 July 1963 DMUs took over more than half of the daily workings between Exeter and Exmouth, with dieselisation virtually complete by the end of the summer service.

In 1963 the line still carried a substantial number of

One of the BR Standard Class 3 engines, No 82024, with a train comprising a rake of recently introduced BR suburban coaches, heads alongside the Exe Estuary heads for Exmouth on 12 August 1960. No 82024 was allocated to Exmouth Junction shed from new in 1954, moved to Eastleigh in September 1962 and was withdrawn from Nine Elms in February 1966. *Terry Gough*

(5519)
2nd-CHEAP
DAY

Exmouth
to
POLSLOE BRIDGE
HALT

(W)
For conditions see over

daily commuters to Exeter in addition to heavy seasonal holiday traffic. That summer there were 31 trains each way on weekdays. This level of service had been introduced in 1957 and represented an almost half-hourly service from Exeter during the day. The Sunday service comprised 18 up and 17 down trains each way.

On summer Saturdays in 1962 Exmouth received three through trains from Waterloo and one from Cleethorpes, all running from Sidmouth Junction via Tipton St John's (Chapter 3.15 and Appendix 3.1). In 1963 the latter train was replaced by an early-morning arrival from Manchester

The once extensive layout at Exmouth station is seen here as one of Exmouth Junction's Standard Class 3 2-6-2 tanks approaches the station's impressive array of signals with a train of suburban coaches in August 1961. A small engine shed was also provided (see photo on page 139). At the time Exmouth received trains from both Exeter Central and from Sidmouth Junction, and during the summer through trains from Waterloo used the latter route. *M. E. J. Deane collection, courtesy of Ian Bennett*

Piccadilly at 6.20am with a return working at 9.18am. The southbound train did not run after 1963 but the northbound departure continued for several more years (Appendix 3.2).

The Exeter to Exmouth line was a surprise inclusion in the Beeching Report, which confirmed that the branch carried more than 50,000 passengers a week and that Exmouth station had annual passenger receipts above £25,000 per year. The only station on the branch with receipts below £5,000 per year was Exton. In the event no closure proposals were ever published and the line is the only one in the West Country where BR voluntarily agreed to retain the passenger service.

With the closure of the line to Sidmouth Junction in 1967 the large terminus station at Exmouth was demolished and replaced by a single platform with no run-round facilities. The double-track section between Exmouth Junction and Topsham was also singled, although a passing loop remains at Topsham. In May 1976 a new station, Lympstone Commando, was opened to serve the adjacent military base, and the old Lympstone station was renamed Lympstone Village. The former halt at Digby was reopened in May 1994 some 380 yards south of the original and named Digby & Sowton. Exmouth trains also call at St James' Bridge Halt,

In the early 1960s a midday train from Exeter Central terminated at Topsham. Here BR Standard Class 3 2-6-2 tank No 82010 arrives with the 1.25pm train from Exeter Central on 12 August 1960. Although allocated to Exmouth Junction from new in 1952, these engines were not permitted to work through to Exmouth until 1956, when bridges on the line had been strengthened. Like other members of its class based at Exmouth Junction, No 82010 ended its days at Nine Elms, being withdrawn in April 1965. *Terry Gough*

DMUs appeared on the branch in July 1963. Trackwork was rationalised in 1967 and the double-track section from Exmouth Junction to Topsham was singled, although a passing loop was retained at Topsham. Here a BR Class 118 DMU stands at Topsham station in the 1980s forming a service to Exeter on 3 April 1986. *Terry Gough*

Class 142 'Skipper' No. 142.019 is seen at Topsham's with the 14.15 to Exeter St. David's on 31 October 1986. The train is waiting at the station's home signal for a train from Exeter to Exmouth to arrive at the opposite platform. The semaphore signals at Topsham have since been removed and the signal box decommissioned. In December 2007 these units, now known as 'Pacers', made an unwelcome reappearance in the area. All had returned north by November 2011 but similar Class 143 units still operate in the area. Photo 215: *Author*

which opened on the LSWR main line as Lion's Holt Halt in 1906. It was renamed St James' Bridge Halt in 1946 to reflect its situation adjacent to Exeter City Football Club's ground.

Although the line is not a Community Rail scheme it is promoted in a similar fashion as the 'Avocet Line', the avocet being a wading bird associated with the Exe Estuary. In the autumn of 2018 the service comprised more than 30 return workings on weekdays, with more than 20 on Sundays, operated by Great Western Railway. Most trains from Exmouth run through to either Paignton or Barnstaple.

Although a Beeching survivor, in 1967 the large terminus at Exmouth was rationalised to a single platform with no run-round facilities. Here First Great Western Class 142 No 142009 waits to depart as the 13.23 service for Paignton on 12 May 2009. *Author*

Topsham remains the only passing place on the Exmouth branch and sees regular Great Western Railway services to and from both Barnstaple and Paignton. Two 'Pacer' units, with No 143618 at the rear, have arrived at the station forming the 13.13 service from Paignton on Saturday 29 December 2019. Leaving the station is the 14.25 service from Exmouth to Paignton worked by Class 153 single-car 'Sprinter' No 153361 and 'Pacer' unit No 143617, seen earlier in the day at Barnstaple. The signal box is no longer operational. *Author*

Western Region Timetable 4 May 1970 to 2 May 1971

By the summer of 1970 only local trains ran between Exeter and Exmouth and the through train to Manchester had been withdrawn. (see Appendix 3) In 2019 trains from Exmouth run to both Paignton and Barnstaple

Table 28

Exeter to Exmouth

Mondays to Fridays

Miles																										
	EXETER ST DAVID'S .. d	06 23	..	07 00	07 20	..	..	..	10 15	..	12 30	..	..	14 33	15 35	16 00	..	17 03	..	18 05	19 00	..	20 07	22 25
0	EXETER CENTRAL .... d	06 28	..	07 04	07 30	08 00	08 28	09 25	10 38	11 38	12 40	13 40	..	14 50	15 40	16 16	16 44	17 13	17 45	18 15	19 04	..	20 23	22 30
¼	ST JAMES' PARK .. .. d	..	..	07 06	..	..	08 30	..	..	..	..	..	..	..	..	16 46	17 15	17 47	18 17	..	..	..	..
1¼	POLSLOE BRIDGE .... d	06 33	..	07 10	07 35	08 05	08 32	09 29	10 43	11 43	12 45	13 45	..	14 55	15 45	16 21	16 50	17 19	17 51	18 21	19 09	..	20 28	22 35
5¼	TOPSHAM .. .. .. d	06 40	..	07 17	07 44	08 14	08 41	09 36	10 50	11 50	12 52	13 52	..	15 02	15 52	16 28	16 57	17 28	17 58	18 28	19 16	..	20 35	22 42
7	EXTON .... d	06 43	..	07 20	07 47	08 17	08 44	09 39	10 53	11 53	12 55	13 55	..	15 05	15 55	16 31	17 00	17 31	18 01	18 31	19 19	..	20 38	22 45
8½	LYMPSTONE .... d	06 47	..	07 24	07 51	08 21	08 48	09 43	10 57	11 57	12 59	13 59	..	15 09	15 59	16 35	17 04	17 35	18 05	18 35	19 23	..	20 42	22 49
10½	EXMOUTH .... a	06 51	..	07 28	07 55	08 25	08 52	09 47	11 01	12 01	13 03	14 03	..	15 13	16 03	16 39	17 08	17 39	18 09	18 39	19 27	..	20 46	22 53

Western Region Timetable 4 May 1970 to 2 May 1971

Until 26 September — **Saturdays**

EXETER ST DAVID'S	d	05 55 06 23 06 55 .. .. .. 09 10 09 56 10 15 11 28 .. 12 30 .. 14 16 14 33 15 20 16 00 .. 17 03 17 19 18 05 19 00 20 07 21 45 ..
EXETER CENTRAL	d	05 59 06 28 07 04 07 32 08 00 08 29 09 15 10 00 10 45 11 32 12 02 12 47 13 27 14 20 14 50 15 25 16 15 16 44 17 13 17 45 18 15 19 04 20 23 21 50 22 55
ST JAMES' PARK	d	.. .. 07 06 .. .. 16 17 16 46 17 15 17 47 18 17 ..
POLSLOE BRIDGE	d	06 04 06 33 07 10 07 37 08 05 08 32 09 20 10 05 10 50 11 37 12 07 12 52 13 32 14 25 14 55 15 30 16 21 16 50 17 19 17 51 18 21 19 09 20 28 21 55 23 00
TOPSHAM	d	06 11 06 40 07 17 07 44 08 14 08 41 09 27 10 12 10 57 11 44 12 14 12 59 13 39 14 32 15 02 15 37 16 28 16 57 17 28 17 58 18 28 19 16 20 35 22 02 23 07
EXTON	d	06 14 06 43 07 20 07 47 08 17 08 44 09 30 10 15 11 00 11 47 12 17 13 02 13 42 14 35 15 05 15 40 16 31 17 00 17 31 18 01 18 31 19 19 20 38 22 05 23 10
LYMPSTONE	d	06 18 06 47 07 24 07 51 08 21 08 48 09 34 10 19 11 04 11 51 12 21 13 06 13 46 14 39 15 09 15 44 16 35 17 04 17 35 18 05 18 35 19 23 20 42 22 09 23 14
EXMOUTH	a	06 22 06 51 07 28 07 55 08 25 08 52 09 38 10 23 11 08 11 54 12 25 13 10 13 50 14 43 15 13 15 48 16 39 17 08 17 39 18 09 18 39 19 27 20 46 22 13 23 18

From 3 October — **Saturdays**

EXETER ST DAVID'S	d	06 23 .. 06 55 .. 08 50 10 15 .. 12 30 .. 14 33 15 35 16 00 17 03 .. 19 00 .. 20 07 .. 21 45 .. .. ..
EXETER CENTRAL	d	06 28 .. 07 03 08 28 09 25 10 38 11 38 12 40 13 40 14 50 15 40 16 44 17 45 .. 19 04 .. 20 23 .. 21 50 .. 22 55 ..
ST JAMES' PARK	d	.. .. 07 06 .. .. 16 46 17 47 .. ..
POLSLOE BRIDGE	d	06 33 .. 07 35 08 32 09 29 10 43 11 43 12 45 13 45 14 55 15 45 16 50 17 51 .. 19 09 .. 20 28 .. 21 55 .. 23 00 ..
TOPSHAM	d	06 40 .. 07 44 08 41 09 36 10 53 11 50 12 52 13 52 15 02 15 52 16 57 17 58 .. 19 16 .. 20 35 .. 22 02 .. 23 07 ..
EXTON	d	06 43 .. 07 47 08 44 09 39 10 53 11 53 12 55 13 55 15 05 15 55 17 00 18 01 .. 19 19 .. 20 38 .. 22 05 .. 23 10 ..
LYMPSTONE	d	06 47 .. 07 51 08 48 09 43 10 57 11 57 12 59 13 59 15 09 15 59 17 04 18 05 .. 19 23 .. 20 42 .. 22 09 .. 23 14 ..
EXMOUTH	a	06 51 .. 07 55 08 52 09 47 11 01 12 01 13 04 03 15 13 16 03 17 08 18 09 .. 19 27 .. 20 46 .. 22 13 .. 23 18 ..

Until 7 June, from 13 September to 4 October and also from 28 March 1971 — **Sundays**

EXETER ST DAVID'S	d	14 10 .. .. 16 35 18 20 .. ..
EXETER CENTRAL	d	14 15 15 15 16 15 17 15 18 45 19 45 20 45
ST JAMES' PARK	d	14 17 15 17 16 17 17 17 18 47 19 47 20 47
POLSLOE BRIDGE	d	14 21 15 21 16 21 17 21 18 51 19 51 20 51
TOPSHAM	d	14 28 15 28 16 28 17 28 18 58 19 58 20 58
EXTON	d	14 31 15 31 16 31 17 31 19 01 20 01 21 01
LYMPSTONE	d	14 35 15 35 16 35 17 35 19 05 20 05 21 05
EXMOUTH	a	14 39 15 39 16 39 17 39 19 09 20 09 21 09

14 June to 6 September — **Sundays**

EXETER ST DAVID'S	d	09 40 .. .. 16 35 18 20 .. .. ..
EXETER CENTRAL	d	09 45 10 45 .. 11 45 .. 13 15 .. 14 15 .. 15 15 16 15 17 15 18 45 19 45 20 45 21 45
ST JAMES' PARK	d	09 47 10 47 .. 11 47 .. 13 17 .. 14 17 .. 15 17 16 17 17 17 18 47 19 47 20 47 21 47
POLSLOE BRIDGE	d	09 51 10 51 .. 11 51 .. 13 21 .. 14 21 .. 15 21 16 21 17 21 18 51 19 51 20 51 21 51
TOPSHAM	d	09 58 10 58 .. 11 58 .. 13 28 .. 14 28 .. 15 28 16 28 17 28 18 58 19 58 20 58 21 58
EXTON	d	10 01 11 01 .. 12 01 .. 13 31 .. 14 31 .. 15 31 16 31 17 31 19 01 20 01 21 01 22 01
LYMPSTONE	d	10 05 11 05 .. 12 05 .. 13 35 .. 14 35 .. 15 35 16 35 17 35 19 05 20 05 21 05 22 05
EXMOUTH	a	10 09 11 09 .. 12 09 .. 13 39 .. 14 39 .. 15 39 16 39 17 39 19 09 20 09 21 09 22 09

Heavy figures denote through carriages;
light figures denote connecting services
For general notes see pages 5 and 6

3.21 Liskeard – Looe (Open)

The line from Liskeard to Looe owes its origin to the Liskeard & Caradon Railway, a tramway that opened to Cheesewring in 1846 to transport copper ore and granite from the heights of Bodmin Moor to the port at Looe. For many years these materials had to be transferred onto barges on the Liskeard & Looe Canal at Moorswater near Liskeard. In 1860 the canal was converted to a railway and became the Liskeard & Looe Railway (L&LR). The line followed the old canal bed and allowed mineral trains to run through to Looe. The first passenger service to Looe ran on the 8¾-mile line in September 1879. Its northern terminus was, however, situated some 300 feet below the Cornwall Railway's main line from Plymouth to Penzance near Moorswater Viaduct.

It was not until 1901 that a short branch was opened that allowed L&LR trains to enter what was now the GWR station at Liskeard. This line left the L&LR main line at Coombe Junction and climbed for 2 miles at a gradient of 1 in 40, curving some 90° towards the north-east as it did so. It then passed under the GWR main line east of Liskeard station before turning a further 180° and entering Liskeard station at a small terminus platform at 90° to those facing the main line. This configuration meant that once a train for Looe reached the station at Coombe Junction it was facing north. It therefore had to reverse to reach Looe on the

Ex-GWR 'Small Prairie' No 4568 arrives at the terminus platform at Liskeard with a train from Looe on 13 July 1955. The engine will have to reverse its train out of the station before it can run round for the next journey to Looe. No 4568 is another example of the earlier Class '4500' engines built with flat tops to their side tanks; it was withdrawn in February 1959.
Frank Hornby

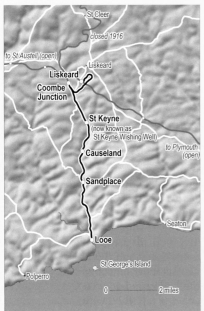

South Cornwall coast, which in the days of steam required the engine to run round its train. The line then ran for 6¾ miles down the east bank of the East Looe River. Intermediate halts were built at St Keyne, Causeland and Sandplace. At Looe only a single platform face was provided. Once passengers had disembarked the train drew forward a few hundred yards on the line to Looe Port where a run-round loop was available for the locomotive. All lines north of Moorswater had closed by 1916.

For many years the L&LR operated the branch with its own 2-4-0 tank engine Lady Margaret and a train of four-wheeled coaches. Built by Andrew Barclay Ltd in 1902, the engine continued to work on the line after the GWR had become responsible for its operation in 1909. After the amalgamation of the L&LR with the GWR in 1923 the GWR numbered the engine 1308 and transferred it to the ex-Cambrian Railways branch to Llangynog; it was finally scrapped in 1948. Once under the complete control of the GWR, the branch came to epitomise the company's

To reach Liskeard the train seen in the previous picture has had to reverse at Coombe Junction Halt; now, having run around its train, No 4568 is seen ready to depart for Liskeard, climbing at 1 in 40 and curving some 270° before arrival at the branch terminus. The viaduct carrying the main line through Liskeard can be seen in the background.
Frank Hornby

summer holiday branch lines. Trains typically comprised two-coach 'B' sets hauled by 'Small Prairie' tanks. As with other ex-GWR branch lines in Cornwall, BR(WR) replaced steam with DMUs at the end of the summer timetable on Saturday 9 September 1961. The introduction of DMUs made operation of the branch much easier, for although the train still had to reverse at Coombe Junction, the driver merely had to walk to the cab at the opposite end of the train. Similarly at Looe the run-round loop was no longer required.

Despite dieselisation there was very little difference between the summer services of 1961 and 1963. Eight trains ran each way on weekdays with an additional early morning train on Saturdays that departed from Looe at 5.45am and 5.55am in the respective years. Seven trains ran on Sundays in 1963, an increase of one over 1961. Connections with main line trains, including the 'Cornish Riviera Express' during the winter of 1962/63, is given in BR(WR)'s Table 81 (see pp. 42 & 43).

The Beeching Report had revealed that the branch carried fewer than 5,000 passengers a week and that only Liskeard and Looe stations had annual passenger receipts above £5,000. Proposals to close the line were published in the autumn of 1965 together with those for St Ives (see Chapter 3.21). In the event the line was saved by Barbara Castle's Transport Act of 1968; this introduced the criterion of social need, which had to be addressed before closure could take place. Because of the poor state of the roads around Looe permission to close the line was refused.

The line continues to run today, operated as part of the Devon & Cornwall Rail Partnership and promoted as the 'Looe Valley' line. This is the largest Community Rail Partnership in Britain and was formed in 1991. It currently involves the local authorities, Network Rail and train operator Great Western Railway. In the autumn of 2019 twelve trains a day ran each way on the line, while eight ran on Sundays until 20 October. Trains still have to reverse at Coombe Junction although only two are timetabled to call there. The line now terminates at the single platform at Looe and there are now no run-round facilities at the station.

Another ex-GWR 'Small Prairie' is seen at Coombe Junction in May 1960. The engine has left its train from Liskeard in the platform and is running round prior to departing for Looe. The track behind the train continues under the viaduct to Moorswater. *M. E. J. Deane collection, courtesy of Ian Bennett*

No 4568 is seen again at Looe after arrival from Liskeard on 13 July 1955. The engine has drawn its train forward in order to run around prior to departure back to Liskeard. The line now ends at the station site that can be seen in the background. *Frank Hornby*

DMUs were introduced on the Looe branch in September 1961, and here a Class 119 three-car unit stands in the Looe branch platform at Liskeard forming the 1.40pm service to Looe on 3 September 1965. *Author*

The introduction of DMUs on the branch removed the need for an engine to run round at Liskeard, Coombe Junction Halt and Looe – the driver merely had to walk from one end of the train to the other. Here the same Class 119 three-car DMU stands at Coombe Junction Halt while he does so before proceeding to Looe. *Author*

The DMU has now arrived at Looe and luggage is being loaded into it from a trolley on the platform prior to departure for Liskeard again at 2.20pm. *Author*

The Looe branch survived the Beeching Axe and today the small terminus station at Liskeard looks much as it did in 1955, although the water tower has long since disappeared. Here, almost 50 years later, Class 153 single-unit 'Super Sprinter' No 153368 stands at the platform forming the 16.54 service from Liskeard to Looe on 10 September 2003. Today Coombe Junction station is considered to be the least used in Cornwall. *Author*

The same 'Super Sprinter', operated by South Wales and West Railways, is seen again on the same day as it runs through the halt at Sandplace with the 16.54 service from Liskeard to Looe. *Author*

Class 150 'Sprinter' No 150238, still in First Great Western livery, skirts the misty East Looe River with Great Western Railway's 10.14 service from Liskeard to Looe on Friday 28 December 2018. The train returned from Looe to Liskeard at 10.44. *Author*

Western Region Timetable 4 May 1970 to 2 May 1971

Table 32 (Second class only)

Liskeard to Looe — Mondays to Fridays / Saturdays From 3 October

Miles	Station		Mondays to Fridays										Saturdays From 3 October									
31	PLYMOUTH	d	..	07 25	08 50	..	12 50	14 07	14 55	17 10	18 50	..	..	07 25	..	08 50	..	..	12 50	14 07	14 55	17 10	18 50
0	LISKEARD	d	06 55	08 10	09 28	11 12	13 22	14 40	16 10	17 48	19 22	..	06 55	08 10	..	09 28	11 12	..	13 22	14 40	16 10	17 48	19 22
2	COOMBE	d	07 04	08 19	09 37	11 21	13 31	14 49	16 19	17 57	19 31	..	07 04	08 19	..	09 37	11 21	..	13 31	14 49	16 19	17 57	19 31
3½	ST KEYNE	d	07 09	08 24	09 42	11 26	13 36	14 54	16 24	18 02	19 36	..	07 09	08 24	..	09 42	11 26	..	13 36	14 54	16 24	18 02	19 36
5	CAUSELAND	d	07 14	08 29	09 47	11 31	13 41	14 59	16 29	18 07	19 41	..	07 14	08 29	..	09 47	11 31	..	13 41	14 59	16 29	18 07	19 41
6½	SANDPLACE	d	07 18	08 33	09 51	11 35	13 45	15 03	16 33	18 11	19 45	..	07 18	08 33	..	09 51	11 35	..	13 45	15 03	16 33	18 11	19 45
8½	LOOE	a	07 25	08 40	09 58	11 42	13 52	15 10	16 40	18 18	19 52	..	07 25	08 40	..	09 58	11 42	..	13 52	15 10	16 40	18 18	19 52

Liskeard to Looe — Saturdays Until 26 September / Sundays 14 June to 6 September only

Station		Saturdays Until 26 September											Sundays 14 June to 6 September only									
31 PLYMOUTH	d	06f10	07 35	08 50	11 08	..	12 01	14 05	..	15 14	17 20	18 55	..	..	09 30	11 30	..	..	15 05	..	17 15	18 20	..	19 25
LISKEARD	d	06 55	08 10	09 25	11 40	..	12 53	14 40	..	15 55	17 57	19 30	..	..	10 00	12 10	..	14 00	15 40	..	17 50	19 00	..	20 05
COOMBE	d	07 04	08 19	09 34	11 49	..	13 02	14 49	..	16 04	18 06	19 39	..	..	10 19	12 19	..	14 09	15 49	..	17 59	19 09	..	20 14
ST KEYNE	d	07 09	08 24	09 39	11 54	..	13 07	14 54	..	16 09	18 11	19 44	..	..	10 24	12 24	..	14 14	15 54	..	18 04	19 14	..	20 19
CAUSELAND	d	07 14	08 29	09 44	11 59	..	13 12	14 59	..	16 14	18 16	19 49	..	..	10 29	12 29	..	14 19	15 59	..	18 09	19 19	..	20 24
SANDPLACE	d	07 18	08 33	09 48	12 03	..	13 16	15 03	..	16 18	18 19	19 52	..	..	10 33	12 33	..	14 23	16 03	..	18 13	19 23	..	20 28
LOOE	a	07 25	08 40	09 55	12 10	..	13 23	15 10	..	16 25	18 27	20 00	..	..	10 40	12 40	..	14 30	16 10	..	18 20	19 30	..	20 35

Looe to Liskeard — Mondays to Fridays / Saturdays From 3 October

Miles	Station		Mondays to Fridays										Saturdays From 3 October									
						♥								♥									
0	LOOE	d	07 30	08 55	10 38	11 46	14 00	15 30	17 15	18 23	19 55	..	07 30	08 55	..	10 38	11 46	14 00	15 30	17 15	18 23	19 55	..
2½	SANDPLACE	d	07 36	09 01	10 44	11 52	14 06	15 36	17 21	18 29	20 01	..	07 36	09 01	..	10 44	11 52	14 06	15 36	17 21	18 29	20 01	..
3½	CAUSELAND	d	07 41	09 06	10 49	11 57	14 11	15 41	17 26	18 34	20 06	..	07 41	09 06	..	10 49	11 57	14 11	15 41	17 26	18 34	20 06	..
5	ST KEYNE	d	07 45	09 10	10 53	12 01	14 15	15 45	17 30	18 38	20 10	..	07 45	09 10	..	10 53	12 01	14 15	15 45	17 30	18 38	20 10	..
6½	COOMBE	d	07 52	09 17	11 00	12 08	14 22	15 52	17 37	18 45	20 17	..	07 52	09 17	..	11 00	12 08	14 22	15 52	17 37	18 45	20 17	..
8½	LISKEARD	a	08 00	09 25	11 08	12 16	14 30	16 00	17 45	18 53	20 25	..	08 00	09 25	..	11 08	12 16	14 30	16 00	17 45	18 53	20 25	..
31	PLYMOUTH	a	08 32	10 11	12 01	12 51	15 55	17 24	18 50	19 36	..	..	08 32	10 11	..	12 01	12 51	15 55	17 24	18 50	19 36	..	..

Looe to Liskeard — Saturdays Until 26 September / Sundays 14 June to 6 September only

Station		Saturdays Until 26 September											Sundays 14 June to 6 September only									
		♦	♦	✕/♦		✕/♦	♦																
LOOE	d	07 28	08 50	10 00	..	12 15	13 26	..	15 20	16 50	18 30	20 15	..	..	11 10	13 10	14 55	..	16 15	18 25	19 35	20 40	..
SANDPLACE	d	07 34	08 56	10 06	..	12 21	13 32	..	15 26	16 56	18 36	20 21	..	..	11 16	13 16	15 01	..	16 21	18 31	..	20 46	..
CAUSELAND	d	07 39	09 01	10 11	..	12 26	13 37	..	15 31	17 01	18 41	20 26	..	..	11 21	13 21	15 06	..	16 26	18 36	..	20 51	..
ST KEYNE	d	07 43	09 05	10 15	..	12 30	13 41	..	15 35	17 05	18 45	20 30	..	..	11 25	13 25	15 10	..	16 30	18 40	..	20 55	..
COOMBE	d	07 50	09 12	10 22	..	12 37	13 48	..	15 42	17 12	18 52	20 37	..	..	11 32	13 32	15 17	..	16 37	18 47	19 54	21 02	..
LISKEARD	a	07 58	09 20	10 30	..	12 45	13 56	..	15 50	17 20	19 00	20 45	..	..	11 40	13 40	15 25	..	16 45	18 55	20 02	21 10	..
31 PLYMOUTH	a	08 32	09b56	11e05	..	13 27	14 30	..	..	17 56	19 41	21f25	..	..	12 20	14 20	16 20	..	17 20	20 05	..	21 48	..

Heavy figures denote through carriages; light figures denote connecting services
For general notes see pages 5 and 6

X From 13 June to 5 September passengers using this service to connect at Liskeard into the trains listed below for destinations beyond Plymouth require to reserve seats, see pages 37 to 53:
10 00 Penzance to Bradford (**Cornishman**)
10 20 Penzance to Manchester
11 35 Penzance to Leeds

♦ From 23 May passengers using this service to connect at Liskeard into the trains listed below for Reading or Paddington require to reserve seats, see pages 37 to 53:
06 35 Penzance to Paddington
08 15 Penzance to Paddington
08 45 Penzance to Paddington
11 05 Penzance to Paddington
12 18 Penzance to Paddington

♥ Passengers using this service to connect at Liskeard into the 10 55 Penzance to Paddington (**Cornish Riviera Limited**) require to reserve seats, see pages 37 to 53
b Until 6 June also 19 and 26 September, the connecting service arr. Plymouth 10 11
e 13 June to 5 September only. On 30 May, 6 June also 12 and 19 September, the connecting service arr. Plymouth 11 20
f 13 June to 5 September only

3.22 St Erth - St Ives (Open)

G.W.R.

LELANT

The station at St Erth, then named St Ives Road, was opened by the West Cornwall Railway (WCR) in March 1852 together with its standard-gauge single-track main line from Truro to Penzance. At the time St Ives was an important port handling copper and tin, together with a thriving fishing trade. However, early attempts to build a branch line from the main line failed and it was not until June 1877 that the 4¼-mile line from St Erth eventually opened. By this time the WCR was leased jointly to the GWR, the Bristol & Exeter Railway and the South Devon Railway, which in 1866 had added an extra rail to create a mixed-gauge line. From March 1867 through trains were able to run between Paddington and Penzance for the first time. The St Ives branch was the last new passenger-carrying broad-gauge line to open in the country and was among the last to be converted to standard gauge; conversion occurred in 1892, together with the whole of what, from 1876, had become the GWR's main line from Penzance to Paddington via Bristol.

The branch line to St Ives followed the western side of the Hayle Estuary to the first station at Lelant. It then slowly climbs, first across the dunes of Porth Kidney Sands then along the cliffside above Carbis Bay to reach St Ives, across the Carbis and St Ives Viaducts (78 and 106 yards long respectively). Substantial stone-built single-platform stations were provided at Carbis Bay and St Ives. The route was single track throughout with no passing places. At St Ives the line continued through the station to the goods yard immediately beyond. The rather cramped facilities at St Erth were improved in 1894 when the station was rebuilt with a separate bay platform for St Ives trains. The main line from Hayle in the east was doubled in September 1899, while the section on to Marazion remained single track until June 1929.

Over the years the mineral and fish traffic declined, to be replaced by holidaymakers.

Ex-GWR 'Small Prairie' tank No 4574, another of the older Class '4500' engines, runs round its train at St Ives after arrival with a train from St Erth on 12 April 1956. The engine was built at Swindon in 1924 and withdrawn in February 1963. *Terry Gough*

In this panoramic view of St Ives station in the summer of 1961 an ex-GWR 'Small Prairie' tank appears to be marshalling coaching stock before departure with a train to St Erth. *M. E. J. Deane collection, courtesy of Ian Bennett*

St Ives became a poplar holiday resort with a branch line typified by ex-GWR 'Small Prairie' tanks hauling one or more two-coach 'B' sets. For many years the local trains were augmented in the summer by through coaches off the 10.30am service from Paddington, the 'Cornish Riviera Express'. As at Looe, DMUs replaced steam at the end of the summer timetable on Saturday 9 September 1961. Connections with main line trains, including the 'Cornish Riviera Express' during the winter of 1962/63, is given in BR(WR)'s Table 81 (see pp. 42 & 43). The through coaches from London off the 'Cornish Riviera Express' reappeared on summer Saturdays in both 1962 (Appendix 3.1) and 1963. The 'Small

DMUs replaced steam on the St Ives branch in September 1961, although the 'Small Prairies' reappeared in the summer of 1962 to work the through coaches off the 'Cornish Riviera Express' from Paddington. By 1965 the run-round loop at St Ives had already been removed as a Class 118 DMU stands in the station forming the 6.57pm service to St Erth on 6 September 1965. *Author*

Prairie' tanks were used again in 1962, but in September of that year the engine shed at Penzance closed to steam. The through coaches ran for the last time in 1963, hauled by NB Type 2 diesel-hydraulics. Since then all passengers have had to change at St Erth. In all, that summer there were 24 departures from St Ives on Saturdays, six more than on weekdays. Twelve trains ran on Sundays.

The history of the line since 1963 follows closely that of the Looe branch. The Beeching Report had revealed that the branch carried fewer than 5,000 passengers a week and that only St Erth and St Ives stations had annual passenger receipts above £5,000. Proposals to close the line were therefore published in the autumn of 1965, together with those for the Looe branch (see Chapter 3.21). This service was also saved by Barbara Castle's Transport Act of 1968, which ensured that social need had to be addressed before closure could take place. In 1970 the future of both lines came under review again when a two-part cost benefit analysis of rail services in Cornwall was carried out. Both lines have nevertheless survived.

In May 1971 the substantial station at St Ives was demolished and the run-round facilities removed to make way for a car park. On a positive note, in May 1978 a new station opened at Lelant Saltings and today this is promoted as a 'park and ride' station, enabling visitors to avoid the narrow streets and limited car parking at St Ives.

Also as at Looe, the line is run today as part of the Devon & Cornwall Rail Partnership and is promoted as the 'St Ives Bay' line. The train operator is now Great Western Railway. There has been a significant improvement in the service in recent years. In the autumn of 2019 28 trains a day ran each way on the line; the first and third ran from Penzance, leaving St Erth at 07.06 and 08.53 respectively, while the last train was at 21.58. A Sunday service of 20 trains ran from St Erth until 8 September,. From 27 October the service was then reduced to 14 trains.

An ex-GWR 'Small Prairie' leaves Carbis Bay with a train from St Ives to St Erth in May 1957. *Ray Ruffell, Silver Link Publishing collection*

Still under the control of semaphore signals, which gives the view a traditional GWR branch-line appearance, BR Class 122 single-unit railcar No 55005 enters St Erth with a service from St Ives on 29 April 1989. *Author*

Two two-car Class 150/2 'Sprinters', Nos 150233 and 150244, operated by First Great Western, leave Carbis Bay as the 12.55 departure from St Ives on 20 May 2009. *Author*

Western Passenger Timetable 4 May 1970 - 2 May 1971

By the summer of 1970 only local trains ran between St. Erth and St. Ives, This compares with one through train from Paddington, was the 'Cornish Riviera Express', during the summer of 1962 (see Appendix 3),

Table 35 (Second class only)   **Mondays to Fridays**

St Erth to St Ives

Miles										B										
0	ST ERTH	d	..	07 20	07 55	08 30	09 20	10 10	..	11 55	13 07	..	14 45	16 00	16 32	17 05	..	18 30	19 20	..	..	..	..
1	LELANT	d	..	07 23	07 58	08 33	09 23	10 13	..	11 58	13 10	..	14 48	16 03	16 35	17 08	..	18 33	19 23	..	..	..	..
3	CARBIS BAY	d	..	07 28	08 03	08 38	09 28	10 18	..	12 03	13 15	..	14 53	16 08	16 40	17 13	..	18 38	19 28	..	..	..	..
4½	ST IVES	a	..	07 32	08 07	08 42	09 32	10 22	..	12 07	13 19	..	14 57	16 12	16 44	17 17	..	18 42	19 32	..	..	..	..

Saturdays   **Until 26 September**

										C							D			
ST ERTH	d	07 20	07 50	08 30	..	09 18	09 55	10 26	..	11 50	13 10	..	14 55	15 51	..	16 26	17 00	17 30	..	18 09	19 12	19 60	..
LELANT	d	..	07 53	08 33	..	09 21	09 58	10 29	..	11 53	13 13	..	14 58	15 54	..	16 29	17 03	17 33	..	18 11	19 15	19 53	..
CARBIS BAY	d	..	07 58	08 38	..	09 26	10 03	10 34	..	11 58	13 18	..	15 03	15 59	..	16 34	17 08	17 38	..	18 16	19 20	19 58	..
ST IVES	a	07 30	08 02	08 42	..	09 30	10 07	10 38	..	12 02	13 22	..	15 07	16 03	..	16 38	17 12	17 42	..	18 20	19 24	20 02	..

Saturdays   **From 3 October**

										B										
ST ERTH	d	..	07 20	07 55	08 30	09 20	10 10	..	11 55	13 07	..	14 45	16 00	16 32	17 05	..	18 30	..	19 20	..	..	..	..
LELANT	d	..	07 23	07 58	08 33	09 23	10 13	..	11 58	13 10	..	14 48	16 03	16 35	17 08	..	18 33	..	19 23	..	..	..	..
CARBIS BAY	d	..	07 28	08 03	08 38	09 28	10 18	..	12 03	13 15	..	14 53	16 08	16 40	17 13	..	18 38	..	19 28	..	..	..	..
ST IVES	a	..	07 32	08 07	08 42	09 32	10 22	..	12 07	13 19	..	14 57	16 12	16 44	17 17	..	18 42	..	19 32	..	..	..	..

Sundays   **14 June to 6 September**

ST ERTH	d	..	..	10 18	..	11 40	..	12 18	..	13 42	..	14 20	..	16 30	..	17 18	..	17 58	..	..	..	..
LELANT	d	..	..	10 21	..	11 43	..	12 21	..	13 45	..	14 23	..	16 33	..	17 21	..	18 01	..	..	..	..
CARBIS BAY	d	..	..	10 26	..	11 48	..	12 26	..	13 50	..	14 28	..	16 38	..	17 26	..	18 06	..	..	..	..
ST IVES	a	..	..	10 30	..	11 52	..	12 30	..	13 54	..	14 32	..	16 42	..	17 30	..	18 10	..	..	..	..

'Sprinter' No 150233 can be seen again on the same day standing in the platform at St Ives waiting to leave as the 12.55 departure. The land formerly occupied by the goods yard is now in use as a car park. *Author*

Western Region Timetable 4 May 1970 to 2 May 1971

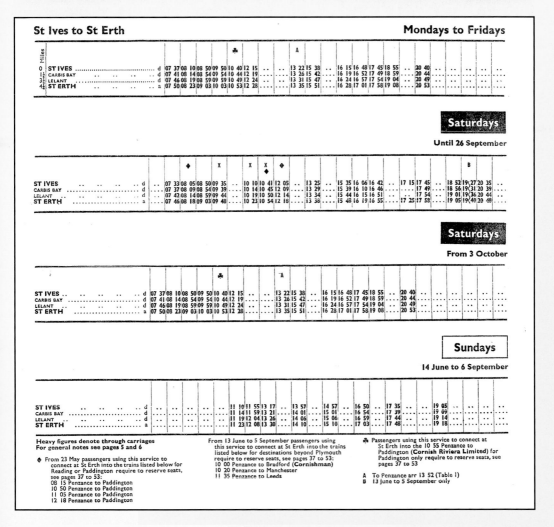

St Ives to St Erth — Mondays to Fridays

Miles								♣		A											
0	ST IVES	d	07 37	08 10	08 50	09 50	10 40	12 15	.. ..	13 22	15 38	.. ..	16 15	16 48	17 45	18 55	..	20 40	.. ..	.. ..	.. ..
1¼	CARBIS BAY	d	07 41	08 14	08 54	09 54	10 44	12 19	.. ..	13 26	15 42	.. ..	16 19	16 52	17 49	18 59	..	20 44	.. ..	.. ..	.. ..
3½	LELANT	d	07 46	08 19	08 59	09 59	10 49	12 24	.. ..	13 31	15 47	.. ..	16 24	16 57	17 54	19 04	..	20 49	.. ..	.. ..	.. ..
4¼	ST ERTH	a	07 50	08 23	09 03	10 03	10 53	12 28	.. ..	13 35	15 51	.. ..	16 28	17 01	17 58	19 08	..	20 53	.. ..	.. ..	.. ..

Saturdays — Until 26 September

							♦		X		X	X	♦							B		
ST IVES	d	.. ..	07 33	08 05	08 50	09 35	..	10 10	10 41	12 05	.. ..	13 25	..	15 35	16 06	16 42	..	17 15	17 45	..	18 52	19 27 20 35 .. ..
CARBIS BAY	d	..	07 37	08 09	08 54	09 39	..	10 14	10 45	12 09	.. ..	13 29	..	15 39	16 10	16 46	..	..	17 49	..	18 56	19 31 20 39 .. ..
LELANT	d	..	07 42	08 14	08 59	09 44	..	10 19	10 50	12 14	.. ..	13 34	..	15 44	16 15	16 51	..	..	17 54	..	19 01	19 36 20 44 .. ..
ST ERTH	a	..	07 46	08 18	09 03	09 48	..	10 23	10 54	12 18	.. ..	13 38	..	15 48	16 19	16 55	..	17 25	17 58	..	19 05	19 40 20 48 .. ..

Saturdays — From 3 October

							♣		A											
ST IVES	d	07 37	08 10	08 50	09 50	10 40	12 15	..	13 22	15 38	.. ..	16 15	16 48	17 45	18 55	..	20 40	.. ..	.. ..	.. ..
CARBIS BAY	d	07 41	08 14	08 54	09 54	10 44	12 19	..	13 26	15 42	.. ..	16 19	16 52	17 49	18 59	..	20 44	.. ..	.. ..	.. ..
LELANT	d	07 46	08 19	08 59	09 59	10 49	12 24	..	13 31	15 47	.. ..	16 24	16 57	17 54	19 04	..	20 49	.. ..	.. ..	.. ..
ST ERTH	a	07 50	08 23	09 03	10 03	10 53	12 28	..	13 35	15 51	.. ..	16 28	17 01	17 58	19 08	..	20 53	.. ..	.. ..	.. ..

Sundays — 14 June to 6 September

ST IVES	d	.. ..	.. ..	..	11 10	11 55	13 17	..	13 57	..	14 57	..	16 50	..	17 35	..	19 05	.. ..
CARBIS BAY	d	.. ..	.. ..	..	11 14	11 59	13 21	..	14 01	..	15 01	..	16 54	..	17 39	..	19 09	.. ..
LELANT	d	.. ..	.. ..	..	11 19	12 04	13 26	..	14 06	..	15 06	..	16 59	..	17 44	..	19 14	.. ..
ST ERTH	a	.. ..	.. ..	..	11 23	12 08	13 30	..	14 10	..	15 10	..	17 03	..	17 48	..	19 18	.. ..

Heavy figures denote through carriages
For general notes see pages 5 and 6

♦ From 23 May passengers using this service to connect at St Erth into the trains listed below for Reading or Paddington require to reserve seats, see pages 37 to 53:
08 15 Penzance to Paddington
10 50 Penzance to Paddington
11 05 Penzance to Paddington
12 18 Penzance to Paddington

From 13 June to 5 September passengers using this service to connect at St Erth into the trains listed below for destinations beyond Plymouth require to reserve seats, see pages 37 to 53:
10 00 Penzance to Bradford (**Cornishman**)
10 20 Penzance to Manchester
11 35 Penzance to Leeds

♣ Passengers using this service to connect at St Erth into the 10 55 Penzance to Paddington (**Cornish Riviera Limited**) for Paddington only require to reserve seats, see pages 37 to 53

A To Penzance arr 13 52 (Table 1)
B 13 June to 5 September only

Further reading in the Beeching Legacy series:

Western Passenger Timetable 18 April 1966 - 5 March 1967
Extract showing train services in the Bristol Division. The former railway lines from Taunton to Barnstaple and between Okehampton and Bude and Padstow are shown as bus routes. These lines did not actually close until October 1966.

Appendix I   **The political background to the Beeching Report**

To put the Beeching Report into context one must go back to the nationalisation of the railways in 1947, when their control was vested in the British Transport Commission (BTC). Over the years successive governments have felt obliged to tinker with both the physical and management structure of Britain's railways. Between 1947 and 1968 there were four major Transport Acts, in 1947, 1953, 1962 and 1968, and in between there were innumerable minor changes to management responsibilities and to the regional boundaries.

Prior to the Transport Act of 1962 the Transport Minister, Ernest Marples, had set up a Select Committee on the Nationalised Industries. The Chairman of the Committee was Sir Toby Low (later Lord Aldington). Its conclusions were generally favourable to the existing organisation of BR. However, a Special Advisory Group, headed by Sir Ivan Stedeford, was also assisting the Minister. Significantly, this 'think tank' included among its members Dr Richard Beeching, a Technical Director of ICI. This committee was much more critical of the existing management structures and operation of the railways, and its advice, rather than that of the Select Committee, was incorporated in the subsequent Transport Bill presented to Parliament towards the end of 1961.

Dr Beeching was appointed as Chairman of the BTC in June 1961. At his first press conference 12 days later he announced that five studies of the system were to be carried out. These involved a detailed examination of the costs of handling the current traffic by existing methods and of traffic flows by both rail and other modes of transport. Other studies were to determine how the handling of passengers and freight might be improved to attract more traffic. In fact, the survey of the density of passenger traffic had already taken place in April 1961. The results of these studies were published in July 1962 and were ominous for the railway system of the day. They showed that no less than 95% of all railway freight was carried on one half of the 18,400 miles of lines then open to traffic, while 30% of the route miles carried only 1% of total freight traffic. Similar figures applied to passenger traffic. In total, British Railways was recording an annual

net deficit of £86.9 million. Maps were produced showing the weekly flows for passenger traffic (Map 1: 'British Railway Density of Passenger Traffic') and freight traffic (Map 2). For passenger lines these were categorised as follows: 0 to 5,000 passengers a week, then up to 10,000, 50,000, 100,000 and 200,000. Map 3: 'British Railways Distribution of Passenger Traffic Receipts' shows the traffic receipts for each station, broken down into £0 to £5,000, £5,000 to £25,000 and more than £25,000 per annum. It also revealed that most branch line and wayside stations had annual revenues of less than £5,000.

The Transport Act of 1962 received Royal Assent on 1 August. Two aspects of the Act are worth noting. The existing BTC, which had overseen the management of road, rail and inland waterways since nationalisation, was now abolished, and separate Boards were set up for each form of transport. Railways came under the control of the British Railways Board, with Dr Beeching as Chairman. The Act also made provision for changes to the existing regional boundaries. This resulted in significant changes in the West Country, where all the former British Railways Southern Region lines west of Salisbury were transferred to the Western Region.

Part I of the Beeching Report was published in March 1963. Although it was heralded as a bombshell by the press, its controversial closure proposals closely reflected the statistics published earlier. The density of passenger traffic revealed by the survey of April 1961 was graphically illustrated in Map I of the Report, which showed that throughout the United Kingdom most secondary and branch lines carried a maximum of 5,000 passengers per week. They included the majority of lines in the West Country, Scotland and Wales. In Wales even major routes such as those from Shrewsbury to Aberystwyth, together with the lines west of Bangor in the north and Carmarthen in the south, could only muster a maximum of 10,000 passengers per week.

Table 4 of the Report, 'Margins of Revenue Over Costs For Low Density Passenger Flows', demonstrated that, with a diesel multiple unit service, 'The revenue earned from up to 6,000 passengers per week is unlikely to be sufficient to cover movement costs alone.' However, when all infrastructure costs are taken into account the Report concludes that, 'Where there is no other traffic, routes carrying up to 17,000 passengers per week may barely pay their way.' By applying these criteria the Report proposed some 5,000 route miles for closure, together with 1,924 stations. The 'Passenger Services to be Withdrawn' were listed in Appendix 2, Section 1 of the Report. In England a number of main lines, including the former Great Central line from London Marylebone to Sheffield, were also included.

A further list of 'Passenger Services to be Modified' was given in Appendix 2, Section 2 of the Report. Part of the Report gave 'More detailed consideration of the main groups of traffic', including the issue of stopping trains. This concluded that, 'Although a high proportion of passenger services operate over lines of low total traffic density, there is also a considerable number of similar services operating over more densely loaded routes. In most cases these services are just as unsound, financially, as those operating over branch lines.' The Report pointed out that in such cases the operating costs were shared with other fast passenger and freight trains. Even so, it concluded that, 'Below about 6,000 passenger miles per week they do not pay their way for their own movement costs, even with short diesel multiple unit trains.' The answer was that such services should also be withdrawn or radically modified. In effect, this meant that on most main lines, especially those running through rural areas, virtually all the intermediate stations serving small towns and villages were to be closed. The Report also questioned the need to maintain duplicate main lines including those from London to Exeter,

Brighton, Birmingham and Manchester.

Despite enquiries at the National Railway Museum and the Public Records Office at Kew, the author has been unable to locate the original data collected in the survey of rail traffic in April 1961. He has therefore had to rely on the information presented in Maps 1 and 3 of the Report. Here the categories for differing levels of traffic identified are very broad-brush but, as this is the only information available, it has been quoted in this book.

Another source of traffic that is examined in the Report is the running of a large number of extra trains on summer Saturdays to cater for holidaymakers. Analysis of this traffic revealed that in 1959 there were 8,900 coaches available for high peak services. Of these, 2,000 were only used on 18 occasions, 2,000 on 14 occasions and 2,000 on 10 occasions a year. The Report calculates that these services lost BR up to £3.5 million annually. A list of these trains to the West Country on summer Saturdays in 1962 is given in Appendix 3.1 together with an analysis of the 'Beeching effect' on the routes and stations served by these trains.

Table 4 of the Report assesses the reduction that the line closures will allow in BR's motive power units. This estimates that 1,174 steam and 55 diesel engines will be rendered surplus to requirements, together with 814 DMUs and 260 EMUs. Twenty-one railbuses would also become surplus. The diesel and electric units were of course deployed elsewhere, enabling BR to rid itself of steam engines earlier than had been anticipated, on 11 August 1968.

Notices proposing the 'Withdrawal of Railway Passenger Services' were soon appearing on the stations affected and as public notices in the press. These advised 'Any user of the rail service which it is proposed to discontinue and anybody representing such users may lodge an objection in writing within six weeks (of the date given in the notice)'. Objections were to be addressed to the secretary of the local Transport Users' Consultative Committee. The notices went on to say that, 'If any such objection is lodged the service cannot be discontinued until the Transport Users' Consultative Committee has considered the objections and reported to the Minister of Transport and the Minister has given his consent. The Committee may hold a meeting to hear objections. Such a meeting will be held in public and any persons who have lodged an objection in writing may also make oral representations to the Committee. If no objections are lodged to the proposal the service will be withdrawn on (the date given on the Notice)'.

Initially objectors at the public meetings tried to show that the statistics used to justify the closure proposal were inaccurate. Much was made of the fact that the 1961 survey had taken place in April, thus ignoring holiday travel. This approach seems to have met with some success to the embarrassment of the railway officials present. The rules were soon changed, which allowed the Consultative Committees to consider only whether public hardship might arise from the closure. In any event, ministerial consent for closure appeared to be automatic. It was hoped that the election of a Labour Government in the General Election of 1964 would result in the whole plan being suspended or at least reviewed. However, despite an election pledge to this effect, when the Labour Government of Harold Wilson was duly elected, little seemed to change.

Although his appointment was for five years, Dr Beeching resigned from the BRB in 1965 to return to ICI. He had just published Part 2 of his Report, 'The Development of the Major Trunk Routes'. This envisaged a further drastic reduction in the rail network to leave just a handful of lines radiating from London as far north as Aberdeen and as far west as Plymouth. In South Wales his 'trunk route' from London ended at Swansea, while in North Wales the railhead would have been Chester. The map published with this second Report does, however, show lines from London to Exeter via Salisbury and from Plymouth to Penzance, which were seen as feeders to the 'trunk routes', which 'would not necessarily be closed'! Strangely, the ex-SR line between Exeter and Plymouth via Okehampton is shown in the same category. Part 2 of the Report was, however, positive to the extent that it proposed further investment in the railways to increase traffic that Dr Beeching felt could be carried profitably. These included the introduction of fast inter-city trains and the development of containerised freight traffic. Ironically, while the unions vigorously opposed the further cuts because of the resulting job losses, additional

investment was opposed by the road transport lobby, which feared that the proposals might be all too successful. As a result, Part 2 of the Report failed to gain Government support.

In 1968 the new Labour Transport Minister, Barbara Castle, included the criteria of social need in her Transport Act of 1968. This allowed loss-making passenger services to be subsidised by the state. By then the closure programme was virtually complete, with only a handful of lines surviving into the 1970s. Nevertheless, the branch-line services to Looe and St Ives were among those to receive a Government subsidy and are still running today.

In October 1970 the Government's responsibility for transport was taken over by the Department of the Environment under Peter Walker (later Lord Walker), the Environment Secretary. Since then the transport portfolio has moved between departments on numerous occasions.

Dr Beeching was made a life peer, as Baron Beeching of East Grinstead, in the Birthday Honours list of 1965. In 1983, not long before his death two years later, he was interviewed by Jim Palm for a BBC local radio station. Among the many questions asked was whether he was disappointed that not all his recommendations had been carried out. Towards the end of the interview he was asked again whether he had any regrets over what he did. His reply was, 'No, none at all, except in so far as I wish I'd got more done.' He went on to say that 'if there are any regrets they are not that I closed lines down but that I left some open that ought to have been closed at that time. And there's still enough for Serpell to propose in the way of closures to bring a good deal of vituperation down on his head.'

The latter comment referred to the Serpell Report on the railways, published earlier that year. This Report, by the late Sir David Serpell, essentially resurrected the proposals contained in the second Beeching Report. Serpell, as an official in the Ministry of Transport, had worked closely with Beeching in the 1960s; in fact, he was an old friend of Beeching, and had claimed in interviews that it was he who had persuaded Beeching to become Chairman of the British Railways Board in 1961. After retiring as a Permanent Secretary, Serpell himself became a member of the BRB between 1974 and 1982. His report for the Conservative Government

Status in 2019 of the stations on lines listed for modification in Appendix 2, Section 2 of the Beeching Report

Name	Listed for closure	Date of closure	Comments
2.1 Castle Cary to Weymouth			
Castle Cary	No	Open	
Sparkford	Yes	3 October 1966	
Marston Magna	Yes	3 October 1966	
Yeovil (Pen Mill)	Yes	Open	
Thornford Bridge Halt	Yes	Open	
Yetminster	Yes	Open	
Chetnole Halt	Yes	Open	
Evershot	Yes	1966	
Cattistock Halt	Yes	1966	
Maiden Newton	Yes	Open	
Grimstone and Frampton	Yes	1966	
Bradford Peverell and Stratton Halt	Yes	1966	
Dorchester West	Yes	Open	
Upwey and Broadwey	No	Open	Also used by Bournemouth to Wemouth trains
Radipole Halt	No	2 January 1984	Structure considered unsafe
Weymouth Town	No	Open	Also used by Bournemouth to Wemouth trains
2.2 Taunton to Exeter St David's			
Taunton	No	Open	
Wellington (Som)	Yes	5 October 1964	
Burlescombe	Yes	5 October 1964	
Sampford Peverell Halt	Yes	5 October 1964	Tiverton Parkway opened on the site of Sampford Peverell Halt in May 1986
Tiverton Junction	Yes	12 May 1986	
Cullompton	Yes	5 October 1964	
Hele and Bradninch	Yes	5 October 1964	
Silverton	Yes	5 October 1964	
Exeter (St David's)	No	Open	
2.3 Exeter St David's to Kingswear			
Exeter (St David's)	No	Open	
Exeter (St Thomas)	Yes	Open	
Exminster	Yes	30 March 1964	
Starcross for Exmouth	Yes	Open	
Dawlish Warren	No	Open	
Dawlish	No	Open	
Teignmouth	No	Open	
Newton Abbot	No	Open	
Kingskerswell	Yes	5 October 1964	
Torre	No	Open	
Torquay	No	Open	
Paignton	No	Open	BR(WR) provided a temporary DMU service until 30 Dec 72 on behalf of the Dart Valley Railway. DVR steam operation started on 1 Jan 73 but regular winter services have not run since. The line is now owned by the Dartmouth Steam Railway & River Boat Company.
Goodrington Sands Halt	No	28 October 1972	Re-opened by DVR 1 November 1972
Churston (for Brixham)	Yes	28 October 1972	Re-opened by DVR 1 November 1972
Kingswear	No	28 October 1972	Re-opened by DVR 1 November 1972

Appendix 2

Status in 2019 of the stations on lines listed for modification in Appendix 2, Section 2 of the Beeching Report

Name	Listed for closure	Date of closure	Comments
2.4 Plymouth to Penzance			
Plymouth	No	Open	
Devonport, Albert Road	No	Open	Renamed Devonport in 6 May 1968
Dockyard Halt	No	Open	
Keyham	No	Open	
St Budeaux, Ferry Road	No	Open	
Saltash	No	Open	
St Germans	No	Open	
Menheniot	Yes	Open	
Liskeard	No	Open	
Doublebois	Yes	5 October 1964	
Bodmin Road	No	Open	Renamed Bodmin Parkway in 4 November 1983
Lostwithiel	Yes	Open	
Par	No	Open	
St Austell	No	Open	
Grampound Road	Yes	5 October 1964	
Truro	No	Open	
Chacewater	Yes	5 October 1964	
Scorrier	Yes	5 October 1964	
Redruth	No	Open	
Camborne	No	Open	
Gwinear Road	Yes	5 October 1964	
Hayle	Yes	Open	
St Erth	No	Open	
Marazion	Yes	5 October 1964	
Penzance	No	Open	
2.5 Par to Newquay			
Par	No	Open	
Luxulyan	Yes	Open	
Bugle	Yes	Open	
Roche	Yes	Open	
St Columb Road	Yes	Open	
Quintrel Downs	Yes	Open	
Newquay	No	Open	

of Margaret Thatcher, in effect a rehash of Part 2 of Beeching's Report, was however a step too far even for the Iron Lady, and his proposals were quietly dropped. He nevertheless appears to have been a power behind the throne throughout the Beeching era.

Today, following privatisation, the picture is very different. There has been large-scale investment in the railways and new stations and a few lines have reopened. The case for reopening the ex-SR line between Exeter and Plymouth is strong due to the regular closure of the ex-GWR line at Dawlish because of flooding from the sea. To date, however, the Government appears rather reluctant to provide the funds for this expensive project!

Appendix 2

Status in 2019 of the stations on lines listed for modification in Appendix 2, Section 2 of the Beeching Report

Name	Listed for closure	Date of closure	Comments
2.6 Yeovil Junction to Exeter Central			
Yeovil Junction	No	Open	
Crewkerne	No	Open	
Chard Junction	Yes	7 March 1966	
Axminster	No	Open	
Seaton Junction	Yes	7 March 1966	
Honiton	No	Open	
Sidmouth Junction	Yes	6 March 1967	Reopened as Feniton in 5 May 1971
Whimple	Yes	Open	
Broad Clyst	Yes	7 March 1966	
Pinhoe	Yes	7 March 1966	Reopened in 16 May 1983
St James' Park Halt	No	Open	
Exeter Central	No	Open	
2.7 Exeter Central to Barnstaple Junction			
Exeter Central	No	Open	
Exeter St David's	No	Open	
Newton St Cyres	Yes	Open	
Crediton	No	Open	
Yeoford	Yes	Open	
Copplestone	Yes	Open	
Morchard Road	Yes	Open	
Lapford	No	Open	
Eggesford	No	Open	
King's Nympton	Yes	Open	
Portsmouth Arms	Yes	Open	
Umberleigh	Yes	Open	
Chapelton	Yes	Open	
Barnstaple Junction	No	Open	
2.8 Exeter Central to Okehampton			
Exeter Central	No	Open	
Exeter St David's	No	Open	
Newton St Cyres	Yes	Open	For Barnstaple line trains only
Crediton	No	Open	For Barnstaple line trains only
Yeoford	Yes	Open	For Barnstaple line trains only
Bow	Yes	5 June 1972	
North Tawton	Yes	5 June 1972	
Sampford Courtenay	Yes	5 June 1972	Reopened for Dartmoor Rambler trains 2006
Okehampton	No	5 June 1972	Summer Saturday/Sunday Dartmoor Rambler trains introduced from 1984

Appendix 3

Through trains using lines listed for closure in the Beeching Report running on Saturdays in August 1962, 1965 and 1970.

Originating station	Time of departure	Region/s	Destination/s	Route
I. Through trains using lines listed for closure in the Beeching Reporton Saturdays in August 1962				
London Waterloo	12.15am	SR	Ilfracombe (1), Torrington (1), Padstow (1) and Bude (1)	Salisbury and Yeovil Junction
London Waterloo	1.10am	SR	Ilfracombe (2), Bideford (1), Plymouth (1) and Padstow (2)	Salisbury and Yeovil Junction
London Waterloo	7.30am	SR	Ilfracombe (3), Torrington (2), Padstow (3) and Bude (2)	Salisbury and Yeovil Junction
London Waterloo	8.03am	SR	Exmouth (1), Sidmouth (1) and Seaton (1)	Salisbury and Yeovil Junction
London Waterloo	8.35am	SR	Ilfracombe (4) and Torrington (3)	Salisbury and Yeovil Junction
London Waterloo	8.54am	SR	Ilfracombe (5) and Plymouth (2)	Salisbury and Yeovil Junction
London Waterloo	9.00am	SR	Exmouth (2), Sidmouth (2) and Seaton (2)	Salisbury and Yeovil Junction
London Waterloo	10.15am	SR	Ilfracombe (6) and Torrington (4)	Salisbury and Yeovil Junction
London Waterloo	10.35am	SR	Padstow (4) and Bude (3) (Atlantic Coast Express)	Salisbury and Yeovil Junction
London Waterloo	10.45am	SR	Seaton (3) and Lyme Regis (1)	Salisbury and Yeovil Junction
London Waterloo	11.00am	SR	Ilfracombe (7) and Torrington (5) (Atlantic Coast Express)	Salisbury and Yeovil Junction
London Waterloo	11.15am	SR	Plymouth (3), Padstow (5) and Bude (4)	Salisbury and Yeovil Junction
London Waterloo	11.45am	SR	Exmouth (3) and Sidmouth (3)	Salisbury and Yeovil Junction
London Waterloo	12.05pm	SR	Ilfracombe (8) and Torrington (6)	Salisbury and Yeovil Junction
London Waterloo	1.00pm	SR	Plymouth (4) , Ilfracombe (9) and Torrington (7)	
London Waterloo	3.00pm	SR	Plymouth (5) , Ilfracombe (10) and Torrington (8)	Salisbury and Yeovil Junction
London Waterloo	7.00pm	SR	Plymouth (6)	Salisbury and Yeovil Junction
Portsmouth & Southsea	9.03am	SR	Plymouth	Southampton, Salisbury and Yeovil Junction
Brighton	11.30am	SR	Plymouth	Southampton, Salisbury and Yeovil Junction
Portsmouth & Southsea	12.15pm	SR	Ilfracombe and Torrington	Southampton, Salisbury and Yeovil Junction
Cleethorpes	7.00am	ER/LMR/ WR/ SR	Sidmouth and Exmouth	Birmingham, Bath Green Park and Templecombe
London Paddington	8.15am	WR	Minehead	Westbury and Taunton
London Paddington	8.30am	WR	Perranporth (Line listed for closure in 1962 and closed February 1963. See Box 2.1)	Westbury, Taunton, Plymouth and Chacewater
London Paddington	10.15am	WR	Minehead	Westbury and Taunton
London Paddington	10.30am	WR	St. Ives (Cornish Riviera Express)	Westbury and Taunton
Wolverhampton Low Level	10.55am	WR	Minehead and Ilfracombe	Stratford-on-Avon, Bristol Temple Meads and Taunton
Swansea High Street	8.50am	WR	Minehead	Bristol Temple Meads and Taunton

Total = 27
(X) = Cumulative number of through trains from Waterloo (seventeen in all) to each destination

Appendix 3

Through trains using lines listed for closure in the Beeching Report running on Saturdays in August 1962, 1965 and 1970.

2. Long distance through trains using lines listed for closure in the Beeching Report in August 1965.

Originating station	Time of departure	Region/s	Destination/s	Route
London Waterloo	1.10am	SR/WR	Plymouth (W1)	Salisbury and Yeovil Junction
London Waterloo	8.00am	SR/WR	Exmouth (W1) and Sidmouth (W1)	Salisbury and Yeovil Junction
London Waterloo	10.00am	SR/WR	Exmouth (W2) and Sidmouth (W2)	Salisbury and Yeovil Junction
London Waterloo	12.00am	SR/WR	Exmouth (W3) and Sidmouth (W3)	Salisbury and Yeovil Junction
Brighton	10.12pm	SR/WR	Plymouth	Southampton, Salisbury and Yeovil Junction
London Paddington	8.15am	WR	Ilfracombe (P1)	Westbury and Exeter St David's
London Paddington	9.50am	WR	Minehead	Westbury and Exeter St David's
London Paddington	10.15am	WR	Ilfracombe (P2)	Westbury and Exeter St David's
London Paddington	11.05am	WR	Ilfracombe (P3) and Bude (P1)	Westbury and Yeovil Junction
Carmarthen	8.00am	WR	Minehead and Ilfracombe	Bristol TM and Taunton
Wolverhampton Low Level	8.00am	LMR/WR	Minehead and Ilfracombe	Stratford-on-Avon, Bristol TM and Taunton
Exmouth	9.20am	LMR/WR	Manchester Piccadilly (ran northbound only)	Bristol TM, Shrewsbury and Crewe

Total = 12
(WX) = Cumulative number of through trains from Waterloo (four in all) to each destination

(PX) = Cumulative number of through trains from Paddington (three in all) which replaced those from Waterloo in 1964

3. Through trains using lines listed for closure in the Beeching Report on Saturdays in August 1970.

Originating station	Time of departure	Region/s	Destination/s	Route
Oxford	7.05am	WR	Minehead	Reading, Westbury and Taunton
London Paddington	8.10am	WR	Ilfracombe	Westbury and Exeter St David's
London Paddington	8.30am	WR	Minehead	Westbury and Exeter St David's

Total = 3

These were the last trains using lines listed for closure in the Beeching Report.
The line to Ilfracombe closed in October 1970 and that to Minehead in January 1971.